M

Make Yo
Damn Movie.

Also by Lloyd Kaufman

All I Need to Know About Filmmaking I Learned from the Toxic Avenger
The Shocking True Story of Troma Studios

Lloyd Kaufman

with ADAM JAHNKE *and* TRENT HAAGA

St. Martin's Griffin
New York

Contents

Acknowledgments

My Own Damn eternal appreciation to Michael and Maris Herz.

My Own Damn gratitude to Elizabeth Beier (my own damn editrix and green-lighting goddess), Jerome Rudes and Fifi Oscard (my own damn wonderful literary agents).

My Own Damn thanks to: Michael Connor (my own damn brilliant editor), Adam Jahnke, Trent Haaga, Gabe Friedman, Megan Powers, Sean McGrath, Doug Sakmann, Brian McNulty, Jamie Greco, Trey Parker, Perry Lerner, Alan Quasha, Jonathan Foster, James Gunn, Fiona Apple, Jean Loscalzo, Eric Raab, Andrew Rye, Frank Reynolds, Sonja Shultz, Julie Strain, Kevin Eastman, Tim Considine, Karen Tepper, John Karle, R. L. Kaufman, Sigrun Kaufman, Susan Kaufman, Charles Kaufman, Lilly Hayes Kaufman, Lisbeth Kaufman, Charlotte Kaufman, and... Jay North, as the Beaver.

Special thanks to: James L. Brooks (for calling attention to my work in *The New York Times*).

No thanks to: Viacom, New Corp, Vivendi, AOL Time Warner, Sony and other devil-worshipping international media conglomerates.

Foreword

by Trey Parker

Lloyd Kaufman had a profound impact on my life. Twice.

The first time was when I was thirteen and I rented a movie called *The Toxic Avenger* at my video store. I'll never forget the way that film inspired me. It made me realize that if a crappy film like that could get good reviews and make it to video stores, I could become a film-maker, too. I knew I could make movies that looked that good even if I was just thirteen. Hell, I knew just about anybody could. I quickly rented more Troma films and started to see their tactic. Quantity over quality. They obviously didn't care what it looked like, they just did it, and kept on doing it . . . just like Merchant and Ivory. Encouraged, I spent every weekend shooting a new, crappy video movie with my reluctant friends with a huge camera with thick cables running to an enormous VCR. When I would direct my thirteen-year-old buddies to just spit out catsup to look like blood, they would complain.

"Dude," they would say, "that'll look stupid."

"No," I would reply, "that's what they do in the Troma movies, and *they* make it to video stores. Don't worry about what the blood looks like, just make the damn movie."

I continued to make tons of short, crappy movies throughout my teenage years, with the important lesson of quantity over quality that I had learned from Troma, and I kept making cheap crappy movies right through film school at the University of Colorado, where I was lucky to find people like Jason McHugh and Matt Stone, who shared my love for cheap, stupid, brilliant crap. Whereas most film students would save up their money and make one big, expensive, great looking film, we would shoot tons of little shitty ones; about three a semester. We didn't care about how they looked, only that they got made. Quantity over quality.

Having such a bulk of material eventually led to us being able to get money to make one big crappy film during our senior year. Thanks to Troma, we were empowered to think "Why *not* make a feature length movie in college with a bunch of rundown equipment? It'll look as good as *The Toxic Avenger!*"

We made the film, an hour and a half piece called *Cannibal! The Musical*, and it was, indeed, as crappy as *The Toxic Avenger*. Maybe crappier.

I believe now that having Cannibal and all our other short films from college is the main reason we found success in Hollywood. We arrived in that town not with one film to show, but dozens. Most important, by making a lot of films in our younger years, (one of those short crappy school movies was the first *South Park*) it helped us to arrive in L.A. with our own unique voice that we had already defined. The studios would eventually corrupt our unique voice, of course, but not until much later in our careers.

You see, Lloyd Kaufman knew years ago what most people are just now figuring out—you don't need a big Hollywood studio to make a movie. With the technical advances in editing systems and digital cameras that's becoming more true every day, it's all about output: output, learn by doing. To hell with whether you should shoot at 5.6 or 5.6-8 split. Fuck all that. Just start making crap. Quantity over quality. The first important lesson I learned from Lloyd Kaufman.

The second lesson came some ten years after the first, when I was twenty-three, and actually had the opportunity to meet Lloyd Kaufman face to face.

It was 1995. At that time, I was living in Los Angeles sleeping on people's floors and running around with Jason and Matt trying to sell *Cannibal! The Musical.*

After its completion, we were rejected at every film festival (except the Denver film festival where my aunt Marilyn worked). Its relative success at small screenings started to make us think more and more that we could actually sell *Cannibal* to a distributor in L.A. We drove out there, and for months met with lots of people who kissed our asses, told us *Cannibal* wasn't right for them, but they'd *love* first rights to our *next* movie.

Then Troma called. They had seen the film and were interested in the distribution rights. I was excited, thinking that things had come full circle. We were told that Lloyd Kaufman himself was going to visit us in L.A. and we would 'do lunch.' It had been almost three years since we had made the film, and it looked like *finally* we were going to make some money off of it.

Lloyd arrived at our rundown apartment wearing a chic blue suit and a very busy yellow tie. If someone asked me to create a cartoon character of a little cliché Jewish, Mel Brooks—type producer from New York, I would have drawn Lloyd, and I would have done the voice just like he does.

"Hi, hi, Lloyd Kaufman from Troma. I *love* your movie, great stuff. You guys are brilliant. So you guys ready to eat lunch?"

"Sure," we said, knowing that doing lunch in L.A. meant a meeting was fairly serious.

"Where should we go?"

"I saw a Del Taco across the street, you guys like Del Taco?"

I remember studying Lloyd's face then, seeing if he, like so many other producers was just trying to put on an "I'm down to Earth" act.

But then I saw it in his eyes: This man really does like Del Taco. He wanted it. Bad. We walked over to Del Taco, anticipating what kind of great offer Troma was going to make us on our movie.

I can replay the whole meeting in my mind as if it happened hours ago. We all placed our food orders at the counter. We quickly realized that Lloyd had no intention of paying for our tacos. In fact, when Jason offered to pay for Lloyd's beef taco with loads of hot sauce, Lloyd's face lit up like a child at Christmas, and he promptly added some guacamole to his order.

We got our food and sat down. The negotiations were about to begin.

Lloyd began the conversation by unwrapping his taco and saying that *Cannibal* was one of the best films he'd seen in recent months and he wanted to distribute it into video stores. Trying to contain our excitement, we settled into the points of the agreement.

"Okay," I believe Jason said, "so how would the deal work?"

"Well, if we ... er ... I mean you can put a bit more violence up front in the movie and fix some of the sound, we'll make a nice video package with the Troma logo in the corner," Lloyd replied, "and hopefully, lots of people will rent it! Then maybe we'll make back all the money we spent on the packaging some day!"

We stopped eating tacos.

"So how much money do we get up front?"

"Oh. Nothing." Lloyd said casually.

"We get nothing?"

"Odds are you'll never see a dime. This is a small movie, and it will take years in video stores just to make back the money we're gonna spend on the new shiny box and posters." I believe he finished off this sentence with another bite into his now rather messy taco with extra hot sauce and guacamole, adding a heartfelt 'mmm' at the end. "Okay," Jason came back shrewdly, "Let me get this straight. *You* want us to give you the rights to our movie, to distribute as you wish, and we make nothing?"

Lloyd was really enjoying that messy Del Taco food; he sort of painted his face with it. He was now sporting a guacamole moustache.

"That's my general offer, yes. It's just sort of how it goes," Lloyd replied, having been through it himself a hundred times, "Not much money to be made in the video business, I'm afraid. Not unless you've got *Gremlins* or something. Mmm, this taco is really good." He did not seem to care that he looked like a "got guacamole?" advertisement.

"Well, then," I think I said, "Why should we even bother giving it to you?"

"Well, I just think *Cannibal* is a really great movie and people should *see* it. I mean, you guys *made* it so that people would *see* it, right?"

This statement hit me like a baseball bat in the face, and was the second time Lloyd Kaufman had a huge impact on my life.

My buddies and I sat silent for over a minute, but in our heads we were all thinking the same thing—*This guy is totally right. . . . This guy with a "got guacamole?" moustache was absolutely right!*

All these years I had been making movies because I wanted people to see them. That was it. We made *Cannibal* in college because we thought it would be funny. We just wanted our friends and family to see it, and to laugh. Just four months in L.A. had made us lose sight of all that, and focus on the money instead.

Thanks to Lloyd it suddenly became crystal clear to me. *Cannibal*, our first feature film, was never going to make us a fortune. But having it in video stores, having people all over the country rent it, and pop it into their VCRs thinking, *"What the hell is this movie?"* as I had done all those years ago with *The Toxic Avenger*, well, that's what it's all about. That's why we make movies. Hopefully, that's the same reason you, dear reader, want to make "your own damn" movie, too.

If you want to make a movie because you want to become rich, go put a thousand dollars down on thirteen black instead. Your odds are way better. You could also try law school or medical school; it will take about the same amount of time to see any profit from your film. You may even want to try selling your sweet ass on the street, odds are you will make more money doing that. If, however, you want to make a movie because you want people to laugh, or cry, or puke—then read on. Nobody knows how to make films and not make any money doing it better than Lloyd Kaufman.

Trey Parker, left, with Matt Stone on the set of Troma's
Terror Firmer.

Introduction

by James Gunn

It was August 1996, we had just completed filming *Tromeo & Juliet*, and the film's associate producer, Andrew Weiner, and I, were the only ones left in the Troma building at the end of a long day. So Andrew and I did what we often did at that time—we snuck into Lloyd Kaufman and Michael Herz's office and messed around with their private stuff. I readjusted two of the Toxic Crusader action figures on Lloyd's shelf so that they were butt-fucking. Andrew pretended to take a shit in Michael's drawer. We sat across from each other in their desk chairs and did mean-spirited imitations of them ("Look at me, I'm Lloyd!" I said. "James, get in here and wipe this dingleberry off my ass!") And then, on this particular evening, Andrew dared me to masturbate in Lloyd's seat.

"That's disgusting," I said. "Sure."

So Andrew went back upstairs to do something important, like draw devils' horns on actresses' headshots, while I stayed in El Troma Presidentes' office. I popped in a videocassette of *Class of Nuke 'Em High*, fast-forwarded to Janelle Brady taking off her top, and commenced to rub one out. This is a difficult feat while giggling, but, eventually, Janelle's luscious puffies defeated my ironic intentions, and I shot my man juice all over Lloyd's desk.

At this point, you may wonder what in the fuck this has to do with introducing *Make Your Own Damn Movie*.

Well, it goes to prove that when you're as cheap as Troma, you don't have any choice but to hire fuck-ups like me, people who masturbate in your office when you're gone. Sure, the chairman of 20th Century Fox has a lot of his own problems—*Glitter*, for instance—but finding mysterious yellow stains on his interoffice memos probably isn't one of them. And that's the first lesson of making low-budget films: *You have to make do with what you got.*

If life gives you lemons, make lemonade. If life gives you assholes, make a Troma movie. Life has been giving Lloyd Kaufman assholes for three decades now, and he's been doing his best with this raw material, somehow orchestrating their limited abilities in such a way as to churn out classics like *The Toxic Avenger, Class of Nuke 'Em High, Troma's War,* and *Terror Firmer.* And by "classics" I mean "Lloyd gave me twenty bucks to call them that." But, really, he needn't have wasted his money—there's no denying the uniqueness, the potency, and, yes, even the *genius* of Troma. Lloyd's blend of slapstick, gore, sex, vaudeville, and nuclear waste has inspired luminaries such as Peter Jackson, Kevin Smith, and Quentin Tarantino. We Tromaphiles are a secret society in Hollywood, numerous, anonymous, and omnipresent. So often I'll meet a studio exec who will discover I worked on *Tromeo & Juliet.* "You did?" she'll say. She'll blush, she won't be able to look me in the eye, and she'll whisper, under her breath: "I *love* that movie." And then she'll shudder uncontrollably. Holy cow, she's having an orgasm!

Take note: This book may not teach you how to make a great film (after all, it's not called *Make Your Own Good Movie*)—the quality is up to you—but it *will* teach you how to make the best film you can within budgetary constraints: You can't afford an expensive car stunt? Just splice in a car flip from an old film.* You can't find the right person for the part? Use the wrongest person you can—someone who can't act at

---

* See the *Sgt. Kabukiman NYPD* car flip used in *Tromeo & Juliet, Terror Firmer,* and *Citizen Toxie.*

all is usually funnier than someone who can act a little.* Don't have enough latex left to make a fake head for a head-crushing scene? Use a watermelon.† Not enough cash for a watermelon? Use a cantaloupe, or a grapefruit. Use a fucking *orange* if you have to! Because, in the end, making a low-budget film is not about *getting it done right*. It's about *getting it done*. We all know so-called "artists" who have ingenious ideas for films, novels, or origami monoliths but who never get up from watching *Friends* long enough to do anything about them. To make a movie one must risk making shit. And Lloyd Kaufman is my mentor and my hero, not only because he has risked making shit, *but because he has actually been making shit for over thirty years*. But it's marvelous shit, and the world is better off because of it. Unless you include *Big Gus, What's the Fuss?*‡ The world's a little worse off because of that.

And don't believe that this book will only be helpful on low-budget films. In my own experience, the only differences between making the $350,000 *Tromeo & Juliet*, the $1 million *The Specials*, and the nearly $90 million *Scooby-Doo* were the size of the paychecks and the quality of the actresses' breast implants. No matter whether it's a Troma movie, an independent period piece, or a studio film, you'll have to deal with crewmembers' griping, arguments between directors and producers, and your idiot pyrotechnic guy accidentally exploding your lovingly crafted five-foot-long Penis Monster before his last shot of the day. Well, okay, that last one probably only happens at Troma. Unless there's a five-foot Penis Monster in the next Harry Potter movie I don't know about.§

Anyway, what I mean to say is my time at Troma taught me everything I need to know about working in the studio system and making low-budget films. I joke around about Lloyd, but the truth is he's a

---

* I love him like a brother, but what would *The Toxic Avenger* be without Mark Torgl's "acting" as Melvin?

† See *Tromaville Café*.

‡ A.K.A. "The 9/11 of Cinema."

§ Wait a second—Harry Potter *is* a five-foot Penis Monster!

good friend and a true visionary and I get giddy every time he sends me a cut of his newest film. When I worked at Troma I was able to learn from Lloyd every aspect of filmmaking, from writing to location scouting to casting to shooting to marketing. Unfortunately, I had to learn the hard way: by actually working at Troma. Now you, the blessed, can learn from Lloyd's wisdom with very little effort at all, by simply partaking of the next few hundred pages.

So say goodbye to your old life, and prepare yourself for a Tromatic transformation. As the serpent said unto Eve, "Eat up, chippie—and welcome to Tromaville."

April, 2002
Los Angeles, California

CHAPTER 1

Let's Make Some Art!

I was surrounded on every side by vermin, roaches, and rat shit. And I wasn't even meeting with executives at Blockbuster.

This was the basement of the Troma Building in New York City. For years, Troma has occupied this four-story building in the part of Manhattan formerly known as Hell's Kitchen.* From this mighty temple, we had steered the mighty ship of Troma through such films as *Tromeo & Juliet, Terror Firmer*, and *Citizen Toxie: The Toxic Avenger Part IV*. The Troma Building occupied a proud, majestic place on the New York skyline. But now, disease and decay had entered the works. Rats threatened the very foundation of the Troma Building.

The Troma Building's basement is Troma's memory center, its archive, its remembrance of things past. In other words, it's where a lot of shit has been dumped and forgotten about over the years. And now, it had been invaded by rodents. No one knew quite where the rats had come from. The Troma Building had remained relatively pest-free for the better part of two decades. It seemed like no small coincidence that the arrival of the rats perfectly coincided with the opening of a brand new McDonald's directly next door to the office. Thanks to that devil-

* In the post-Giuliani, Disneyfied New York, it's commonly known as Mickey's Asshole.

worshipping, burger-shilling corporate clown, Troma was lousy with humongous, voracious rodents that knew no fear. And now, everything in our basement was contaminated by rat shit and had either been partially eaten by the rats or was in imminent danger of being so.

Now ordinarily, ridding the basement of rats the size of baby coyotes would be a job for anybody but me. After all, I am president and cofounder of the fucking company. You don't see Harvey Weinstein in the flooded basement of Miramax trying to salvage old promotional T-shirts and baseball caps from *Playing for Keeps*.* But, after years of doling out the most backbreaking, humiliating, odious tasks imaginable, I had finally stumbled across a job so disgusting and wretched that *nobody* would accept it. Even our interns (who are, by their very nature, subjected to more humiliation than our regular employees simply by virtue of the fact that they are unpaid) refused to take it on.

The choice was simple. Either we seal the basement forever like some old, abandoned mine that's been tapped out or rendered unsafe and just write off thirty years of Troma history (an option that was seriously pursued by a small handful of Troma employees who were always looking for an excuse to blow something up) or I had to go down there and deal with the rats myself. The history of Troma was in that basement. A shit-stained, fucked-up history it may be, but it was a history that Michael Herz and I had built. I couldn't ask anyone to defend that history but me.†

Armed with a shovel (which I cleverly figured would serve double duty as both shit scooper and rat bludgeon), I swung wide the steel doors that led to the cellar. I switched on the single 40-watt bulb that provided what milky light the basement offered. I could see four or

---

* For you trivia buffs, *Playing for Keeps*, the sole directorial effort from the mighty and powerful Weinstein brothers, is about a bunch of teens who dream about building a rock 'n' roll hotel. I can neither confirm nor deny the rumors that the Weinsteins were, at this stage, modeling their careers after Troma by making a film not unlike *The First Turn-On*, which predated *Playing for Keeps* by a good three or four years.

† Of course, I could and did ask many other people to defend that history but after being told repeatedly to shove it up my ass, I had to rationalize something.

five rats stop what they were doing, look me in the eyes, then lazily make their way deeper into the basement. Presumably these were mere sentries, going off to let the others know that some asshole was about to interrupt them.

I continued into the darkest recesses of the basement. I walked the rickety pallets to the far door, the door that led into the real heart of darkness. Rat Central. A filthy, damp, pitch black storage area that contained those weird items that tread the fine line between garbage and artifact. Too precious to throw away, but far too useless to ever hope of using again. All around me, I could see the physical reminders of my thirty years with Troma. There was a box containing production schedules and the shooting script from *The Battle of Love's Return* (1971). I thumbed through the papers, trying to decipher the notes I'd written to myself almost thirty years earlier. It just seemed like gibberish now and I wondered if I'd ever been able to read them. That would explain a lot about that movie. Stacked nearby were molding stacks of posters from *Troma's War* (1988). There were all kinds of posters from dozens of different movies but it seemed as if you couldn't turn around without seeing a *War* poster.* There were decomposing boxes full of *Squeeze Play* T-shirts (circa 1980), the computer monitor with the smashed, bloody severed head of Capulet from *Tromeo & Juliet* (1996), and the costume for Tromie, the Nuclear Squirrel† from *Class of Nuke 'Em High* parts 2 and 3 were precariously balanced like gar-

---

* The explanation for this optical illusion is that there were actually three different poster designs for *Troma's War*. The first poster bore the movie's original title, *Club War*. Apparently we thought this was such a brilliant title that we would have to use it eventually and kept the posters just in case. The second poster, a satire of the *Platoon*‡ poster was deemed "too cartoony" by theater owners who refused to hang the posters in the front of their cinemas. The final, more traditional poster satisfied theater owners but they didn't have to hang around long anyway because nobody went to see *Troma's War* when it was originally released. You may be thinking, "Gee, Lloyd, that's a shame but what the fuck does that have to do with me and my movie?" Well, when we get to the chapter on promotion and publicity you'll see exactly what it has to do with your movie and you'll thank the good lord up above that you spent the time and energy reading this footnote.

† We'd tried to make Tromie a live character at events and conventions, like Toxie, Sgt. Kabuki-man NYPD, and Killer Condom Man. But after a couple dozen interns passed out from dehy-

goyles atop unmarked boxes. I turned and nearly tripped over a pair of metal film cans, coming ominously close to landing face-first in a mound of petrified rat shit. I examined the can and was not in the least bit surprised to discover that I had almost fallen over the work print of *Big Gus, What's the Fuss* (1973). My worst movie, arguably the most heinous atrocity ever committed to celluloid, continued to find novel ways to injure and humiliate me. It was the only thing I'd found down here that I thought deserved to be locked away and left to collect dust and feces in this dank basement.

As I cast my eyes over the collected Tromabilia, all of a sudden I knew with the certainty usually reserved for either the very pious or the very insane that spread out before me was what my thirty plus years in movies boiled down to. All the hours spent on set, all the disappointment when something didn't go according to plan, all the elation when something turned out better than hoped, all the money-men I'd had to fellate . . . and what had it got me? An extremely limber throat and tongue and a basement full of neglected crap that was slowly being transformed into a public toilet for every sewer rat in Manhattan.

I bent over with my shovel in one hand and an open garbage bag in the other. As I attacked the rat-crap with my shovel, the ancient turds exploded into thick, heavy clouds of dust. The dust immediately coated my ears, eyes, nose, and throat.* I kept shoveling and, squinting through the putrid dust, saw a huge rat lazily walk past and, I swear to god, salute me with a Bronx cheer, just like the mouse in *Tom & Jerry* cartoons. *Tom & Jerry* had been a huge influence on the Troma style of

---

dration and mild heat stroke, people started referring to Tromie as a deathtrap instead of a costume. If not for this minor setback, Tromie would have continued to be a valuable part of the Troma Team instead of the source of an amusing but false urban legend revolving around an intern who died a spectacularly gruesome death during a Troma parade.

‡ Editor's Note: *Platoon*'s director, Oliver Stone, worked on Kaufman's *Battle of Love's Return* and *Sugar Cookies* before going on to make good movies.

* A personal note to the medical examiner who performs my autopsy. The black crud lining my lungs isn't tobacco or asbestos. It's microscopic particles of rat shit. That ought to save you some time.

violence. The debt I owed to this thing's animated counterpart didn't prevent me from taking a swing at it with my shovel. The rat seemed unconcerned by this attack and, after staring at me for a few uncomfortable seconds, disappeared between some boxes.

As I returned to my shoveling, I wondered, when all is said and done, why the fuck was I even bothering to make movies? It's certainly no way to make money. Harvey Weinstein and I started in the business at around the same time. Now people flocked to him like flies to shit, while I was actually down in the shit. It was getting to be virtually impossible to even get our movies seen. The vast majority of movie theaters in the U.S. are now once again owned and operated by the major studios, who seem intent on forcing the same Tom Cruise blockbuster onto every screen and driving the theaters into bankruptcy (both moral and financial). Smaller mom-and-pop video stores were being pushed out of business by Blockbuster and one or two other giant chains that impose an economic blacklist on Troma and other independent studios.* And every day seemed to bring news of another independent studio going out of business. The "lucky" ones merely lost their independence and were absorbed into a gigantic, devil-worshipping international megaconglomerate. More often than not it seemed the only way to make money at this was to sell out your ideals and give up your independence. But it's not always about money. The late, lamented, legendary Sam Arkoff, cofounder of American International Pictures, once told me that the biggest mistake of his life was selling AIP to Filmways (which was later bought by Orion which later went through a spectacular bankruptcy that has fucked up the distribution of hundreds, if not thousands, of movies).

If it's not money, I thought to myself as a rat the approximate size and color of a kielbasa ran across my feet, leaving a trail of fragrant droppings, *maybe I'm doing it for the respect and admiration of others.* Yeah, sure. I

---

* EDITOR'S NOTE: Clearly this is Mr. Kaufman's opinion. While it is true that a buyer at a major video chain had verbally committed to stocking *Terror Firmer* and her order was subsequently mysteriously cancelled with no explanation, there is no evidence to support a "blacklist."

couldn't even command enough respect to get my own goddamn employees to do the scut work around the office. Maybe I'd vomited green Bromo Seltzer on camera once too often to be a truly effective leader.

Scraping the shit off my feet, I saw another large, immobile rat on the floor next to me. The rats knew they had control, so it wasn't at all unusual that it wasn't moving. But this one looked far too comfortable. It was either completely at home or dead. "Lucky fucker," I muttered and enviously kicked it to make sure it was dead. As my foot hit fur, the rat burst open. Hundreds of spiders erupted from their corpse-nest, swarming every which way. Confronted with a plague of rat-born spiders, I did what any pillar of manly American fortitude would do. I squealed like a prison bitch and slammed my shovel down again and again, hitting the floor, my feet, the dead rat, the walls, and, I'm fairly sure, at least a couple of spiders.

Exhausted, I leaned against the wall. A particularly brave rat, unphased by my spectacular display of martial arts, peered at me from atop a box of SGT. KABUKIMAN FOR PRESIDENT pins from 1992. I recognized the contemptuous look in its eyes from dozens of surly production assistants over the years. Whatever my reasons may have been for starting to make movies, the cold reality was that this is what it boiled down to. There was no glamour when I made movies. There was nothing but hard work to be assigned and, more often than not, returned to my lap. This was the world of filmmaking that I knew. No limousines. No craft services. No imported bottled water to wash the starlet's hair. Just a neverending basement full of shitty, moldy rot that had to be cleaned out. Why the fuck was I doing all this?

DISSOLVE TO:*

Thirty-six hours later in the magnificent town of Sitges on the Mediterranean coast of Spain and I have my answer. Every October,

---

* Dissolve (verb): 1. The most common reaction of human flesh to toxic chemicals, as evidenced in *Class of Nuke 'Em High*. 2. In film, a transition between scenes where one shot fades

Lloyd Kaufman receives a "lifetime achievement" award in *Citizen Toxie*. This scene was cut from the film because it was just too damn unbelievable—even for Troma.
(Doug Sakmann)

the city hosts the Sitges Film Festival, one of the most comprehensive and prestigious horror, science fiction, and fantasy film festivals in the world. I've been fortunate enough to have movies I've directed invited here several times. In 1996, Sitges showed *Tromeo & Juliet* and in 1999, we brought *Terror Firmer** here. This year, they were hosting the world premiere of *Citizen Toxie*. Not only had the festival flown me over for the occasion, they'd also brought along Heidi Sjursen, who plays Toxie's blind wife Sarah in the movie, and Gabe Friedman, the movie's editor. Now it's one thing for a film festival to fly in the director or the star of a movie. But if you think it's commonplace for a festival to fly

---

away while the next fades in simultaneously. Commonly used to demonstrate the passage of time or the editor's love of clichés.

* EDITOR'S NOTE: Readers interested in what sort of person this Lloyd Kaufman is are advised to watch his "performance" as blind director Larry Benjamin in *Terror Firmer*. While this is not the first time he has appeared on film, Kaufman's previous directors (who have included John G. Avildsen in *Rocky* and Trey Parker in *Orgazmo*) are usually smart enough to severely limit his screen time and number of lines. The director of *Terror Firmer* was obviously an idiot.

in a movie's editor, guess again. Editors are notoriously pale, shaky guys who rarely see the light of day. The inhuman amount of hours they spend locked away watching the same footage over and over again causes them to have social graces that are rudimentary at best and a bizarre, unpleasant omnisexuality that makes it very difficult for them to see other people in the flesh without becoming visibly and embarrassingly aroused.

Citizen Toxie was playing in an amazing 3,000-seat cinema that ranks among the best I've ever seen. I took the stage to introduce the film and immediately remembered why the fuck I bothered making movies. Here was an auditorium full of enthusiastic men and Gynos* who were genuinely *excited* to see a movie. Even more astonishingly, they were excited to see a *Troma* movie. Here were people applauding and chanting "Troma! Troma! Troma!"† Here were fans dressed as Toxie, Kabukiman, and the Tromettes. Not because anyone asked them to, but because they wanted to. One group of fans had started their own website, Villacabras.com, and arrived at Sitges with their own Toxified bottles of champagne called Tromanpagne. Another Spanish fan club, Fester, had made their own Troma T-shirts using images and lines from the script of *Terror Firmer*. I was gratified and amazed at all the effort the fans had put into showing us their appreciation. Heidi and Gabe were completely overwhelmed. They had no idea Troma had such a far reach.‡

I was inspired not only by my renewed connection with the audience but by the other films screening at the festival. Finally, audiences

---

* With movies like *Bloodsucking Freaks* and *Terror Firmer*, Troma is obviously incredibly politically correct, so in Tromaville we use the word "Gynos" to describe non-male gendered peoples. The term "woman" is unacceptable because it contains the root "man" and "girl" is as demeaning in its own way, so we use the term "Gyno-Americans." Since I was in Spain at the time, here I use the universal "Gyno."

† Or possibly "Toga! Toga! Toga!" Either way, at least they were clapping.

‡ Gabe was also overwhelmed by the unusual sensation of having women hit on him. It was a very special time to be with the boy.

Guerilla marketing at the Cannes Film Festival whilst "campaign for shaved armpits" reaches climax (*From left to right*). Terry Firmer (super Tromette), Sgt. Kabukiman NYPD, Heidi Sjursten (star of *Citizen Toxie*), Troma volunteer, Toxie, and Troma head of production Doug Sakmann. Unfortunately this picture was taken two weeks after the Cannes Film Festival in Newark, New Jersey.

were given the opportunity to see amazing, brilliant movies they'd never have a chance to see through ordinary channels. At Sitges, it was possible to go on a three-day movie binge, watching ten films a day with each one better than the last. Movies like Geoffrey Wright's uncut version of *Cherry Falls*, Santiago Segura's *Torrente*, Shinya Tsukamoto's *Tokyo Fist*, and Alex de la Iglesia's *Common Wealth*. Seeing these masterpieces in such incredible surroundings with audiences who appreciated them was as invigorating as seeing the movies in my youth that first inspired me to be a filmmaker.

Finally, I'd found the reason I continued to make movies despite the many, many reasons I could come up with for trading in the whole goddamn thing and trying to do something vaguely productive with my remaining years like becoming an air-conditioner repairman. Days earlier I'd been risking the plague in ankle-deep rat shit, now, here I

Tromettes publicize Troma movies at the Cannes Film Festival. Troma-tic tip to aspiring filmmakers: Tell the Tromettes you are gay and challenge them to "in" you!!! (Tartan Burgess)

was, surrounded by people who appreciated what I'd been doing, enjoying free drinks and pot. And I knew that as long as there were people with a passion for watching movies, I would retain my passion for making them.

Over the past three decades, I've directed, produced, written, shot, and/or distributed hundreds of movies and, believe it or not, not all of them received standing ovations, glowing reviews, and orgasmic audiences at prestigious film festivals. In fact, more than a couple died painful, humiliating, protracted deaths. Some of them deserved it. Some of them, I think, deserved better. None of them, good or bad, were easy to make. If you're looking for a book that will help put you in touch with your inner genius and make only good movies while avoiding the bad, keep on a-lookin' (and if you find one drop me a line at lloyd@troma. com. I can use all the help I can get). What this book *will* help you do is avoid having two days worth of abandoned footage because, for whatever reason, everything fell apart on you at the last minute.

To make your own damn movie, you have to be equal parts dictator and diplomat. You must be both the visionary storyteller addressing the audience at the film festival and the dickhead shoveling rat shit out of the basement because nobody else would and everything would be lost if it didn't get done. You must be both extravagant artist and penny-pinching asshole. It isn't easy, it isn't always fun, and if you're looking to get rich quick by making the next *Blair Witch Project* then you'd might just as well stop right now. The odds are stacked heavily against you ever making a dime directly off your masterpiece.

So, knowing full well that the road you're about to embark on is long and painful, will probably require you to be publicly humiliated on more than one occasion, and will require your total obsessive attention for more than a year, is it worth doing? Absolutely. Writers know the satisfaction of completing a story. Musicians know the satisfaction of completing a song. But filmmakers know that they've brought people together and created something bigger than any of them could have done individually. They have orchestrated an experience that no one involved will ever forget.* They have created something that will have a life long after they're gone. They have made some art under circumstances that would send most people into therapy for the next five years. In the end, it isn't about money ('cause it probably isn't out there) or fame ('cause some of the people who do end up knowing your name or face will hate your fucking guts) or free dope and booze at film festivals ('cause . . . well, maybe it *is* about the free dope and booze a little bit). It's about capturing a vision and sharing it with those willing to watch. Sooner or later, your vision *will* connect with someone and when that happens, it makes all the rodent fecal matter you've gone through worthwhile. Even the time you had to take a diarrhetic shit in a paper bag.†

THE MAN IS INSANE, BUT IN A GOOD WAY
Trent Haaga

Inspiring chapter, isn't it? One of Lloyd's greatest strengths as a person and a filmmaker is the ability to make something as horrendous as killing rats with a shovel seem noble, if not down-

---

* Of course, Hitler did precisely the same thing.
† Don't worry. We'll get to that part soon enough.

right romantic. This is how he managed to lure me into two feature films, a television series, countless hours of office work in
the "mighty temple" that is the Troma building, and, finally, the
book you hold in your hands.

My name is Trent Haaga and I'm a Troma-holic.

As I said, Lloyd is a truly inspiring guy. Sure, I question his
mental stability. But he's inspiring nonetheless. When Lloyd
came to me with the proposal for this book, his dreaded two-
page contract in hand, I almost declined to be involved. A book
is a bigger project than a movie in some ways and, as usual, there
wasn't much money involved. But then I harkened back to my
humble beginnings as the lone weirdo, skateboarding, punk-rock
movie freak in my dismally small midwestern hometown. Troma
films were an inspiration for me to get the hell out of bumfuck.
Lloyd was living proof that you could thrive in the cutthroat
business of filmmaking without having to sell your soul or compromise your artistic integrity. He was living proof that you
could still love *Mad* magazine and punk rock music, could still
keep your middle finger firmly extended toward the establish-
ment while doing what you loved. Ten years ago, I was the guy
who would've rushed right out and bought this book* and it
would've inspired me to go out there and Make My Own Damn
Movie. How could I say "no" to being involved?

In my long four-year career with Troma (I know four years
doesn't sound like much, but one Troma year is equal to approximately 10 human years—which makes Lloyd over 250 years old,
for those of you counting) I have endured verbal, mental, and
financial abuse. I've been spit, shit, and puked upon and ass-
raped more than once. I've narrowly avoided prison time and

---

* And, knowing Troma, I will probably *still* have to rush out and buy a copy of this book.

severe beatings at the hands of angry crew members and, most horrifically, I've had my crotch fondled by Lloyd Kaufman (see *Troma's Edge TV*, episode #5). All of these experiences became my film school and, although I'm not rich by any means, I've managed to eke out a living as a writer, producer, and an actor due to the things that Lloyd Kaufman taught me. I'm living proof that you, the reader, can follow the steps in this tome and go from a how-to book reading film enthusiast to a bona fide filmmaker. It's going to take a lot of hard work, cajoling, begging, and debasement . . . but it can be done.

All right. Enough with the Lloyd worship. I've acted for the guy, I've produced for him, I've written for him, I've hosted a TV series for him, and I've been his office bitch. I'm not just here to champion the guy. Sure, he's a genius, but he's also one of the hardest employers to work for I've ever had. And he also tends to have selective memory when it comes to some subjects. I'll be popping in periodically to remind him of some stories and to give you some insight on what it's like to make your own damn movie when you're not the director, but part of the crew.

CHAPTER 2

Raising Money or Mastering the Ancient Art of Fellatio

I've always received a fairly large number of calls, letters, and face-to-face encounters from fans that border on the erotic and homoerotic, but ever since e-mail took off, that number has skyrocketed. After all, my e-mail address is posted all over the internet. And even if it wasn't, it doesn't take a genius to figure out lloyd@troma.com. Hell, it's already been in this book twice and this is only page 14. Needless to say, I'm probably the most accessible head of any film studio. Much to my employees' dismay, it's virtually impossible to not get ahold of me.

Of all the e-mails I get, most of them are along the following lines:

hey asshole,

just wanted to remid [*sic*] you that you are not fooling anyone. you are a hack and your movies are stupid and boring. you've got nerve to call youself an artist you parasite. i hope you live long enough to see payback for all the people you've ripped off.

sincerely,

amy taubin*

---

* Amy Taubin is a highly respected film critic for the *Village Voice* and while I can't say for certain that this e-mail came from *the* Amy Taubin, it certainly sounds like something she'd say.

Of the nonthreatening e-mails I get, most of them fall into the next category:

Dear Mr. Asshole,*

I've been watching Troma movies since I was dick high. I love them all. I have an idea for a really kick-ass movie that I want to make but don't know how to start. How do I raise money for my kick-ass movie?

I get the feeling that most of the people who ask this question are hoping on some level that when I respond, I'll send them the number and password to a secret Swiss bank account that exists solely for independent filmmakers. The fact is, there is no right or wrong answer to this question. Everyone struggles with this problem and everyone finds his or her own way around it.

Sam Raimi shot an 8mm short for no money and took it around to local people he figured had money (mainly dentists† and doctors) to get the money to make *Evil Dead*. Chad Ferrin, director of the Troma movie *Unspeakable*, sold his house to make his movie. Robert Rodriguez subjected himself to paid medical experiments to finance *El Mariachi*. These three guys risked humiliation, homelessness, and hideously deforming side effects to raise money for their projects. Each of them decided in the end that getting their stories told on film was the most important thing in their lives. You will need that conviction every step of the way. A lot of people will only tell you about the constraints under which they are placed by a low budget. I, on the

---

* Note the respect with which the true Troma fan treats me.

† I have always found dentists to be an excellent source of investment money, particularly for movies that are somewhat Tromatic. I'm not sure why this is, although if you spent your days staring into the gaping, smelly mouths of rich old ladies, you'd probably be pretty eager to invest in a movie featuring big-breasted women wearing very small clothes. Another benefit for me is that the dentist's life experience dealing with gum disease, impacted wisdom teeth, and swollen, infected canker sores has prepared them well for whatever disgusting and repulsive thing I might want to put on screen.

other hand, have always found it liberating. The more money people put into a film, the more concerned they become over what happens to it. Unless your last name is Spielberg, Lucas, or possibly Hitler, you will find that the more money you have to work with, the less creative freedom you have.

Unfortunately, you are going to need some money in order to make your movie. The easiest way to get money is to come from a wealthy family. No matter how disapproving they may claim to be of your project, your parents are a much surer bet for some easy cash than a complete stranger. Assuming that you either do not have or are not on good terms with some fantastically rich relative, you will need to find some other way into people's wallets. The most common of these is convincing people with money that your project is a worthwhile investment.*

The road to getting investors is a tricky one. There are a lot of complicated legal issues involved that you've probably never even thought about, particularly if you're a young person who hasn't had to deal very much with shit like taxes. If you think the Nasdaq is a creature from the cantina scene in *Star Wars*, you might want to do some financial research before heading out to raise funds.

When Michael Herz and I raise money for a movie, we form what's known as a limited partnership. A limited partnership provides two big advantages for our investors. First of all, they receive certain tax advantages in the likely event that the movie loses money. The investors are also protected legally under a limited partnership. Basically, they themselves are not personally liable for what is done with their money under the terms of that partnership. So, if somebody gets maimed or killed on the set, the investors are not responsible and can't be held accountable (dammit!). We are. It's our fault

---

* Investment (noun): A valuable asset (usu. money) that is exchanged in expectation of a projected profit at a later date. Many young filmmakers mistake an "investment" for a "gift."

and if anybody gets sued, it's going to be me, Michael, and whatever dumbfuck was directly responsible for causing something to go wrong.

Limited partnerships are among the most straightforward methods of legitimate entrepreneurial endeavors.* But the laws governing them vary from state to state. In New York, for instance, you are only allowed to solicit money from a handful of people (I believe it's fewer than twenty), all of whom are supposed to know each other. You are not allowed to call every name in the phone book and ask for $5 from each of them.† Still, a limited partnership is the least expensive legitimate way to accept under a million dollars. Just be careful and familiarize yourself with your state's laws. The forms for limited partnerships are easy to come by: A quick internet search can help locate them. New York's Practicing Law Institute (PLI) publishes these forms and others in massive books that may also come in handy later in production as a heavy object to drop on your head when you're looking for a way to commit suicide that will look like an accident. I would reprint the New York form here but it runs thirty pages. My contract with St. Martin's limits me to about 300 pages and my editor believes that reprinting the form would be even more boring than whatever I could come up with.‡

Once you have an investor on board, you can use that person to find others. One dentist with money to invest in an independent film probably knows like-minded people (like dental hygienists, floss manufacturers, etc.) who might also be interested. We often throw a cock-

---

*There are, of course, many illegitimate methods which are considerably more straightforward, like accepting a bag of nonsequentially numbered bills that you just happen to find in locker number 1802 at Grand Central Station. For more information on these methods, I suggest researching the Mafia or contacting your local congressman.

† If you run into trouble on this score, simply say you were soliciting sex, not money. The State of New York actually encourages people to phone up complete strangers and solicit sexual favors.

‡ EDITOR'S NOTE: I may be forced to reconsider my position on that point.

tail party at the home of our primary investor.* That person would invite a bunch of likely prospects, we'd trot out our little dog-and-pony show and wow them with our pitch, and maybe by the end of the night we'd have one or two more investors signed on. As a bonus, you might get to hear some pretty gruesome stories about painful dental procedures that can inspire another movie.

Besides dentists and oral surgeons, some filmmakers will enter into partnerships with their cast and crew. This might be a swell idea if you're working with a group of spoiled rich kids who honestly don't care what happens to their parents' money, but it does have some significant drawbacks. For one thing, you're going to be working closely with these people. If they think they've invested more in your movie than you have simply by virtue of their monetary involvement, you could run the risk of losing control on the set. In my own experience, I know full well that most of the people I'm working with are going to hate my guts by the end of production. You don't want your investors angry with you before you've even finished principal photography. The last thing I need is to be harassed over money by some incensed key grip.†

Forming a limited partnership will also be the first time in the filmmaking process that you will need to consult with a lawyer (although it will not be the last). You'll need the lawyer to go over the forms and contracts to make sure everything's on the up and up. The one thing you *don't* need at this point is an entertainment lawyer. All you're doing right now is raising money and forming a limited partnership, so your family lawyer is more than qualified to handle this. This isn't rocket science and your chances of running across an honest lawyer are greatly increased if you look outside the entertainment industry.‡

---

* It's a good idea to clear the party with the investor first, though. Don't just break into their house and raid their liquor cabinet.
† Key Grip (noun): The film set's official compulsive masturbator. Don't worry. Every movie has dozens of unofficial "key grips" as well.
‡ Eric Przybisiki, Troma's director of legal affairs, has just offered me $50 to delete this sentence. I'm not going to do it because he works for Troma and, therefore, doesn't have $50.

Honesty may be a strange thing to discuss in a book devoted to filmmaking but I believe it's vitally important. While it may be a lot of fun to consider bilking the old war widow down the street out of her last $10,000, doing so can actually land you in jail. While it's certainly possible to create great art in prison, it's uncommonly difficult to make a great movie in prison. So be honest with your potential investors. One of the reasons Troma has survived for so long may be that Michael and I have always been completely forthcoming with our investors. We advise them that investing in any movie is risky and investing in a low-budget Troma movie is particularly risky.* We tell them there's every possibility they might not see any return on their investment and they should only invest money they can afford to lose. Tell your investors right up front that if they're looking for an investment that has a better-than-average chance of producing a return, they're probably better off investing in General Electric. They're more likely to get their money back and they get the satisfaction of knowing they've contributed to the pollution of the Hudson River.

Of course, you might decide to forgo the entire process of looking for investors by applying for a grant. That's certainly a viable option and there are plenty of places to turn, from the National Endowment for the Arts to all manner of corporate foundations and fellowships. Depending on the movie you want to make, however, this option might not work. If you've got your heart set on making a movie about sex with farm animals and you've applied for a grant from the National Donkey Fucking Foundation, you might have no trouble at all. But if you've applied to the Endowment for the Humanities with the same script, you'll probably run into trouble.

Early in my career, I did a free budget for Barbara Kopple's pro-

* Of course, Herz and I are pathetic failures, as evidenced by my paltry advance for this book. So you should guarantee your investors a 2,000 percent return on their investment within two weeks of the film's release. Fuck the war widows! Lie your ass off! In the words of Max Bialystock in *The Producers*, get that money!

ducer that was to be included with their application for a grant.* She told me there was no real secret to getting these grants. She told the various foundations what they wanted to hear and it didn't hurt that what they wanted to hear was coming from the lips of a black woman. Now even though I am a black woman, I'm unable to do that. I don't have the patience (or the cynicism) to please anybody. And which fucking foundation am I going to ask for a grant from, the National Association for the Advancement of Fart Jokes? But if this method suits you, then by all means pursue it. You'd have to be some kind of idiot to turn down free money.

"All right, Kaufman," you say. "So I've gone to every dentist in town and I'm being totally honest with everyone about all the risks involved in investing in my kick-ass movie. All I'm getting is a whole bunch of thanks but no thanks. Sure, I'm going to heaven but in the meantime my movie's going nowhere! Thanks a whole fuck-of-a-lot for the advice, shithead!"

If this is the case, now's the time to appeal to their benevolence. When you're talking about making a movie or any sort of artistic expression, a lot of philanthropic individuals may not necessarily think in terms of financial profit. They'll feel like they're part of the creative process, allowing a young genius (that's you) to blossom under their benevolent patronage. Granted, this technique works a lot better if you live anywhere in the world other than New York or L.A., where everybody and their pedigreed schnauzer has lost money investing in a movie. But if you live in Pocatello, Idaho or someplace, it's definitely worth a try. Besides, if you strike it big and start collecting awards and big paychecks, then they'll be able to say they were in on the ground floor and they knew you back when you were serving dip cones at the

---

* Barbara Kopple is the director of such classic documentaries as *Harlan County U.S.A.* and *American Dream* and if you didn't know that, stop reading this right now and go rent those movies immediately.

Tastee-Freeze and telling everybody who'd listen about your brilliant idea for a kick-ass movie.

It's very possible that you may have missed the fact that at the tail end of that run-on sentence, I buried the only useful tip that anyone will ever give you about raising money for an independent film. For those of you who are just flipping through the pages, convinced that there will not be a single piece of worthwhile advice in this book, here it is again.

TELL EVERYBODY WHO WILL LISTEN ABOUT YOUR BRILLIANT IDEA FOR A KICK-ASS MOVIE.

Unless you have amazing psychic abilities, there is no way you can predict who is going to come through for you and give you the money you so desperately need.* When I was trying to secure financing for *The Battle of Love's Return*, I went through all the usual channels, pitching the movie to every well-off person I could think of. I was still coming up short. I was beginning to think my movie would never get made.

One evening, after a particularly fruitless day of attempting to squeeze blood from stones,† I went to the movies.‡ As I left the theater, I ran into Garrard Glenn, a classmate of mine from Yale. Garrard asked me what I'd been up to lately, as people do when they unexpectedly run into people they know and are forced to be polite.

At this point, I had a decision to make. Do I (a) assume Garrard's

---

* If you do have amazing psychic abilities, you shouldn't be wasting your time on something as frivolous as making movies. There's real problems in the world, you fucker! And you could make a difference if you weren't such a shallow, self-centered cocksucker who only wants to use their freakish gifts to entertain people! You goddamn son of a bitch! I hate you!!!

† Speaking of stones, I was later able to talk my childhood friend Oliver Stone into helping me raise money for *Sugar Cookies*, the only X-rated film in history to ever lose money. This may explain why he is no longer my friend.

‡ Have you ever noticed that when you tell stories that revolve around going to the movies, there's always some asshole whose only question is, "What did you see?" While I don't remember exactly what movie I saw that night, I suspect it was *L'Avventura* by Michelangelo ~~Andiono~~ . . . ~~Antonio~~ . . . ~~Antaliono~~ . . . I saw *The Erotic Adventures of Back-Door Sally*, okay?

just being polite and give the standard, noncommittal "not much" answer that most people are looking for when they ask this question? Or, (b) should I tell Garrard exactly what I'm doing, which is running around making appointments with dentists, trying to get money for my kick-ass movie? Figuring that at worst, Garrard will get a glazed look on his face and regret coming over to say hello, I plunged into my spiel about *The Battle of Love's Return*.

To my surprise, Garrard's eyes did not glaze over. Instead, he became genuinely interested and told me that he had wanted to become involved in a movie project. This was news to me. I wasn't even aware that Garrard liked going to the movies, much less that he wanted to work on one. As it happened, Garrard not only became a producer on *The Battle of Love's Return*, he raised money for my next movie, *Sugar Cookies*, as well. Pretty good for a chance meeting with somebody who would've been one of the last people I'd have thought to approach for backing.

Sooner or later, you will have to ask yourself how badly you really want to make your movie. You run the risk of losing friends, alienating complete strangers, and humiliating yourself in ways you never imagined possible . . . not to mention the very real possibility that if things don't work out, you may never have a painless visit to the dentist ever again. But the big question is always how big a schmuck are you willing to look like in order to get your movie made? Is there a line that you won't cross? 'Cause if there isn't, there's plenty of money to be made in the sex industry and you might be able to finance your movie a lot quicker. Back in the '60s, some of my father's friends would hire graduate students from a prominent Upper West Side university in New York. These girls said they were financing their college education, making around $200 a night, roughly the equivalent of $2,000 these days. That's a pretty good gig by anybody's standards. Before you dismiss the idea completely, just think how many people in Hollywood have sucked and fucked their way to the top. If it's good enough for them, maybe it's good enough for you.*

But while you're compromising your dignity and maybe your morals in your quest for money, don't be a completely selfish asshole. Don't risk more than you can honestly afford to lose. If you're married and/or raising a family, your movie probably isn't worth losing your house and security over. Sometimes it's possible to borrow money directly from a bank and, if you're extraordinarily lucky and catch them on the upside of a boom/bust cycle, they may take a gamble and accept your film as collateral. But more often, banks want something of bona fide tangible value, like your house or your scrotum.

It isn't just banks that threaten the homes and welfare of independent filmmakers. Many gamble it all on something called a negative pick-up deal. Usually what happens here is that the filmmaker enters a deal with a distributor, gets a small advance and the promise of participation in the projected future profits. It's extremely rare for this kind of deal to bear fruit.

In the late 1980s, my brother Charles wrote and directed a brilliant movie called *Jakarta* starring Chris Noth.† Troma coproduced the movie with an Indonesian guy and, thanks to my brother's talent,‡ the movie turned out quite well. MCEG paid Troma two million bucks

---

* I'd like to take this opportunity to deny the rumor that I myself tried sucking dick for nickels down at the bus depot back in the early days but failed because my lips and mouth were not as soft and sweet as my potential benefactors were used to. However, the person who prevented me from entering a life of bargain blow jobs turned out to be a dentist. He helped save me from the horrors of gingivitis and even pointed me toward a couple potential investors for *The Battle of Love's Return*.

† Noth had already appeared in a movie I'd directed called *Waitress!* Not long after *Jakarta*, he would end his promising career in Troma movies by starring on such TV shows as *Law & Order* and *Sex & the City*.

‡ Not to mention my sister Susan, who was the movie's art director. See the next chapter, Hiring Your Crew, for more information on saving money by exploiting . . . I mean, hiring your family.

for the international distribution rights to *Jakarta*, leaving us to distribute it throughout North America.

The Indonesian coproducer was dazzled by the money and figured all he had to do was throw together a flick with a couple of car crashes and he'd make two million bucks. Who needs Charles Kaufman and who needs Troma? So he mortgages his house to make another movie and enters into a negative pick-up deal with MCEG. He hires *Jakarta*'s cameraman to direct the new movie and ends up, perhaps not too surprisingly, with a piece of shit. MCEG takes a look at the awful new movie and tells him to go fuck himself, they had their fingers crossed on the deal and they're not going to pay him.

At this point, the Indonesian coproducer calls us in tears, crying that he's on the verge of losing his house and that MCEG refuses to honor their deal. Because we're nice (meaning stupid) guys, we decided to help bail him out. We signed over the U.S. distribution rights to *Jakarta* and got stuck with a shitty Indonesian movie called *The Stabilizer* that we have never made a dime from. And while this guy was able to keep his house, my brother's movie, and arguably his career, got royally fucked and *Jakarta* has never been properly seen in this country.

To add insult to injury in all this, the year after this whole debacle, MCEG threw a lavish party in Cannes for *Jakarta*. None of us were invited to this shindig. The good news is that MCEG went bankrupt not too long afterwards and my brother Charles has since become a legend in San Diego with his bakery, the Bread & Cie. Next time you're in San Diego, stop in and pick up an olive loaf.

"All right, pal," you now interject. "I'm toeing the line, being honest and straightforward with people, and even found a few willing to cough up some dough. I've sold all the bodily fluids I have access to and turned a few tricks, but I'm still short by several grand. What the fuck am I supposed to do now, big shot?"

At this stage of the fund-raising process, it might be a good idea to come to terms with the cold reality that you might not be able to raise all the money you wanted to. The good news is you can always cut corners. Take a look at your script and see what you could possibly live without.

Also, keep in mind that making a movie is a *loooong* process. The only thing you really have to worry about at this stage is raising enough money to get your movie shot. Post-production will take several months and you can always return to raising money at that point. And don't forget the importance of bargaining. You may be able to get vendors and labs to give you their services at cost in exchange for a credit. If worse comes to worst, you can always go into debt to the lab. There are worse things than having a lab take possession of your film for a while.

If you play your cards right, however, it shouldn't come to that. There are also distributors like Troma who can provide you with finishing funds. We've done that for a number of movies, including *Decampitated* and *Sucker: The Vampire.** The important thing to remember is that once a movie is shot, it usually ends up getting finished one way or another. If you can raise every dime for every stage of the film this early in the game, great! Congratulations and more power to you. But if you can't (and it's very very possible that you can't), don't let it stop you. Focus on getting your movie shot. The rest will work itself out in time.

I could drag this chapter out with boring stories about how one person or another got money for their movie but it wouldn't be particularly interesting or instructive. What worked for one person isn't necessarily going to work for you. It really isn't relevant to you how I raised the money for *Citizen Toxie* because odds are pretty good that your first movie isn't going to be the third sequel to a well-known superhero movie. Just remember the following points:

---

* *Sucker* was written and directed by Hans Rodionoff, who was able to use his completed, distributed film as a calling card and has gone on to write the screenplay for the movie version of Marvel Comics' *Man-Thing*. There is little to no truth to the rumor that Hans's own man-thing had anything to do with Troma distributing his film.

Back in their formative Yale days, Lloyd Kaufman and Michael Herz (with guitar) would sing Yale anthem "Boola Boola" before "script conferences." (Doug Sakmann)

1. Talk to *everyone*. Particularly dentists, orthodontists, and peri-odontists.
2. Sell the things you own that are worth money and you don't really need. Many vital organs come in pairs for this very reason.
3. You can always cut corners. In many ways, that's one of the traits that defines an independent filmmaker.
4. Be nice to your parents. It's much, much easier to save money if you're living at home rent-free.
5. Attempting to double your budget by taking your investors' money to Atlantic City is *not* considered a sound investment.
6. Neither is Las Vegas.

Michael Herz and I learned points five and six the hard way. Fortunately, with the recent proliferation of casinos on Indian reservations, there is new hope. We have developed a system which we are confident will result in a windfall of gigantic proportions. Although our system has not paid off yet, that's no reason it shouldn't work for you. Take a trip out to the country and hit those crap tables! Your investors will thank you later.

Okay, let's pause for a moment to be reasonable. It may appear that the advice in this chapter is somewhat discouraging. While Hollywood's definition of "low budget" is downright criminal, even my definition of "low budget" may seem unattainable for 90 percent of you out there. Sure, $350,000 is low budget compared to $6 million, but what if you live in a place where there are only two dentists in town and they're partners? Where do you come up with that kind of dough when every one of your friends, neighbors, and family members are buying cigarettes with money they got by selling food stamps? If you live in New York City and happen to be walking around (unemployed but still having enough money to go to the movies) the odds are good that you're going to bump into/pass on the street *many* folks who are millionaires. And a small percentage of those millionaires may be able to lead you to other millionaires.

But let's assume there aren't *any* millionaire investors in your hometown. Good movies *can* be made for the cost of a car. New York filmmaker Chris Seaver is only twenty-four years old and has shot about fourteen feature films.* The biggest budget he's worked with was probably $1,000 or so and his films are incredibly entertaining and certainly belie their budgetary restraints.

---

* Chris was also able to get me to act in his film and I put him in touch with Debbie Rochon, who also agreed to appear in Chris' movie for nothing, thus immediately giving his movie some esoteric production value. Ramzi Abed got me and Mark Borchardt from *American Movie* to appear in his movie *The Tunnel* and all it cost him was the price of an airplane ticket from New York to Texas. Ramzi's movie has been accepted to numerous prestigious film festivals, in part because he was able to get Mark and I involved.

At this point it seems as if you'll never make a movie because I've been talking about lawyers and investors and limited liability. Ignore this for now. If you have to make your film for $250, just make it. I've been making movies for more than thirty years now and the budgets I work with are pathetic compared to the budgets of people I started out with like Oliver Stone and John Avildsen. Even so, I realize that $350,000 is still a lot of dough by most people's standards. Do not let one hurdle stop you indefinitely. Move on no matter what the personal cost and get that movie made. Don't be discouraged by money. As you'll see by the rest of this book, getting money will be the least of your worries.

500 Useless Screenwriting Books Boiled Down to One Short Chapter

So you've sold your Mom's soiled panties on eBay and have raised enough cash to shoot your opus. I'll assume that since you're reading this book you've already got some sort of idea. Now all you need to do is slap it onto some paper and thrust it into the hands of the people you're going to be working with. Many screenwriting instruction books will spend a lot of time telling you how to format a script. They'll tell you an improperly formatted script with misspelled words and improper grammar will never get your script past stage one in Hollywood. But you're not in Hollywood, so don't worry youself aboout the misteaks what yo7u made. Hand write your script on a cocktail napkin with crayons if you have to. Just get the damn thing written and make sure it's got a beginning, a middle, and an end.

In a "typical" Hollywood screenplay one page equals one minute of film, thereby making the ideal screenplay length about 90 to 120 pages long. This is only a rule of thumb however, as a single line in a Troma script which says "the hard-bodied lesbians with rivers of passion flowing between their legs make sweet sapphic love" may take up to 32 minutes to portray faithfully on screen. Conversely, a page-long description of an alien environment may become a ½-second shot when we find that the painted macaroni noodles glued onto construction paper can't quite live up to a viewer's scrutiny.

Another "rule of screenwriting" is "to thine own self be true"* (or, in the simplified parlance of today's scriptwriting guides: "write what you know"). This may be not just the greatest advice a struggling screenwriter can receive, it may be the best advice anybody doing anything can receive. You may be asking yourself, "If this is true, Lloyd Kaufman, what the hell do you know about hard-bodied lesbians with rivers of passion flowing between their legs or the true effects of defenestrating yourself into a barrel of toxic waste?" Well, what I didn't know about lesbians and hideously deformed creatures of superhuman size and strength I made up for with my excellent knowledge of being an unloved ninety-eight-pound loser who couldn't get laid to save his life and still lived at home with his mom. The best movies ever made—fantastic and violent and sexy or not—are loved because of their pathos. Great stories come from great characters and great characters are familiar to the viewer in some way. Your screenplay can be as fantastic and "out there" as you want it to be. But relate parts of the movie to your own obsessions and interests. Every movie I've made, no matter how bizarre or outlandish it gets, has been centered in themes and issues that are of real importance to me. Always base at least some of your story on something that you can relate to—the script I'm currently working on is about zombie chickens with a human hero who has a tiny, tiny penis.

Maybe you've got a good concept and want someone else to sweat over things like formatting and having to type every single letter in the damn thing. No problem—"real" screenwriters are often willing to work for nothing or close to nothing in exchange for a credit on a

---

* Coined by popular screenwriter William Shakespeare in his seminal work *101 Surefire Screenplay Ideas*, also known as *Hamlet*.

If you wish to read an amusing caption for this publicity still, please see my first book, ALL I
NEED TO KNOW ABOUT FILMAKING I LEARNED FROM *THE TOXIC AVENGER* (see page 300),
published by Penguin Putnam, available at *www.troma.com* or fine bookstores everywhere.

real, completed movie. I haven't actually put a piece of paper in a
typewriter since . . . well, since you wrote scripts on a typewriter. I
got Trent Haaga, coscreenwriter of *Citizen Toxie,* to do about ten
drafts of the script for a mere $750.00.* While this amount may
seem exorbitant by your particular standards, I got a feature film
script for .002 percent of the film's budget! In other words, as vital as
it is, your screenplay can be one of the least expensive components
of your film.

It's possible you may feel a twinge of guilt over exploiting someone's talent and reducing him or her to a state of indentured servitude. You shouldn't. While you can't offer cold hard cash, you're
giving them a tangible, finished film for which they will have a valuable screen credit and, if they promise to share their flabby, pale

---

* He received some other "good and valuable" consideration, such as my bringing him chocolate bars to the set when he had exceeded eighteen hours of consecutive on-set work.

writer's body, maybe even their name on the poster. And if the writer's talented, she'll be able to parlay her time in the trenches into honest-to-god jobs that actually pay paper money. James Gunn wrote *Tromeo & Juliet* and within two years made the logical progression from writing one of the most obscene films ever made to writing the script for the live-action adaptation of the beloved children's cartoon *Scooby-Doo*.

Should you let the budget that you've attained dictate the grandiosity of the screenplay that you write? Common knowledge says that if you've got a five-dollar budget, you shouldn't attempt to recreate the Roman coliseum games in all of their splendor and glory. But common knowledge is for assholes. I say that if that's the story you *really* want to make, a box of assorted animal crackers can be bought for $.98, monofilament can be pilfered from your Dad's fishing kit, and those little green army men can be easily turned into gladiators with the aid of a handy disposable lighter.*

Many screenwriting books will refer to the screenplay as "a set-in-stone blueprint for your film." Adhering to this definition is one of the biggest mistakes first-time filmmakers make. They think that if something's in the script, they have to shoot it, even if it sucks. In reality, the script should be a mere flow chart of your film, one of the most flexible aspects of the entire production. The script isn't finished until you are literally unable to make any more changes; that's when you've struck your composite print.† If you find a new location, your script should be able to accommodate it. If an actor you've hired really sucks, you can change her lines or eliminate the character altogether. If another actor breaks her leg in the middle of production, you should be able to work it into the story.‡ If you

---

* See the discussion on inexpensive special effects in Chapter 9.

† Composite Print (noun): a print upon which sound and picture are married . . . and can fornicate legally.

‡ Simply add some dialogue: "What happened to your leg?" "I broke it on the way over here."

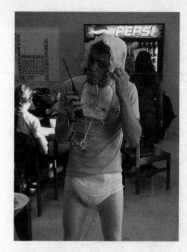

Always efficient, Trent Haaga performs his duties as AD whilst urinating during the filming of *Citizen Toxie*. (Doug Sakmann)

hire Robert Downey Jr. as a well-respected and levelheaded lawyer, make him a well-respected druggie lawyer rather than firing him when he gets caught sucking dick for rock across the street from Troma's Los Angeles office.* Even after you've finished principal photography, keep writing. Lines can be added or changed throughout the editing stage. Don't worry about synching the dialogue up with the actor's lips, toss them in whenever they have their face turned away from the camera. Keep a microphone handy while you're mixing the sound so you can record whenever inspiration hits you. The script should be a living, breathing thing that you can slowly choke the life out of throughout every stage of the filmmaking process.†

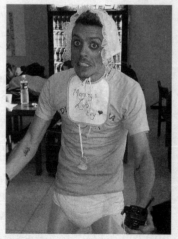

Always efficient, Trent Haaga performs his duties as AD whilst defecating during the filming of *Citizen Toxie*. (Doug Sakmann)

* See chapter 11, "Marketing, Publicity and Distribution" if you're lucky enough for something like this to happen.
† *Terror Firmer* was actually one of the first films ever to be written, shot, and edited entirely in post-production.

Lloyd Kaufman demonstrates the approximate speed of the hand job he expects to receive after the wrap from his obviously delighted AD/writer/actor Trent Haaga.
(Doug Sakmann)

Treating the script like an amorphous blob of Silly Putty® will drive some of your cast and crew insane at first. As the director, you will have to reassure them all that you're not going to go to Movie Jail if you change dialogue between two takes of the exact same shot. This technique is particularly frustrating to assistant directors, whose job it is to try to keep everything organized, under control, and running on schedule. In 1995, after twenty-five years of filmmaking I finally figured out a way around this problem when I made James Gunn assistant director on *Tromeo & Juliet*. I perfected the process a few years later on *Citizen Toxie*, when I made my main writer, Trent Haaga, assistant director and featured actor. This triple duty required him to craft dialogue and run the set while dressed in a diaper and baby bonnet with a pacifier hanging around his neck, getting rid of any last illusions of dignity or respect the other cast and crewmembers may have had for him. The system worked quite well and Trent appears to have made a complete recovery.*

I WAS A TROMA SCREENWRITER
Trent Haaga

Having suffered this particular form of abuse, I can vouch for Lloyd's acumen in this chapter. Writers, especially those writers who haven't had their work adapted yet, are willing to do damn-near anything for damn-near nothing to get a writing "gig." Lloyd called me to the Troma offices one fine day in 1999 . . .

"As you know, Trent, we go into production on *Citizen Toxie* in a month. This one's gonna be our biggest picture yet! Michael has promised me $500,000 for this one! No expense is gonna be spared!"

"Great, Lloyd! I'm ready for this one! I've been looking forward to the fourth installment of your wildly popular series ever since you put out those two shitty sequels!"

"Good, Trent. I knew you were on board! There's only one problem. We don't have a script. I need you to write it."

The sound of a thousand singing angels fills my ears. I'm being asked to write a Toxic Avenger *movie!!!!*

"Lloyd. I'd be honored. I've wanted to do this since I was a kid! You've made my dreams come true!"

---

* TRENT HAAGA RESPONDS: I am working on this book from a bed in a secluded upstate group home. They pipe soothing chamber music in through hidden speakers and I am only allowed to eat with a plastic spoon. They have removed the TV from my room because watching movies upsets me. It's quiet here. Everything stays the same. I am in a happy place.

"Good, Trent. Good. I've got a meeting with the investors in twelve days. I need a script before then."

The singing angels screech to a halt with the sound of a needle flying across a record.

"Twelve days? But, Lloyd, I'm going on my honeymoon tomorrow! That means I've got to have a finished screenplay by the time I get home!"

"I understand, Trent. But I need that script and I need it in twelve days. How hard could it be? I know that it's gotta have a good Toxie and an evil Toxie so that Toxie can fight Sgt. Kabukiman NYPD.* And we need something about the evils of plastic surgery in it. And hit the controversial abortion button. And a Columbine High School slaughter scene. And penile implants. All *you* need to do is make it have a beginning, a middle, and an end. Oh, and figure out how to put that *Kabukiman* car flip from 1989 in there, too.† I paid way too much for that stunt to only use it three times."

"Okay, Lloyd. My wife's got to understand, right? This is a chance of a lifetime, right? I'll bring you a script on time."

Lloyd smiled and whipped out another one of his two-page contracts. I perused it.

"Lloyd?"

"Yes, Trent?"

"This contract is for $750. In three installments of $250. I

* When Penguin-Putnam sent Lloyd on his first book tour, he would invariably be asked by a fan who would win if Toxie and Kabukiman got in a fight. While most people spend hours and hours contemplating whether or not God exists, Lloyd became obsessed with trying to figure out how such a contest of champions could become a reality.
† Astute Troma fans will know that the car flip shot for the movie *Sgt. Kabukiman NYPD* has been used and reused in *Tromeo & Juliet*, *Terror Firmer*, and now, *Citizen Toxie*. As time goes by and the car in the scene gets older, it gets harder and harder to

don't even get the last check until the film is done. I can't even cover my rent with this amount."

"I know and I'm sorry, Trent, but times are tough."

"But you said that no expense was going to be spared and that this was going to be the biggest Troma picture ever."

"Oh, it will be. But all of that money's got to go up on the screen, right?"

I know that there are other writers out there who would've held out for more money or time. But I also knew that Lloyd would simply assign the task to somebody else (or even worse, write it himself) if I didn't do it. Like I said at the beginning of the book, one of Lloyd's greatest skills as a filmmaker and businessman is his ability to make it seem like *you* should be paying *him* for performing just about any odious task in the name of creating art.

My honeymoon scrapbook is now filled with photos of me sitting on the beautiful, pristine Caribbean beaches . . . with my face buried in a notebook. I returned to New York City tanned and not nearly as laid as I wanted to be. But I had the first draft of *Citizen Toxie*. It was a huge script, chock full of interdimensional travel, high school shoot-outs, massive stunts and gore effects, explosions, and penile implant awareness. Sure, it was massive in scope. But this was going to be Troma's biggest picture ever! In Hollywood, my script would have needed a budget of at least $60 million. Any other independent film studio would

---

film original footage that matches this scene. The car we used in *Citizen Toxie* doesn't even come close to resembling the original vehicle. Despite advances in automotive design, Troma will no doubt continue to use the *Kabukiman* car flip for years to come. Troma's commitment to recycling and other environmental issues has earned praise from such tree-humpers . . . I mean, environmental activists as the EPA and the Earth Communications Office (ECO).

have budgeted at least $6 million. But Troma ended up shooting it for $350,000—less than the cost of the original *Toxic Avenger*, which was made twenty years earlier. And we didn't have to sacrifice any of the spectacle or action that was in the script. How'd we manage to perform such a feat? By following the production guidelines in this book.

CHAPTER 3

Meet Your Future Victims!—
Hiring The Crew

The other day I was riding the subway here in New York. The other passengers and I were riding along, minding our own business, when the connecting door between cars slammed open and in rolled a ragged-looking homeless guy* with no legs.

In true New York fashion, the guy rolled himself to the middle of the car and, in a loud, clear voice, called out, "Ladies and gentlemen! I apologize for interrupting your pleasant ride but a minute of your time is all I ask. I want to work but I can't. Biology and the prejudices of others have conspired to keep me from realizing my full potential. Won't you take a moment please, look inside your heart and help someone less fortunate than yourselves? If you can't spare any money, maybe you can spare some food. If you can't spare some food, God bless you just the same. Thank you for your time!"

Having delivered his speech (and very well, I might add . . . he'd obviously rehearsed many times before), the homeless guy rolled from person to person, occasionally picking up some money, occasionally

---

* I don't actually know for certain whether this guy was homeless or not. It would be more accurate to just call him a beggar but that makes it sound like I was strolling through Whitechapel on the trail of the Ripper.

some extra food from somebody's lunch, occasionally just being ignored. As he passed me, taking with him a buck and my sincere thanks for a truly award-worthy performance, it occurred to me that that guy is me. And you. And any other low-budget independent film-maker trying to get something for nothing. We are the destitute of the film world, rolling through crowds, trying every way imaginable to get people to take pity on us and lend a hand.

Now I don't usually like to pass myself off as an expert on any-thing. There's always somebody to challenge your claim and I simply don't have the patience, energy or hubris* to worry about such things. However, there is one aspect of filmmaking that I firmly believe I am as well-versed in as anyone and that's hiring a crew. Not only am I able to get people to work dirt cheap, but I have to do it all the time. Most filmmakers develop relationships with key crewmembers over the course of their careers, forming a production team that works together over and over again. In my case, by the end of principal photography, most of the crew is so pissed off at me they never want to see me again. Consequently, I find myself hiring a crew from scratch on practically every movie I make.†

The first-time filmmaker tends to have one of two attitudes toward hiring a crew, neither of which is entirely correct. Some people will think it's a daunting task tantamount to assembling an army from scratch. Others won't be daunted nearly enough, thinking all they need to do is get their buddy Scooter to borrow his Uncle Jeff's used cam-corder from 1988 and start shooting. It is certainly possible to capture sound and image on videotape this way and create something that

---

* What I lack in hubris, I more than make up in hummus.

† EDITOR'S NOTE: Kaufman has been clinically diagnosed as suffering from paranoid schizo-phrenia and firmly believes that everyone who deals with him eventually grows to despise him. The truth is that Kaufman continues to work with many members of the same production team film after film, including director of photography Brendan Flynt, editor Gabe Friedman, and therapist Dr. Herschell Bernardi.

technically satisfies the definition of a moving picture. But your audience's cinematic experience will be greatly enhanced if you go to the time, effort and, yes, expense of hiring a small crew.

If you've ever sat through the credits of a film, you've probably wondered what the hell all those people could possibly have had to do with the movie.* Well, about 90 percent of them stand around scratching their asses, smoking cigarettes, and complaining about the food. Even Troma productions have suffered from some of the same bloating. Of course in our case, we're not paying these people exorbitant wages. Mostly these are fans who swore they would give their testicles or uterus (or, if nothing else, the testicles or uterus of someone very dear to them) for the opportunity to work unpaid on a Troma movie. Exactly what illusions they were operating under when they made this oath, I can't be sure. In any event, once they're on the set most of them demonstrate that they're just as good at scratching their ass and smoking cigarettes as any highly-paid studio employee.

In my experience, on a low-budget, independent film, the bigger your crew gets, the less effective they will be and the less control you will have over them. And most people who volunteer to do anything at all for a movie aren't capable of doing much. They're willing to do anything because they've never done anything. They have no skills in any one area, so all they're really good for is moving boxes and maybe driving cars. Don't discount them, though, because you'll need some people like this. Their enthusiasm and energy can compensate for the fact that the closest they've ever been to a movie set is seeing a commercial for the Universal Studios tour.

At first, all of your unpaid volunteer workers will be considered

---

* With me, this usually happens because I've fallen asleep during the main feature and woke up disoriented and confused, thinking perhaps I've died and the names scrolling along the screen are people I knew in life and this is the low-budget version of having your entire life flash before you.

Special effects genius Tim Considine (in sunglasses). The man with the mullet haircut is not holding a special effect. He was, in fact, born with a head on his right arm. Troma is an equal opportunity employer. This man was one of the best grips in the business. He also gave great head . . . as you can see.

Production Assistants (or PAs). With any luck, some of these people will have a modicum of smarts to go along with their excitement. The best of these PAs can be elevated to other positions. Remember to keep your budget low, however. I've promoted exceptionally talented unpaid PAs all the way up to line producer in some cases. Of course, once they stop being a PA, you ought to pay them a little something. You might not want to tell them they've been promoted until the last week or two of shooting.

It may also become necessary for you to limit the number of PAs you take on. A couple dozen are great but a hundred of 'em is just dead weight. On *Citizen Toxie*, we had sixteen people quit in one day. We kept on shooting as if nothing had happened. In fact if anything, we were more efficient after the mass exodus because we had fewer people to move around and keep track of.

The good news is that it's taken twenty-seven years for Troma to build a fan base of eager volunteers willing to attach themselves to our

Here I am at one of my happiest moments during *Toxic Avenger II*. Unfortunately, the happy times ended when we screened *Toxic Avenger II*.

productions for no apparent reason. Odds are you won't have the problem of having too many crew members on your first film, unless you, like me, are amazingly good-looking and charismatic, exuding an animal magnetism that attracts people to you like fat guys to a lunch buffet at a pizza place. Not only is it logistically desirable for you to keep your crew small, it's probably an economic necessity that you do so (see Trent sidebar).

THE TOM SAWYER THEORY OF HIRING PRODUCTION ASSISTANTS
Trent Haaga

Please pay attention to the fact that you can make a movie with a very small crew. I've never understood why Lloyd, who seemingly watches every penny spent on the set, will reply to every letter sent by a fan who wants to work on a Troma film with something like "Hey, we're doing a film this Autumn and you should come out. If you find a way to make it to New York, you can work on the film!" There is no screening process for PAs on a Troma film. If you're an escaped serial rapist and you show up at the doorstep of the production offices and say "I'm here to work on the film," you're guaranteed a floor to sleep on and a cheese sandwich for lunch. Sometimes this method works wonderfully, like in the case of Caleb Emerson.* Caleb showed up on the doorstep of the *Citizen Toxie* production offices with one pair of shorts and a *Cannibal Holocaust* t-shirt. He looked like a psychotic six foot four inch Amish guy. He didn't know a soul in New York and had to sleep on the floor of the unheated office. Caleb became invaluable to the production and can be seen as the Diaper Mafia punk who gets smothered with his own shit-filled diaper. On the same day, another guy showed up who looked well-educated and clean cut. He was some rich guy's son. He appeared to be nonthreatening and expressed an interest in working on the film. The fucker ended up losing us a location and being one of the only injuries on the set because he didn't listen to his AD. You'll read more about this punk later on.

I guess there's a method to Lloyd's madness. A sort of shotgun theory. If you hire twenty-five or thirty production assistants, you're probably going to have two or three decent crew members who'll stick it out to the end and become assets to the production. The volunteers travel from all over the world to help

* Caleb is a Rhode Island filmmaker whose movie, *Red's Breakfast 2* was one of the highlights of the first TromaDance Film Festival in Park City, Utah.

out on the movie and, while they might not know jack and/or shit about the nuts and bolts of filmmaking, some of them might just add something to the mix that's intangible and more valuable than money, knowledge, or skill. The rest of the layabouts will eventually disappear once they realize that making a film is hard work. This is precisely what happened on *Citizen Toxie* when we had the "great walkout" (which I prefer to think of as the "great cleansing") and we lost sixteen employees in one day. The end result is exactly as Lloyd describes: we were a tighter and more constructive crew once the cancer had been removed. I'm sure that all sixteen of those spineless wimps have *Citizen Toxie* on their résumés right now and are probably working as high-paid production managers on big-budget Hollywood pictures.

The old adage "you get what you pay for" came to mind many times when I had to deal with the mentally and emotionally unstable production assistants that Lloyd hired on *Citizen Toxie*. I didn't understand why Lloyd wasted his time doing the elimination process while we were shooting. Wouldn't it be wiser to interview production assistants and only hire the good ones for a little bit of money, thereby eliminating the transport and feeding of the wasted flesh? It was as I counseled a bawling, drooling, obviously traumatized PA on *Citizen Toxie* that I realized Lloyd's genius: spend your time interviewing your assistant director and production manager and let *them* deal with the PAs.

For your shoot, you probably want to keep the volunteer help to a minimum, especially if you don't have the time or manpower to weed out the weak links during production. Spend the time in pre-production to talk to these people and hire the people you believe will be most stable and diligent. Cheese sandwiches may not seem like much of a financial sacrifice to make for free help, but the worst of these guys'll end up costing you more than they're worth in the long run.

Theoretically, it's possible for you to shoot your movie with a skeleton crew of only four people*: the director of photography, a camera assistant, a gaffer, and a sound recordist. Theoretically, it's also possible for perfectly normal, well-adjusted people to go completely around the bend on their first film and end up blowing their brains out. To avoid this, there are a couple of people you should hire first. They will help you hire the rest of your crew and, if they're good at their jobs, they'll make your life much easier. If they suck, you'll still want to blow your brains out but not before you make these fuckers suffer for the hell they put you through.

PRODUCTION MANAGER

This can be a tough slot to fill because whoever does this job actually has to work and not just dick around being "artistic" all day. The production manager has to solve problems. If you're shooting a scene that requires a six-foot jade donkey phallus, the production manager has to make sure it's there when you need it. If you're shooting on location, the production manager has to make sure everybody knows where it is, how to get there, what time people need to be there, how long you're allowed to shoot there, every last detail. The production manager is involved in

---

* Eventually you're going to need a fifth person: the editor. But for this chapter, we're focusing on the actual production of the movie so we'll return to the subject of finding editors in homeless shelters and through the Men Seeking Men personal ads in the chapter on post-production. However, if you already have someone in mind, you should by all means include them in the process as early as possible. Especially if they understand they're not getting paid until they actually do some editing.

things like budgeting and scheduling, things that require an obsessive eye for detail and a mind like a computer, aware of every dollar that's spent.

For this job, you'll want to find a kid who can think, has common sense, and is burning with energy devoted solely toward your movie. The best production managers simply smother every job with their time and energy and shit gets done.* On a low-budget, independent film, you probably don't want to hire an older person to be your production manager because they most likely aren't going to have the fire inside that the position requires. If they're middle-aged and are still willing to work inhuman hours for peanuts, there may well be something seriously wrong with them. They're obviously incapable of making it any farther than they have already.

Caroline Baron worked on *The Toxic Avenger* as an unpaid intern, then found herself promoted to production manager because the incompetent assholes that preceded her either got fired or quit. She went through hell on that movie, organizing forty-two locations, working twenty-hour days, scheduling car chases, head-crushings, and multiple fight scenes. Caroline went on to work for Disney and recently had an independent movie she produced shown at Cannes. I know she values her Troma experience and feels that it prepared her for anything and everything that she would deal with later. Nevertheless, I still have pangs of guilt over the day I blew up at her for taking an afternoon off during production for an emergency dental visit. In retrospect, her freakishly swollen mouth should have been some kind of tip-off that she genuinely needed the time off.

When we made *Sgt. Kabukiman NYPD*, we had the backing of some significant Japanese investors so we decided we'd better not fuck around. We decided to hire a "professional" production manager. Big mistake. "Professional" production managers (i.e., people who are have done the job for major studio productions) do not work. They

---

* In fact, your production manager should be able to tell you exactly how much shit gets done, because one of their jobs is making sure you've got toilet facilities on set.

just throw money at every single problem until the problem goes away. We paid this guy $2,000 a week and not only in my opinion did he do absolutely nothing, he turned around and hired his girlfriend at $600 a week to do nothing with him. We (and you) need somebody who can fix things without spending a nickel.

I've worked with production managers both outstanding (Caroline Baron on *Toxic Avenger* and Franny Baldwin on *Tromeo & Juliet*, for instance) and retarded (I have been asked by the National Association for the Advancement of the Developmentally Disabled to not name names in this book). The good news is you probably already know somebody whose personality makes them perfect for the job. The bad news is they're probably not going to want to do it. Being a production manager really sucks, so you'll have to be as persuasive as you've ever been to convince him or her that you can't make your movie without 'em. Hypnotism is a viable option in cases like this.

ASSISTANT DIRECTOR

Speaking of jobs that suck the shit right out of a dead nun's ass, assistant director (or AD) is right up there. Perhaps on your movie it won't. You may be a benevolent leader who feeds stray puppies and kittens on your set and is so beloved that each and every member of your cast and crew would gladly take a bullet for you. You might have fistfights break out over who gets the privilege of being your assistant director. But more likely, you'll find that face-to-face with the pressures of daily production, even Gandhi can turn into a Mussolini.

Instead of having me tell you what I think an assistant director should do, let me turn the floor over to the person who most recently held that job: Trent Haaga, cowriter, feature actor, and assistant director on *Citizen Toxie: The Toxic Avenger Part IV*.

TRENT HAAGA: I never meant to be an Assistant Director. Wasn't it enough that I was willing to write Citizen Toxie *in a prohibitively short amount of time while having to watch my new bride frolic in the warm surf? Wasn't it enough that I was willing to leave that new bride for a month to sleep on the floor in Poughkeepsie, New York and run around in an adult diaper?*

We had an AD during pre-production. He was a nice guy who had all of the proper (and ridiculously expensive) scheduling software. He spent most of his time hunched over said computer "breaking down" the script. Lloyd hated him. Two days before we went into production Lloyd told Patrick Cassidy, our production manager, to fire the AD. But it didn't quite work out that way. He quit before we had the chance. As he was quitting, he told us, "You guys are nice and everything. But this movie's never gonna get made. You're all insane. Especially Lloyd." He walked out of our lives with the schedule and breakdown in his computer, never to be seen by us again.

The next day Lloyd, Patrick, and I were coming back from a scouting trip to Poughkeepsie. Lloyd was driving as he usually does, with about .005 percent of his brain on the winding country road ahead. Patrick had finally succumbed to the eighteen-hour days of pre-production and had passed out in the front seat. A thin line of spittle dangled from his bottom lip. Lloyd spoke up as he fiddled with the radio dial, narrowly avoiding an oncoming truck. I don't know how Patrick managed to sleep with Lloyd behind the wheel.

"Trent? You know how at the beginning of a shot they yell 'Roll sound' and 'Roll camera'? That kind of thing?"

"Sure, Lloyd. I've been on a few shoots. I know the protocol."

"Good, Trent. Good."

"Why do you ask, Lloyd?"

"Because you're going to be the new assistant director for this film. And that's what they do."

Oh, god, if only it had been that simple. Usually on a shoot, the schedule is made weeks in advance and it becomes the bible by which the rest of the production proceeds. Our schedule had walked out the door with the quit/fired AD. We were a rudderless ship sailing into dangerous territory, and Lloyd was asking me to take over the wheel. (An interesting note: Lloyd was paying the original AD $600/week to do the job. I was making about $300/week to line produce. Lloyd gave me a $50/week raise to add AD to my list of jobs, thereby saving himself $550/week— this is how you watch your budget in Tromaville.)

While the line producer or production manager must deal with location, equipment, and transportation issues, the AD is left with a much less pleasant task: he or she must deal with the human element of making a film. Maybe this sounds easy to you. Maybe you're a people person. But when your cast and crew is made up of underage alcoholics, fidgety "performers" who are starved, heat-exhausted, filthy from lack of showers and forced to sleep on deflated air mattresses and armies of extras who are gathered from the local homeless shelter, the task of the AD is daunting if not downright dangerous. As the assistant director of Citizen Toxie, *every day was a careful process, balancing the needs of the cast, the crew, the director, and the citizens of Poughkeepsie, New York.*

During my stint as the assistant director, I witnessed full-grown men crying like babies. I broke up fistfights. I sent people home and begged people to stay. I thwarted several assassination attempts on Lloyd's life. I yelled, screamed, begged, pleaded, negotiated, cajoled, debated, demanded, charmed, whored, and pimped . . . anything to get the film in the can. I spent many mornings gathering the cast and crew for impromptu "cheerleading" sessions in which I reminded them that we were making film history and that while their pain was temporary, the film would last forever.

One day we were shooting a large crowd scene outside of a school. It was a full day of shooting and we had the location for a limited time, so our day began around 5:00 A.M. By 7:00 A.M. we had managed to gather a pretty impressive group of local homeless people and prison escapees ready to act their hearts out. The scene required the Toxic Avenger to come out of a smoldering building to the jeers of the agitated Tromavillians outside. Dave Mattey, the imposingly large actor who played the Toxic Avenger, was supposed to be in his Toxie makeup and on set by now but Dave was running late that day and was still in the makeup chair. Lloyd assumed that Dave was throwing his weight around, being the lead actor and all. Dave felt that the four-hour turnaround between shooting days was a bit abusive and had decided that he needed an extra hour of sleep since we had kept him in full makeup for about seventeen hours the day before. In essence, they were both right. But it wasn't my job to make moral judgments on the set. We had a film to shoot. The three-hour process of transforming Dave was still underway, but the rest of the cast and crew were ready to shoot. More important, Lloyd was ready to shoot. As the

AD, I had to help make a crucial decision: how to start the day's work without our lead actor. Lloyd, ever the quick thinker, suggested that we take one of the more muscular Poughkeepsie locals, throw a Toxie stunt mask on them, and start the day. That is exactly what we did.

Dave showed up in full makeup and costume about forty-five minutes later to find the cameras rolling and another Toxic Avenger in his place. Needless to say, he was very unhappy. I think it had something to do with the fact that the new Toxie had a crappy mask on, was about a foot shorter than the 6' 2" Dave, and was black. He seemed to think that such a stopgap measure would lessen the film's production value. Lloyd argued that lessened production value was better than no film at all. Once again, both sides of the argument could be seen as equally valid . . . if this were a regular shoot. But I had to side with Lloyd. The rules are made up as you go along when you don't have millions of dollars for holdups like this. We had the location for a limited time and Lloyd and I had come up with the best solution given the situation.

This friction between Lloyd and Dave had been brewing throughout the production. Dave felt Lloyd was too hard on his inexperienced and underpaid cast and crew and that, despite a successful thirty-year film career, he constantly cheapened the film by cutting corners and moving ahead. Dave was very vocal about his beliefs since he was the main character and felt that he had some say in the production. Lloyd, on the other hand, felt that Dave was causing dissent among the ranks and was complaining for no reason—we told each and every crew and castmember a million times that this would be one of the most miserable, grueling, and depressing experiences of their lives, so everyone had been forewarned. What Dave didn't know was that Lloyd could (and would) replace him with a shorter black guy with a crappy mask for good if he didn't get in line.

We didn't have the time or wherewithal to hash out Dave and Lloyd's differences. I didn't want to lose Dave as an actor (because with my luck, Lloyd would've made me play Toxie), but I certainly didn't want to piss off Lloyd. As I said, Lloyd could and would have fired Dave on the spot. And Dave could and might have snapped Lloyd like a bent, twisted fifty-four-year-old twig if things got too ugly. As the AD, it was my job, my duty, to smooth out relations between the two, get Dave in the next shot, and continue with our day's work. To tell the *honest-to-god truth, I don't even remember how I resolved this situation. All I do know is that I solved all problems like this with extreme diplomacy. Like I said, my brain is somewhat damaged from the entire experience due to sleep deprivation and nutrient deficiency, but it probably went something like this:*

(Dave Mattey appears as the cameras roll on the impostor Toxie.
He towers over me.)

DAVE: Trent! What *the fuck* is that black guy in the crappy mask doing in front of the camera?

TRENT: Oh, hey Dave. We, um, we were just shooting the master shot while we waited for you.

DAVE: You're kidding me! That guy doesn't even *look* like me! Where's Kaufman? I'm gonna give that fucker a piece of my mind! Doesn't he know he's making a piece of shit film when he does stuff like this? I'm gonna kill that guy! This is totally unprofessional!

TRENT: C'mon, Dave, you and I both know that he's senile and incompetent. But we're in this together, man. We've got to humor him. He'll be dead in a couple of years anyway. It's not worth the hassle. Let's just get you in front of the camera, okay?

DAVE: Fuck that! He owes me and his whole crew an apology! And I'm not gonna get in front of the camera until he reshoots this scene with *me* in it!

TRENT: Okay, Dave. You're absolutely right. I'm gonna go and talk to Lloyd right now.

(I weave my way through the drunken and heat-exhausted crowd of "actor persons" and confer with Lloyd.)

LLOYD: Oh, I get it. *Now* the fuck shows up. I hope he enjoyed his extra hour of sleep, the bastard. This is totally unprofessional!

TRENT: I know, Lloyd. He's been nothing but trouble from day one. You're right to hate him. But you know how these *actors* are. We've gotta humor him, you know? It's not worth the hassle to fire him. Let's just get him in front of the camera, okay?

LLOYD: Fuck that! He owes me and the whole crew an apology! I'm gonna keep shooting the picture without him until he shapes up, goddammit!

TRENT: Okay, Lloyd. You're absolutely right. I'll go and talk to Dave right now.

(I once again weave my way through the belligerent crowd.)

TRENT: Dave. It's all worked out. Lloyd says he's sorry. Now let's get you in front of the camera and roll, okay?

DAVE: What about the last shot with the other guy in it?

TRENT: Don't you worry, Dave. It'll get fixed in post.

DAVE: You know I'm only doing this because I like you, Trent. I know that Lloyd'll ride you into the ground if you don't stay on schedule.

TRENT: Thanks, Dave. Someday we'll be big-time actors and directors and we'll be able to pay Kaufman to be our coffee bitch.

(Now I run over to Lloyd again.)

TRENT: Lloyd. It's all worked out. Dave says he's sorry. Now let's roll the camera, okay?

LLOYD: He's not gonna pull any more of that prima donna shit on us again?

TRENT: Don't you worry, Lloyd. I'll make sure it doesn't happen again.

LLOYD: You know that you're learning valuable lessons from this, Trent. If you let the actors step all over you, the PAs are next.

TRENT: Thanks, Lloyd. This movie'll be over soon and then when we do another one Dave'll come begging to be in it.

LLOYD: Yeah. And I'll make him my coffee bitch.

TRENT: Okay, everybody! Let's get ready to shoot!!

There were about a billion other distasteful tasks and narrowly averted disasters on the set of Citizen Toxie, *but to outline them would require several more chapters and would probably deter you from ever attempting to make a movie on your own. Just remember that you need to find an AD who is good with people and has the ability to lie, cheat, steal, and bargain coupled with the overwhelming desire to get the film shot at any cost. The funniest thing about the entire* Citizen Toxie *fiasco is*

Michael Herz, in joke glasses and fake beard on the Japanese set of *Toxic Avenger II*, will kill Lloyd Kaufman for including Herz in this book.

that there is no credited AD on the film!! *All the work I did was for naught. I didn't even get the fucking* credit *for doing the most horrible job on the set! In the end, I did get the film shot at any cost. And the cost was my credit. Fuck you, Lloyd.*

Another reason to hire your production manager and AD early on is they will be able to help you hire the rest of your crew. Once you start hiring the rest of the crew, you will quickly figure out if you've got capable hands in the production manager and AD slots or if you need to perform an emergency head-from-ass procedure. There exists a network of mediocrity in the movie industry (maybe in every industry, for all I know). Good people know other good people but stupidity breeds stupidity and bad people will only know other bad people to hire. I have never had bad crew members mistakenly introduce me to someone who knows exactly what they're doing. The first person you and your team should seek out is . . .

THE DIRECTOR OF PHOTOGRAPHY

The director of photography (or DP or, if they're insufferably pretentious, the cinematographer) is the person you're going to be working most closely with during production, so choose wisely. Be as selective as you would be choosing a spouse, life partner, or sexual surrogate. A good DP is worth their weight in goldfish crackers.* A bad one will turn your dream project into a nightmarish battle of the wills.

The one fight you are virtually guaranteed to have during production is with your DP and it will be a fight between The Shot and The Story. The DP isn't going to care about your story (not at first, anyway). All he will care about is composing the perfect shot and in their quest to do so, he will bring production to a standstill. A weak filmmaker will allow this to happen. He will be persuaded by the DP's insistence that the only way to convey a certain character trait is to wait until precisely 4:37 P.M. when the sun will hit the actor person at a perfect 45 degree angle which, when properly diffused by a W8 warming filter and offset by a deep amber gel mounted nine feet above and to the right, will instantly communicate everything about the character's motivations.

It's easy and tempting to allow control of the movie to slip out of your hands and into the paws of the DP, especially if you don't know the first thing about photography. If you *do* know how to operate a camera, you should try to do it yourself as much as possible. On my earliest movies, we really couldn't afford a DP better than myself. Not that I was any great shakes . . . on *Squeeze Play* we just pointed a light in the general direction of what was going on and shot. But I learned and improved and, eventually, when I could afford to get a better DP, I hired him. Even so, I constantly look through the camera to make sure

---

* This may not seem like much to you now, but when we address the issue of feeding your cast and crew you will come to understand just how valuable goldfish crackers really are.

that the DP is doing what I'm asking for and I always operate the second or third camera myself. Also, I'm pretty good at handheld camera work (if I do say so myself), so usually I operate the camera whenever we're shooting handheld.

Even with video playback (which we can't afford anyway), it's impossible to know what you're going to end up with when you're shooting unless you're actually operating the camera yourself. You may notice something in your peripheral vision while you're shooting that you'll need to adjust. Video playback can't help you with that. Video is also a major distraction on the set, creating a colossal cluster-fuck as everybody and their uncle gathers around to watch the playback instead of working and setting up the next shot.

Let's suppose for a second that you've never even touched a camera. You don't even know how to make the film move through it (Is there a button? A crank? Magic words?). Now if the DP really wants to seize control of your movie and turn it into a demo reel showcasing his virtuoso camera moves, he has a whole encyclopedia of technical jargon he can pull out to baffle you. Don't let yourself be intimidated. You have to convince him that telling the story is the primary concern. If the movie sucks because the actors got burnt out waiting for the shot to get set up or because the images seem completely disconnected from the story they're ostensibly telling, nobody is done any favors.

On the last several films I've made with Brendan Flynt, he'll set up the shot and fiddle with the lights for awhile and eventually I'll stop him and tell him time's a-wastin'. We've got to shoot now. *This second.* Because we've worked together for awhile now, he now realizes that I'm not going to stop with just one take. So after we do the first take, I work with the actors and Brendan goes back to tweaking the lights. By the fourth take or so, I've usually gotten what I want and Brendan has what he wants.

Because the DP is such an important collaborator, a lot of first-time filmmakers have one picked long before they go into production. If they know what they're doing, great, you're ahead of the game. But if they don't know what they're doing* or, better yet, you're just some average schmuck who wrote a screenplay out of a genuine love of movies and not because you've spent the last four years of your life at USC studying cinema, then you're gonna have to go out and look for somebody to shoot the picture.

Fortunately, this is where you can benefit from the arcane union rules and racist and sexist policies that dominate the Hollywood studio system. You may be able to find someone who's been shooting commercials or porno movies for god-knows-how-long and is aching for the chance to shoot a feature film. Often these guys who have been toiling in the salt mines of advertising for awhile have been well paid for selling their souls. Some first-time filmmakers may think this prices them out of reach but the opposite is true. If they've been making $4,000 a week, hopefully they've saved up a little and can now afford to take a substantial pay cut for the opportunity they've been waiting for. Never forget that the offer of a feature film on their résumé is just as valuable a commodity as cold hard cash.

You can also find people who've been camera assistants on major studio films but have been unable to negotiate the union minefield and make the move to DP. Our DP on *Sgt. Kabukiman NYPD* was one of the finest assistants in the union. Of course, union guys working on a nonunion film like yours could get into a shitload of trouble. That's when it's time to play Fun with Pseudonyms. For instance, Jimmy London, DP on *The Toxic Avenger* and other Troma films, is a card-carrying union member under his real name but he got his big break with Troma when he assisted me on *Waitress!*, eventually becoming Troma's DP on movies such as *Troma's War*. Even though he hasn't worked for us in years, Jimmy could be kicked out of the union and blacklisted for

---

* Some ways to tell that your DP doesn't know what they're doing: they keep looking through the big glass circle instead of the small one. They take light readings by staring directly into the light source and calculating how long it is between the time they start to see spots and when they stop seeing anything at all. If they refer to the camera as "mommy" and are occasionally discovered dry humping it when they think nobody's around, they may know what they're doing but you might want to consider replacing them anyway.

A delighted Michael Herz (in joke glasses and fake beard) beams satisfaction at Lloyd Kaufman (*far left*).

life if I told anyone that Jimmy London's true identity is James Lipton, host of TV's *Inside the Actors Studio*.

If you know *anybody* working even tangentially in the movie or TV business, they should be able to find one or two people looking to make the big leap from assistant to DP or from commercials to features. Most of these guys aren't exactly shy about expressing their displeasure with the work they're stuck doing. Maybe you think you don't know anybody in the business (most of the people who think this live somewhere other than Los Angeles or New York City). Local TV stations are often swarming with cameramen who would kill for the chance to work on a feature. Assure them that it needn't come to that but they should definitely keep that level of enthusiasm and, who knows, you might just find a use for a killing machine on set. You can also post notices on the Internet, on Websites devoted to hiring film crews or in discussion groups and bulletin boards.

If you can't find a pro willing to work with you, you can always hit the film schools. Now that Film and Television is as common a major as Swine Husbandry (though not nearly as respected), most every state

in the union has a film department at one university or another.*
Unfortunately, most film students will have no practical experience
whatsoever, yet despite this they still think the $40,000 a year they've
been shelling out guarantees that they now know everything there is to
know about filmmaking. For instance, on a Troma set we instill an
almost religious reverence for the equipment into our crew. Without
these fundamental tools, we're fucked. There is no movie. During the
shooting of *The Toxic Avenger*, I saw a film school kid set an Arriflex
camera on a greasy, bloodstained restaurant floor. This kid's daddy
would have had to pay a shitload of money for this camera if anything
had happened to it. Not only did I tear the kid a new asshole (as I am
wont to do), I actually made him cry. I hope that I instilled that kid
with such terror of equipment mishandling that today, if he so much
as sees his grandmother leave a disposable camera in direct sunlight,
he suffers a post-traumatic stress disorder breakdown.

Speaking of equipment, it is always preferable to hire a DP who owns
his own.† Not only will you save money, you'll save yourself time and
headaches by having a DP who's working with equipment they're familiar with. And if the equipment breaks down, you don't have to waste a
lot of time trying to get ahold of the asshole that rented it to you. The
yelling can begin immediately with the frustration at its peak level.

Whether or not your DP owns their own stuff, you should make
sure you're on the same page as far as the amount of stuff they're
going to use. The director of photography's job is to paint with lights.
You want to be damn sure that he can paint economically. This doesn't
mean your movie has to look shitty or cheap. This means you and your
DP have to be creative, turning necessity into a virtue. Remind your
DP that Hitchcock was famous for such sparing lighting techniques as
creating pools of light . . . and everybody rips off Hitchcock!

---

* Some schools even make this book required reading. Avoid these schools at all costs.
† By this, I mean lighting and film equipment. I don't care where he gets his own personal
equipment.

Ask to see your department heads' equipment lists immediately. Some people will want to be "ready for anything," which simply means they do not want to have to think and plan what they're going to do. If their equipment list starts to look like that of the Israeli Army plotting an invasion of Syria, put the kibosh on their delusions of grandeur right away. Look at it as a luxury to keep the equipment as light as possible. While bigger productions have the curse of having to negotiate two-ton trucks full of shit that may or may not get used, you'll be blessed with being able to move quickly and easily with all your equipment stored safely in the back of one shitty bread van.*

In 1979, I was production manager on a big-budget sci-fi movie called *The Final Countdown* that starred Kirk Douglas and Martin Sheen. The production of this movie was loaded down with enough equipment to shoot half a dozen movies simultaneously. The gaffer and the grip had their own trailer-trucks full of shit. They owned the trucks and insisted that the production rent them or they wouldn't work on the movie. And the only way we could get the DP we wanted was to hire these guys I felt were assholes and, therefore, rent their trucks full of shit. Somehow we had to get these trucks on board the aircraft carrier where we were shooting. We ended up using a huge industrial crane to hoist the beasts onto the carrier. Afterward, both guys complained that the crane had bent the trucks. It didn't matter that we didn't want their fucking trucks in the first place and the only reason they had been brought on board was because they had insisted on it. They demanded to be compensated for the damage. On *The Final Countdown*, 90 percent of the crew's energy was devoted to complaining about the food and damage that they'd done themselves, leaving about 10 percent to be put toward making a good movie. Not

---

* If you take just one piece of advice from this book, make it this: make sure you've got a spare tire for your vehicles. I can't tell you how many times the presence or absence of a spare has saved or fucked a day's shooting.

coincidentally, *The Final Countdown* was the last outside job I ever took. This was where I realized I would never be happy in filmmaking unless I was in control.

Once you've hired your DP and feel reasonably sure that he knows what he's doing, you can safely delegate the hiring of the other members of your indispensable skeleton crew to him.* These three will be working closely with the DP, just as the DP works closely with you so it's important that the DP finds people he's comfortable with. Once again, you will have to shell out some money for these folks but you're not going to be able to make your movie without them.

CAMERA ASSISTANT(S)

Technically, this person assists the camera *person* and not the camera itself. Although two hands are sufficient for most of life's little necessaries (eating, washing, self-pleasure, etc.), more are needed to get a motion picture shot. Until genetic engineering catches up and perfects the octo-DP, you will need to hire one or more camera assistants. While you or your DP are busy actually operating the camera[†] and the DP is fucking around with the lights long after it looks fine to you, the camera assistants are responsible for little things like making sure there's film in the camera (very few cameras work well without film loaded correctly).

The number of assistants you will need or desire depends on the magnitude of your production. I generally use three. One acts as focus-puller, one acts as loader, one acts as clapper, and all three trade off as

---

* I'd appease the politically correct among you by saying "or her" but statistically, gyno-cinematographers are about as rare as watchable Steven Spielberg films. In the sexist world of moviemaking, women are encouraged to be designers and production managers (presumably because these jobs require a lot of heavy lifting), but don't gravitate towards cinematography. If I knew any gyno-DPs, I'd get rid of the sweaty bohunks I've used in the past in a heartbeat.
[†] On big productions, the DP does not actually operate the camera himself. The camera operator does that. If you can afford to hire both a DP and a camera operator and all these other people, then you should buy copies of this book by the dozens and give them out to all the members of your cast and crew as gag gifts.

the DP's spunk-depositorium.* When we shot *The Toxic Avenger Part II* in Japan, the focus-puller (who was one of the best I ever worked with) was also the grip, which put him in charge of moving the camera around between shots. This would never happen in America but it isn't as though there's an *International Rules of Play* book for moviemaking.

The camera assistant is also in charge of writing camera reports for both the processing lab and the editors. They write down every single shot, whether it was any good or not, if there were any anomalies that took place, things like that. Good script notes are essential. If you're watching dailies and every so often you see a cloudy vision of Jesus fill the screen, you can go back to the script notes and discover that Jesus only appears whenever you use the 25mm lens. These notes can also save you money on telecine costs. If you only transfer good takes to video for editing, it takes less time and costs you less dough.

GAFFER

Slang term for an elderly man and, more important in this case, the guy who's in charge of the lights, putting them where the DP tells him. It's also a fancy-schmancy term for the chief electrician. Yes, you need one. It is remarkably difficult to make a film without electricity.

"Listen pal," comes the retort from budget-conscious filmmakers around the world, "Maybe back in your day when you had to hand-crank your motor-car and street lamps ran on gas you needed a gaffer. But in today's modern society, electricity is everywhere! I'm shooting most of my movie at my parents' house anyway! I can do very nicely without a 'gaffer' thank you very much."

Fine. Knock yourself out. When you blow every fuse in your par-

---

*I know, these all sound dirty but they're all genuine bona fide movie terms. Focus-puller— the person who manually adjusts the camera's focus during filming. Loader—the person who loads film into the camera. Clapper—the person who operates the slate held up at the beginning of the shot with vital information like scene number, take number, etc. Spunk-depositorium—the person who receives the semen discharged after sexual release, usually orally or anally.

ents' house with all the lights and shit you've got plugged in everywhere or when the one klieg light you've got set up overheats and starts a fire in the rumpus room, don't come crying to me.* The lights and equipment used to make a movie aren't like a couple of desk lamps. You need a gaffer to make sure everything's wired correctly, to make sure the lights are operating and focused. And if you're going to do anything even remotely complex like a tie-in to a fuse box, somebody on your crew should be a licensed electrician and that somebody should probably be the gaffer.

The ranks of the gaffers are also good places to pull DPs from.† Gaffers already know their way around lights and that's half the battle right there. A gaffer with an itch to move up to DP can be extraordinarily gifted. Ralf Bode was a gaffer on movies like *Cry Uncle* and *Joe* before he moved up to become an immensely talented DP, shooting *Saturday Night Fever*, among others.

Your gaffer can also pull double duty as key grip.‡ This puts him in charge of the Moving Shit Around Department, adjusting lights, and laying dolly tracks for the camera (or if you don't have actual dolly tracks, maintaining the shopping cart you stole from Safeway to stick the camera in. Another good makeshift dolly is a wheelchair, so keep an eye out for parapalegics and, if it looks like you can take him, grab that chair!).

SOUND RECORDIST

It is 100 percent possible to make a perfectly acceptable movie without one of these headphone-wearing, coffee-swilling society rejects. But, the audience for silent films was pretty well tapped out about

---

* No, seriously. Don't come crying to me. Call 911 if you've got a fire, for Christ's sake!

† *The Ranks of the Gaffers* is also the title of an uncommonly good British adventure film from 1931 directed by Alexander Korda. (EDITOR'S NOTE: No, it isn't.)

‡ As we have seen, many movie terms sound like they should be dirty. Key Grip, Best Boy, Skin Flute Operator, Snake Wrangler, etc. This is simply because the film industry was founded and continues to be run by pedophiles, rapists, and compulsive masturbators. Troma, of course, was founded and continues to be run merely by compulsive masturbators, thus explaining our outsider status in mainstream Hollywood.

eighty years ago and you'll most likely find it just as difficult to record every line of dialogue in post-production, so you'd might as well bite the bullet and record your sound during production. By the way, when you do shoot a scene without recording sound, it's called shooting MOS. This stands for Mit Out Sound* or Money's Out, Soundguy, which is usually why you have to shoot MOS in the first place.

The sound guy's job is pretty self-explanatory, but it's more than just hitting the RECORD button on a tape deck. They have to check and maintain sound levels, be able to figure out what the best microphone is for a particular shot, and work with the DP to keep the mics out of sight. Oh, and they should probably remember to hit the RECORD button as well. And, like the camera assistant, they need to keep a log of which takes are good for sound. Ideally, you would like to use takes with good picture *and* sound, so you want to match up the two elements. Or you can just loop good sound from one take over good picture from another take and hope nobody notices the difference.

The one thing you should drill into your sound recordist's brain is not to waste time on set. He should be ready to go the second you and the DP are ready to shoot. If there's a problem on the set with lights or focus or some other camera problem, I'm willing to wait. But you should never, ever have to wait for sound.

If it's possible, try to find a sound recordist who doesn't mind being his own boom mike operator, as Evan Messaros, our sound guy, often did on *Terror Firmer*. It can be done easily, they have the headphones so they know the best Mike placement, and they eat less food than a sound guy *and* a boom guy. If that's not going to work, then you can carefully pick a boom guy from the production assistants. However, this is an important job so don't just close your eyes and pick at random. The

---

* "Mit Out Sound" is often (and annoyingly) said on-set in a piss-poor German accent. The assholes that do this probably do not realize that they're imitating director and cinema martyr Erich Von Stroheim and, if you tell them, they probably won't care. I only bring it up myself because my editor at St. Martin's bet me that I couldn't squeeze twenty footnotes into a single chapter. Just two more and I'm drinking for free!

boom guy has to be strong enough to hold the Mike up out of frame for long periods and smart enough to remember where the fuck he had it during the last take. A lot of filmmakers will allow the boom to drift slightly into frame, assuming that it will be cropped out when the picture is matted at 1.85:1. That's nice but when your movie plays overseas or, even more likely, on TV, it's going to be framed at 1.33:1 and you'll look like a dick because of the amateurish boom mike dangling at the top of the screen. You should always keep the boom mike completely out of the "full" aperture. It's only a couple inches more anyway and my wife has always assured me that a couple inches more doesn't make any difference at all.

With these key personnel lined up, you are ready to begin shooting your movie. Of course, most movies get made by more than seven or eight people. Even the briefest glance at the end credits of a movie will prove that it isn't just the same few names repeated over and over again. Depending on the size of your budget and/or how many people you can sweet talk into working for free, you may find yourself with a bigger crew. Here are a few credits you might wish to offer in lieu of cash.

PRODUCTION DESIGNER/ART DIRECTOR/SET DECORATOR

These are the guys responsible for the "look" of a movie. They do things like build sets and make sure there isn't a copy of *Shaved Beaver* magazine in a room that's supposed to belong to a seventy-eight-year-old woman.* You're probably not going to have to worry too much about building elaborate sets. Your sets are more than likely going to be found locations and the set decoration will end up being whatever's there. If you need to shoot a seventy-eight-year-old woman's room, you'll probably just find a room that belongs to a seventy-eight-year-

---

* Unless, of course, it's a character trait and there's supposed to be a copy of *Shaved Beaver* there.

To insure 100% accuracy, actual severed heads of rare yellow-back dolphins live in the Troma special effects sweatshop. Nine-year-old Inga from a third world country, New Jersey, earns 39¢ a day for designing Dolphin Man. (Tim Considine)

old woman and shoot it as is. When you're through, please feel free to send me her copy of *Shaved Beaver.*

While I give all the designers on my movies virtual carte blanche to do whatever they damn well please, I make sure to approve every design element before we shoot. Make sure the designers show you everything. Their ideas are usually great and can spark more ideas for you in rewriting the script (which of course you will still be doing even after the camera is rolling).

DUMPSTER DIVING FOR FUN AND PROFIT
Jean Loscalzo

Jean Loscalzo was production designer on Terror Firmer, *where she had to create man-eating escalators and apartments for sexually confused hermaphroditic serial killers as a matter of course. Here, Jean reveals how you can whittle down the budget of your design elements to around $1.98.*

In low-budget filmmaking, a pile of dirt takes on many new levels of style.

Working with Troma was a challenge every day; a life lesson and magic show rolled into one. My first challenge was hiring an unpaid art crew. Dig deep. Search the city for creative people who have always wanted to work on a movie. Key word here is "work." Fire anyone who cannot keep up his or her end of the workload. Any slacker will only create unrest within your crew and annoy you in the process. You are nothing without your crew. I managed to obtain a tireless crew with endless vision and physical strength, topped off with an eccentric sense of humor and respect. We were one happy little family. Independent film Troma-style is its own kind of war. Gather your soldiers and let them know how fantastic they are every day, and steal any PA that shows any creative talent and intelligence.

Troma is not your conventional type of project. Any given day can consist of sanding knives and razor blades to ripping apart raw and sometimes rancid animal parts or constructing a set to look like an escalator devouring a 400-pound man. We took our jobs very seriously. If you do not love your cause, you're doomed and lazy. Our production office was in a fourth-floor walkup in Hell's Kitchen. We carried the whole front end of a car up those steps because we thought it vital to a specific scene. We used the sanitation schedule so we could get vans on prime pickup days and preroute our garbage picking. When one of the art crew discovered the CBS dumpsters, we celebrated our victory with a fifteen-minute break. We picked up trashed prime-time sets and reconstructed them to build one of ours. Lumber is not cheap.

You can save a lot of money on set-building and dressing by getting the right location. It is so important to fight the good fight for any location you feel will complete your vision. Good locations will save you on aesthetic value and can make or break a scene. And as far as props go, anything can be a prop if, when presenting it to the actor person, you convince them of its importance and how special they are to possess it. Let them do the rest. They don't have to know it came out of the trash.

The art department was always cleaning up bodily fluids. Not only did we make the feces and the vomit but we also cleaned it up. I think cleaning the maggot-infested Porta-Jon was the worst thing I had to ask them to do. Fortitude is an understatement. I just wanted to hug them and tell them how sorry I was.

Which brings us to Popo. Popo was the puppet I reconstructed from an old Charlie Chaplin doll. I replaced its human features with those of a wild boar and assorted reptiles to make it scarier. We were always looking for Popo. He would disappear all the time. I remember digging through the cargo van screaming his name and begging him to come out so we could shoot his death scene. It was like he knew or something. No joke, we never found him at the end of the shoot.

COSTUME DESIGNER

Again, not something you're probably going to think about too much unless you're shooting a historical drama or something. Your own need for a production designer or costume designer will depend on the size and scope of your project. It's not so much a question of paying them a lot of money. You can find excellent designers willing to work for little or no money by placing notices on the Internet or in theater and film departments at universities. But you will have to allocate a budget for them to work with.

The main job of the costume designer on a Troma film is to wash the blood, spunk, sweat, and skid marks out of the costumes. The costume designer is also responsible for breaking down the script into script-days to make sure the characters are wearing the same thing from shot to shot. And while most of the costumes in *Terror Firmer* were the actors' own clothes, the cast had to surrender their belongings to the costume designer for the duration of the shoot so that some moron couldn't ruin a day's shooting by forgetting to wear the same shitty T-shirt for scene thirty-eight that he wore in scene thirty-nine a week ago. On *Cry Uncle*, we had a sequence where a character walked across a room. During the first part, he wore a blue suit. We forgot that and, weeks later, when we shot the rest of it, he was suddenly wearing a green suit. John Avildsen, the director of *Cry Uncle*, noticed this in dailies and ordered the scene reshot. I, on the other hand, would not have bothered to reshoot the scene. John Avildsen has won an Academy Award. I have watched the Academy Awards on TV while eating cheese doodles and drinking gin.

Both the costume designer and the art director are involved in maintaining continuity. If you have a "hot" set that you're going to be using for a few days, that set needs to not be fucked with. On *Citizen Toxie*, people kept sleeping on the bed and couch in Toxie's shack despite the multiple signs and warnings that the place was off-limits. This had a lot to do with the fact that they were the only beds and couches these people had seen in weeks. Most everybody had been sleeping on the floor of the giant warehouse we were using as a barracks. So, while I could understand conceptually their attraction to the shack, their desire to sleep on something softer than concrete kept fucking up our set. The joke was on them, however, because the couch and mattress were found on the street outside a crackhouse in Poughkeepsie. Apparently a lifetime of skin rashes was worth a few nights of sleeping on an actual bed.

Oftentimes the costume designer and art director will maintain continuity by taking Polaroids immediately after a take. This practice usually goes to shit on a Troma movie because Polaroid film is too expensive. You'll want to hire designers with a photographic memory so you don't have to use actual photographs.

Continuity is also one of the main concerns of our next victim . . .

SCRIPT SUPERVISOR

In less enlightened times, this was the "script girl," a term I only use today when the person hired for this position is male. This person is really there for the editor's benefit, so whoever your editor is can pick a production assistant and train him or her to be their script monkey.

The script monkey keeps track of what has been shot and in what order and notes any changes made to the script. On Troma movies, we change the script all the time, sometimes in the middle of a shot. This drives the script supervisor nuts, and their final copy of the script ends up filled with tiny, handwritten attempts at writing down spontaneous dialogue and improvs until it resembles the notebook of a homeless schizophrenic person. The script supervisor almost always ends up quitting, often spectacularly.

Good script notes are absolutely essential so you should have the script monkey start practicing as soon as possible. At Troma, we film everything, including the rehearsals. The rehearsals aren't just for the actors, they're also for the crew. The filmed rehearsals are ideal places for the script monkey to practice his new calling.

PRODUCTION OFFICE COORDINATOR

Like any organization, your production will need a base of operations. One location where people can call to get directions, contact folks, and complain about how poorly everything is being run. The production office coordinator takes a lot of abuse and sleeps in the production office, if at all. It's a fairly awful job but absolutely vital if there is to be any communication between your production and the outside world.

CASTING DIRECTOR

The casting director organizes auditions and makes recommendations on who should be cast in what part. I'll talk more about the casting process in the next chapter but for right now, just know that a good casting director will help you tremendously, especially if you're going to be looking at actors without much experience.

LOCATION MANAGER

This is the person who makes sure there's someplace to take a shit when you're out shooting on location. This is another position to promote a competent production assistant into. I will go into nauseating detail about what location managers are forced to do and how they should do it in Chapter 7.

PROPMASTER

Obviously, the person in charge of rounding up the props. This is something most anybody can do, unless you're planning on handcarving a bunch of graven images for your big cult scene. Just make sure whoever does this has an eye for detail. Even if the prop is only mentioned once in the script, they need to be able to pick it out and make sure it's there on the day you need it. If you're shooting a knife fight in the middle of the desert and your propmaster forgets the knife, it's gonna be a real pain in the ass trying to find one.

LINE PRODUCER

On major studio productions, the line producer supplies the stars with high-grade cocaine. Basically, there's nothing a line producer does that a good AD or production manager couldn't do instead, but it is a fancy credit to use to reward and motivate people who have done exceptionally good work for nothing. Franny Baldwin is credited as line producer on *Tromeo & Juliet* because she was an amazingly good production manager. Associate producer is another great credit to reward the truly dedicated. Andrew Wiener was an associate producer on *Tromeo & Juliet*. He started as a production assistant with no experience at all, then quickly become location and unit manager.

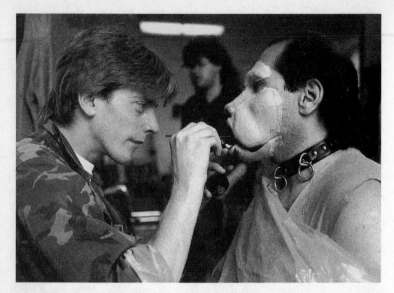

Because the ill-paid, ill-fed Troma cast and crew are constantly bitching, veteran Troma special effects artist Tim Considine is inspired to create "bitch man" for *Toxic Avenger II* and *Toxic Avenger III, Last Temptation of Toxie.*

EXECUTIVE PRODUCER

Executive producers are people who did fuck-all on your movie but you've got to be nice to them for one reason or another. This is a perfect title to give to rich people who want to give you money.

CREATIVE CONSULTANT

These are people you don't have to be quite as nice to as the executive producers but you still want to stay on their good side. This is a good credit to give to people you're trying to sleep with.

DIRECTOR'S FLUFFER

I personally find it much easier to direct if I have a constant erection. The director's fluffer makes it possible for me to do my best work. This is usually the highest paid position on the set.

MEANWHILE, BENEATH NEW YORK CITY . . .

The subway pulled into my station and, as I was getting off the train, I saw the homeless guy again. Turns out he had a pair of legs after all. He was standing on the platform, the little makeshift dolly he'd been using to wheel himself around on propped up against his seemingly healthy legs. He was counting the money he'd brought in and throwing out the bananas and bottled water he'd collected from the kindhearted people who took him at his word that food would be a perfectly acceptable alternate to cash.

I thought to myself, "Now there's a low-budget independent film-maker. He starts off hobbled, chopped off at the knees. He goes out there in front of complete strangers with a story. He does whatever it takes to get people to see things his way and, through the generosity of these people, gets his feet back under him. Now, he's ready to make a movie . . . or score some heroin."*

Without a doubt, your biggest task throughout every stage of the production will be bringing everyone in line with your vision. You must do whatever it takes to get people to give you everything they've got with virtually nothing in return but the promise of a good movie at the end of the journey. It's absolutely vital that you make everyone from the DP to the editor to the unpaid production assistants as passionate about telling your story as you are yourself before you even shoot a frame of film.

You will have to explain to every member of the crew that on your movie, it isn't about the food. The food will be spare and occasionally revolting. It isn't about perks like accommodations or travel arrange-ments. You're going to be sleeping an hour a night on surfaces that are so uncomfortable your spine will be permanently misshapen. It's all about the movie. It's about coming together and creating something as a team, something bigger than any of you individually. It's about com-

---

* By now, the homeless guy had noticed me staring at him with this weird, half-assed grin on my face so I decided I'd better get the hell out of there. And that's 20! I'm gonna wrap this chapter up pretty quick, 'cause the drinks are on St. Martin's Press!

municating your vision . . . first to your collaborators, then, together, to the world.

VIDDY WELL, LITTLE BROTHER
Trent Haaga

Okay, I think it's about time for me to quickly jump in here and say *for God's sake, shoot your film on digital video*!!! Lloyd started making movies in the '60s, so he thinks "video" is just the name of the captain on a crappy SF TV show he watched while he was pouring Rice Krispies into his sister's diaper. He can appreciate a shot-on-video movie and Troma just produced the DV feature tentatively titled *Tales From the Crapper*, but it's extremely unlikely that Lloyd himself will ever stop shooting on 35mm film. But for you, the first-time filmmaker who does not yet have thirty years of experience under his belt, do yourself a huge favor and go with digital video. You'll still need most of the crew discussed in this chapter, but it's a lot less time-consuming and expensive to take advantage of this new technology. I know, I know. You want to make a *film*, not a *video*. But anything shot on digital video can be transferred to any film format you can think of. Even Troma has purchased a high-end digital video camera for the amount of money it costs to *rent* a 35mm camera for three weeks. And there are many, many other advantages to shooting digital. Not only is stock cheaper, but there's no processing cost, no telecine cost (telecine is transferring your film negatives onto ¾" videotape so that the editors can digitize it and begin the editing process), you can review your footage immediately, and even reloading the camera takes a fraction of the time. Most important, it takes a hell of a lot fewer lights to make digital video look great and there are no costly film prints to deal with.

I just finished producing three digital video features at about $35,000 each. This includes the cost of post-production. The cameras we used were able to shoot in a 16 × 9 widescreen format. Our entire stock budget per picture was about $800 for 16 hours of footage. We used standard fluorescent lights for many of the scenes (and they turned out to be some of the best scenes in the films—low light levels give video a semi-grainy look). We used a process called "film look" that added even more grain and contrast to the picture. I've been told the first film sold 18,000 copies to Blockbuster video, earning around $250,000. *Terror Firmer* cost about $300,000 to make. Sure, it's played in cinemas across the United States and at prestigious film festivals throughout the world, but it's going to take a lot of foreign sales and Web site orders before it makes back its cost. Even if Blockbuster had bought 18,000 copies of *Terror Firmer* (which they didn't because they're a puritanical, right-wing, devil-worshipping conglomerate), it wouldn't cover the cost of production.

The digital video math is simple: the lower your budget, the fewer copies you have to sell to make profit.* The quicker you make a profit, the quicker you can start production on your next film. With the money we made off of the digital movie, we could afford to make a low budget picture on film. We didn't because the executive producer needed some quick cocaine

* EDITOR'S NOTE: This is true from an economic perspective, but Kaufman believes that having a low budget allows you to unburden yourself of monetary concerns and take greater artistic risks. This belief has led to Sam Grogg, dean of AFI's Center for Advanced Film and TV Studies, to say in an issue of *Creative Screenwriting* magazine, "Lloyd Kaufman represents one of the true, great auteurs." In return for working with a low budget, Kaufman has total control of his movies, a luxury that only a few contemporary directors like Woody Allen and Martin Scorsese enjoy. Of course, this is the only luxury that Kaufman has in common with Allen and Scorsese, but it is not an insignificant one.

money or something . . . but the point is that digital video is the way to go if you are working with a low budget. Show nine out of ten people on the street something that's been shot digitally and they'll swear they're watching film. Theaters are beginning to project digitally. *Tales From the Crapper*, Troma's DV feature was fucked up the first time around and had to go back for significant reshoots, but even this process is cheaper and easier with DV. Pretty soon, Hollywood productions will be shot on video and the distribution of film will cease to rely on making and shipping cumbersome film prints made out of unstable petroleum by-products. You can not only be cost-conscious, but part of the wave of the future by going digital.

CHAPTER 4

Get Your Wimmen Nekkid and Other Invaluable Casting Tips

In my last bestseller,* *All I Need to Know About Filmmaking I Learned from the Toxic Avenger*, I spoke at great length about the trials and tribulations of working with actors. For those of you who were unable to purchase a copy due to the overwhelming demand for the book, I'll repeat the most important lesson contained therein:

MOST ACTORS SUCK

However! A very, very, very small percentage of them are among the greatest people in the world. There are even a handful of big-time movie stars (like Oscar winner Jon Voight) who are genuinely good, decent people. If you cast your film well, you will weed out the actors that suck and use the 1 percent that give you everything they've got and more besides. I've been lucky enough to build an ensemble of actors out of the 1 percent and these people have become lifelong friends. Actors like Will Keenan, Mark Torgl, Yaniv Sharon, Debbie Rochon, Joe Fleishaker, Jane Jensen, and others have continued to be a part of the Tromaville Players, despite opportunities to make a shit-

* Sales tracking provided by the Florida electorate.

Lloyd Kaufman's two newly adopted daughters, Tracey and Allison, use the *Terror Firmer* comic books to cleverly conceal Aristotle's *Poetics* on the set of Troma's *Edge TV.*
(Doug Sakmann)

load more money than we could ever even pretend to offer them. There is no reason that you can't build your own recurring ensemble of gifted and generous actors. But first, you have to get people to the door of your casting ~~couch~~ . . . er, office.

Troma's basic theory of casting is to make the audition process as difficult as humanly possible without getting punched in the face. You may think this is a joke.* But I swear to whatever god you're comfortable with that, not only does it work, it's necessary. Troma movies require actors who are completely fearless, totally committed, and willing to do absolutely anything on camera. That could be anything from getting completely naked and running through the middle of Times Square to pissing and shitting themselves after their head is crushed.† The casting process should be a microcosm of the production of the

---

* For that matter, you may think my whole career is a joke. I guess I can't argue with that, but I'm dead serious about Troma's theory of casting.
† We do not, however, insist that our actors provide their own piss and shit. A trained crew of defecators is always standing by, ready to assist.

film. You need to find out what these people will and will not do. People who will not do something need to be eliminated. Don't hide anything from them. If there's nudity, *tell them*. If a part requires long, difficult, uncomfortable makeup applications, *tell them*. At this stage of the game, you should describe your production as the fifth concentric circle of Hell. If anything, make it sound much, much worse than it will actually be. That way, your cast can be pleasantly surprised when it all turns out okay.

Getting people to audition for your film is relatively simple. Ask anybody on the street if they'd like to be a big, famous movie star and every single one of them will respond with a resounding and emphatic "Yeah, I guess, why not." Filmmaking, particularly outside of Los Angeles and New York, is very glamorous to most people. You may know that the process is rife with neurosis, stress, fatigue, filth, and gastrointestinal distress, but the rest of the world doesn't. To paraphrase a movie whose title I can't remember,* "If you make it, they will come."

The first step in the audition process is the open call. This is traditionally the most amusing part of the process, as well. Here, you get anybody and everybody from all walks of life and give 'em sixty seconds to do whatever the fuck they feel like. As with every audition, you should videotape the entire thing. I learned this, and a lot of other things, from John Avildsen when I helped him cast *Cry Uncle*. When I worked on *Joe* in 1970, he had the idea to film the auditions and rehearsals on Super-8. We switched over to video on *Cry Uncle*. Around the same time, I was hanging out with Andy Warhol's Factory crowd. Warhol always carried an Instamatic camera with him and photographed everything. Ever since, I've carried a camera with me most everywhere I go. Now that video cameras are about as small as a Wrap-Around Sally rubber vagina, I've started to carry one of those with me as well.† By keeping a camera with you all the time, you're prepared for

---

* It may have been something called *Field of Creams* starring Troma regular Ron Jeremy.
† By "one of those," I'm referring to the video camera. I've been carrying Wrap-Around Sallies with me for decades now.

those moments when you just happen to see the perfect location or (and this is more pertinent to our discussion here) the perfect actor.

During your auditions, don't just lock the camera down and forget about it. Hopefully your movie will consist of more than just medium shots from fifteen feet away, so your audition tapes should, too. Use the camera to get in there and really look at these people. If there's anything particularly unusual or distinctive about their look, focus on that. Explore the bodies of good-looking guys and gynos. But I'm getting ahead of myself. First, you need to get the bodies in the room.

If you live anywhere near a metropolis, you can place advertisements in an industry trade magazine like *Backstage* or *Variety*. For the 99 percent of the planet that doesn't live in or near a large city, any classifieds section of a local newspaper will do. Most places have classified mini-papers where you can advertise anything for free—just look for key words like "saver," "penny," or "cheap ass" in the title. The Internet might be another good place to list (usually free), but then you're dealing with an international audience. Flying in actors from other regions isn't an option for a big and powerful motion picture company like Troma, so it's probably out of the question for you, too.

But don't worry, I have had the most success at casting by using one of the cheapest methods available: posting flyers. For the last thirty years, for every movie I've done, from *Battle of Love's Return* to *Citizen Toxie*, the cheapie flyer has been my primary means of obtaining a cast. A simple piece of paper with the words "YOU CAN BE A MOVIE STAR" posted throughout a local college campus, video store or old folks home will result in a line of nubile undergrads, zit-faced teenage loners, and geriatric hotties outside your door. Don't be afraid to get creative with the flyers, either. In 1967 on *The Girl Who Returned*, I wanted a wide range of people to choose from but knew that since this was my first film, people weren't necessarily going to come out in droves just to be in my movie. So I made up flyers that read, STANLEY KAUFMAN IS CASTING FOR A NEW MOVIE. Stanley is my first name (I was named after my father) and, coincidentally, Stanley Kauffman is a highly regarded film critic from *The New Republic*. Not a lie, not a hoax, simply a mild exploitation of a fortuitous association and most people's inability to spell. It worked, too. I got a pant-load of shitty actors of all ages and sizes willing to work for free in my half-assed, 16mm, Bolex-shot* film.

While most of the people that show up at your casting office after seeing your flyer won't be professional actors, don't let this stop you from auditioning them. Many great films have been made with "non-actors," from *Class of Nuke 'Em High, Part 3: The Good, the Bad, and the Subhumanoid* to *The Bicycle Thief*. If a character in your film is a homeless one-armed black castrato with a Ph.D. in astrophysics and a facial tic, there is a person out there who *is* that character. In Hollywood, they'd pay Mel Gibson† $20 million, erase his arm with CGI, and hire teams of black castrati and astrophysicists to train him for six months. And, whether or not the studio was able to purchase an Academy Award to give Mel the stamp of approval, his performance would never come close to the real thing.

Of course, your quest for realism isn't going to amount to squat unless you communicate what you're trying to accomplish with your crew. For a scene in *The Toxic Avenger* that required a guy to have his arm torn off, I had the brilliant idea of casting a bona fide amputee. After a long and arduous search, I found Larry Sutton. He wasn't a professional actor. He was an IRS agent who wanted to act and was willing to have his handicap immortalized on celluloid. However, the overeager special makeup effects crew decided to create a fake arm-stump anyway. Without my knowledge, they tied his real arm behind his back, put the fake stump on his shoulder and rigged the fake arm

---

* This means it was shot on a Bolex camera, a type of 16mm camera that was quite high-tech back when it was introduced in the 1930s. When I got around to using one, it was already the kind of camera you found lying around your grandparents' attic, covered in dust and rat piss. This should not be confused with a Botox-shot film, which would mean that it stars Michael Douglas.

† Because the very first thing to be changed would be the character's ethnicity.

up on that side of his body, completely defeating the purpose of casting Larry in the first place.

You, as the independent filmmaker, have the advantage of spending as much time as possible finding the perfect cast. You don't have the time constraints that a "real" production company has. This can be used to your advantage in the casting process. Take your time. Find the right people for the job. Sometimes the right people, like Larry, aren't professional actors. Joe Fleishaker is a 500-pound computer programmer, yet has turned in brilliant performances in everything from *Troma's War* to *Citizen Toxie*. Trent Haaga was also some kind of computer hotshot* when he wandered into the Troma offices and Will Keenan suggested we audition him for the role of Jerry in *Terror Firmer*. Of course, there are probably outstanding amateur actors who are not computer geeks. But a lot of these techno-types have made a lot of money in the real world and are more than willing to take a pay cut (down to about zero dollars an hour) in order to live their dreams of being a movie star.

I WAS A TROMA ACTOR or HOW I FLUSHED A PROMISING AND LUCRATIVE COMPUTER CAREER STRAIGHT DOWN THE CRAPPER
Trent Haaga

This is something that I know a little bit about, as acting is to blame for my involvement with Troma.

I was a Tromite like you, working a shitty job and dreaming about someday being able to make my own damn movie (hell, I was willing to make somebody else's damn movie, for that mat-

---

* Designing Web sites or something like that . . . I'm really not sure. I try not to pry into personal details that I probably won't understand.

ter). Being a Tromite (and some sort of computer geek, as Lloyd said), I went to Troma's Web site.

BE AN ACTOR-PERSON IN OUR NEW FILM! it said. There was a phone number. I had never acted before, never even thought about it. But I had seen some of the acting in Lloyd's films and figured he had no aversion to hiring amateurs. Besides, it was a call for extras—how good did I have to be? I called the phone number and a production assistant told me the address of the production office (actually an old, dilapidated karate studio with rotting, sweat-stained foam rubber stapled all over the floor). I went there after work and was delighted to be auditioned by none other than Tromeo himself, Will Keenan. Since I wasn't an actor, I had no headshot or résumé. Will told me not to worry about it and to just do something for the camera. I proceeded to tell the story of how I lost all of my friends in high school when I repeatedly exposed them to multiple Troma films and they quit hanging out with me. "Lloyd," I said, "you owe me for losing cherished friends due to my overwhelming Troma support. I'd love to be an extra. But if you could kill me in this movie, I'll name my firstborn child after you." (As I write this, my firstborn is incubating in my wife's tummy. I lied, Stanley Lloyd Kaufman, Jr., I lied.)

I got a "call-back" a day later and went back to the karate studio. Will Keenan handed me some "sides" and said, "Here's a scene for a guy who gets killed . . . But would you mind reading for one of the lead roles?" Shit, man, just getting called back was cool. But getting to *read* for a guy who gets killed and even a lead role? This is the kind of story I could tell young Stanley Lloyd when he asked me how he got such a shitty name. Once I read the lines for the "Jerry" character (who I eventually ended up playing in the film), I knew that I *had* to have the part and that I would do anything for it.

Did I say I'd do anything? It was true. Lloyd had me come back to the karate studio *every day* for about three weeks. He'd have me read with one person, then another, then wait around for four hours, then send me home without a clue as to whether I had the part or not. The boss at my regular job was beginning to get annoyed at my long lunches and early departures, but I kept coming back, hoping for the proverbial green light. The role of Jerry required me to be in a sex scene. I was brought in every day for a week to strip down and make out with some naked girl I had just met—I know it sounds awesome, but it can be pretty weird. Especially when you've only been with your wife for a decade and there's a handful of people standing around videotaping it. Still, Lloyd led me along with no indication as to whether I'd get the part or not. In the end, I think it was definitely the fact that I put up with so much shit that got me the part, not my "acting ability," "screen presence," or "chemistry." To tell the truth, Lloyd didn't want to hire me because I wasn't a real actor and I didn't physically fit the part as he imagined it—a fat, bearded makeup effects guy.* Will Keenan repeatedly went to bat for me.† That, coupled with my overwhelming desire to be in a Troma movie, is what got me the part. In the end, Lloyd ended up with an actor who stayed behind with the crew and

* LLOYD KAUFMAN RESPONDS: I don't remember ever wanting a fat, bearded guy for the role of Jerry. I wanted a good-looking leading man type. What happened was that all the other people we read for the part were either extremely gay or couldn't act at all. Despite the fact that Trent was and is extremely gay, he was a good enough actor that he was able to hide it well enough that his sex scenes with Alyce LaTourelle were believable. No, my memory is that I wanted Trent to play Jerry from the moment his lips first met mine and we succumbed to passion amidst the sweat-stained foam rubber in the karate studio.
† If only Will had bothered to fight for something worth fighting for, like better food or humane working conditions.

hauled garbage every day because he loved being there so much. As for my performance, I did the best I could. As for my on-set attitude, I like to think that Lloyd got his $150 worth from my twenty-eight days of work.

By the time we actually got to shoot, Lloyd had rehearsed and re-rehearsed all of us so much that he didn't need to work with the actors on set and could concentrate on more pressing matters like finding someone to clean out the prop porta-potty that someone had defecated in despite all of the signs posted on it that said it was a prop. Lloyd was a great director to work with as long as you had been hired to do a part. Many of the roles ended up going to whoever was unlucky enough to be standing around. For a great example of Lloyd's directing style with the untrained and unrehearsed actor, see the infamous "Joey the PA" scene in the documentary *Farts of Darkness* on Disc 2 of the *Terror Firmer* DVD.

Anyway, once you've papered the kiosks, store windows, bulletin boards, telephone poles, car windshields, and ladies rooms of your town with flyers, it's time to meet the teeming hordes of wannabe Brendan Frasers and Julia Robertses. Those who fancy themselves "professional" actors will most likely come prepared with a résumé and a head shot.* That's swell but you should make everybody, sea-

---

* A head shot is an 8 × 10 photo of the actor in some inane pseudoglamorous pose that you would never, *ever* want them to adopt in your movie. A head shot is *not* a bloody, gaping head wound. I was disappointed when I found out, too. The second word gets out that you are casting a movie, you will be mailed hundreds of thousands of head shots . . . more than enough to wallpaper the padded cell you will find yourself locked in after your movie's wrapped. More often than not, you will call these actors in only to discover that the beautiful, blemish-free Greek goddess in the airbrushed head shot only looks good from the neck up. Below the neck, she suffers from elephantiasis of the ass. The head shots are useful only for filing . . . *not* for making decisions.

You can see how flexible an actress *The Toxic Avenger*'s Andrea Miranda was. It's a shame Hollywood never took advantage of her ass . . . ets).

soned pro or rank amateur, fill out a form as soon as they arrive. The form should ask for all the general info you'd usually find on an actor's résumé (height, weight, age, some means whereby you can communicate with them on the off chance you think they're any good) but it should also ask more probing questions. Troma's form asks things like, is nudity a problem?* (this results in some great responses when you're auditioning fat slobs and eighty-year-old women) and, can you provide any special wardrobe or costumes?†

---

* If their response to this question is, "Nudity is acceptable if done in good taste or the script calls for it," reject them immediately. They will back out of the nude scene when the time comes, I guarantee it. If they say, "I love it" or "It makes me hot," boy are you lucky! Fuck the movie! Ask them out on a date or something, you dumb shit!

† Remember to keep revising the script throughout. If a really good actor comes in and tells you they're a fireman and can provide you with fireman uniforms and a hook-and-ladder truck, see if there isn't someplace to work that in. Fire trucks are big, expensive, and they've got lights and sirens on 'em so they look neat on screen. I always like movies with fire trucks in them.

FIRE TRUCK LOVE
Trent Haaga

Lloyd really does love movies with fire trucks in them. There's an entire deleted scene in *Terror Firmer* where we talk about shooting a scene with a fire truck in it. I think Lloyd's love comes from the fact that a fire truck in a film is a sign of high production value.

While shooting a scene in *Citizen Toxie*, we accidentally set off the building's fire alarm with our smoke machine. As soon as the alarms went off, Lloyd began to yell like a drill sergeant for us to take the camera out to the street corner. Within minutes, we had a handful of fire trucks pull into the building's lot with their sirens and lights blazing. The camera was already there to catch the action. Instant production value.

At this first audition, give your potential stars sixty seconds to do whatever they want to do. If they use the first chunk of this valuable time to say something like, "My name is Janet Finkleburger and I'm an actress," I usually stick them in the actor-person* file. However, each and every time you see these people, whether it's the first or the forty-first audition, ask them to take a few seconds and say their name and phone number on camera. This way, when your crack-addicted PA fucks up the notes he/she/it is supposed to be diligently taking, you'll still be able to contact the people you want. Also, you might want to date some of the cuter Gynos or guys who audition for you and this is a convenient way to get their number.

---

*On less enlightened productions, actor-persons are referred to as "extras." On a Troma set, we do not use this demeaning term, believing that if we cannot acknowledge their valuable contribution through amenities such as food and toilet facilities that aren't made out of paper, the least we can do is give them some respect.

Some of the things you should look for in the initial audition are energy, creativity, and screen presence. It's extremely difficult to gauge a person's acting ability based on sixty seconds of anything. You might have somebody come in and do sixty seconds of *Hamlet* that blows you out of the water, but when your script calls for him to tell a joke about a rabbi, a gorilla, and a six-inch pianist walking into a gay bar, he suddenly becomes as stiff as a six-inch pianist and as unnatural as if he'd learned the lines phonetically. A lot of the best actors I've worked with won me over in their very first audition by doing something out of the ordinary. Jane Jensen auditioned for *Tromeo & Juliet* wearing a plaid schoolgirl skirt and Oxford shirt and recited dialogue from *The Toxic Avenger*. Will Keenan had read an interview where I was asked whether I was open to script contributions from cast and crew. I replied that I'd let the pizza delivery guy contribute jokes if I thought they were funny. Will came into his first audition for *Tromeo* with a pizza box and delivery cap so I'd remember him and call him back. Actors have a very limited amount of time during this first audition to make a good impression (or even a bad impression for that matter . . . you'll probably see so many people that you'll simply forget most of them even existed). Anything they can do to stick out in your memory is welcome.

After the first round of casting, take your collection of tapes and review them with your casting director (if that isn't you), your screenwriter (if that isn't you), your producer (if that isn't you), and your DP (if that isn't you) . . . basically, any of your key personnel. Try to involve as much of your team as you can in the audition process. They will all be looking at different aspects of each person and their opinions will be of untold value. But while you should listen to and appreciate their opinions, in the end you'll need to do what you believe. When we were casting *Tromeo & Juliet*, both James Gunn and Andrew Weiner were initially against casting Jane Jensen as Juliet. The person they wanted was also a good actress but had bigger breasts and a zaftig look, but I stood firm in my conviction that Jane was perfect for the part. Eventually, I think James and Andrew saw that I was correct even though they still believe I'm gay because of my fondness for women with trim, athletic bodies and small breasts . . . and possibly because I'm always dropping the soap whenever the three of us shower together. I also held out for the lithe, small-breasted charms of Alyce LaTourelle in *Terror Firmer*, a decision that was not met with unanimous agreement by Will Keenan and the rest of my team but ultimately resulted in a terrific performance. With both Jane and Alyce, I went with the best actress. Of course some times, you should tell yourself to shut the fuck up and listen to other people. Unfortunately, Michael Herz, my partner at Troma and co-director of many Troma movies, including *The Toxic Avenger Parts 1–3*, has asked . . . well, demanded really . . . that he not be mentioned in this book. Michael has always shunned publicity, particularly of the sort I seem to generate, so as much as I'd like to and informative as it would be, I swore to Michael I would not mention the time when Michael decided not to cast future media queen Madonna for a major part in our movie *The First Turn-On*. Despite the fact that Madonna told Michael that she would do *anything* to be in a Troma movie, Michael felt she seemed more "Italian grandmother" than the "Jewish princess" we were looking for. Yes, out of respect for Michael's wishes to remain anonymous and out of the limelight, I cannot tell you that story or any other stories about Michael Herz, not even the incident where we were locked up in a Japanese prison and Michael made me his bitch, making sweet sweet man-love to me long into the night. I have made a solemn vow to my lifelong friend and partner, Michael Herz, that I will not so much as mention the name Michael Herz in this book. Don't worry, Michael. Your secrets are safe with me.*

You will probably run into some actors who are intimidated by auditioning in front of a large group, especially if you're doing a nude

---

* If I *was* allowed to say anything about Michael, these stories would be found in Chapters 6, 8, and 9, and on a special, password-protected Web site, www.secretsofmichaelherz.com.

scene. Get rid of them immediately. If they can't do this shit in front of five or six strangers, how the fuck do they expect to do it on set in front of dozens of drooling crew members, castmates and investors, not to mention the many hangers-on and rubberneckers who invariably pop up during the filming of fucking scenes . . . oops, sorry . . . sex scenes . . . I mean, "love scenes."

Oh, yeah . . . so the first round is over and you're looking at the tapes of people doing their sixty seconds . . . right. Now, get rid of the ones you hated and call back the interesting ones.* The rest of the auditions should be more structured than the improvisational free-for-all you hosted at the open call. Starting with the first call-back, the auditioners should read pages from your script.† Sometimes when you're calling back actors, they will ask to see the scenes they will be reading in advance. I have met filmmakers who won't let any pages from their script out of their possession until the last possible second. This is the behavior of an asshole. If you're lucky enough to have actors with enough initiative to want to prepare, by all means let them take the pages home to do just that. Your script may be brilliant but it isn't the plans and locations of top-secret missile silos defending this great nation. With all your actors, encourage improvisation as much as possible. Some of the best ideas come from actors going off-script during auditions.

The call-backs should test not only the auditioners' acting ability, but also their dedication to your project. If you think you'll be ready for the actor at 3 P.M. make him show up at 1 P.M. Make all the auditioners wait together and have someone observe how they get along.

---

* And don't worry about offending the ones you didn't like. Just say, "Sorry but we've decided to go in a different direction but we'll keep you in mind for future projects." It's the diplomatic way of saying "You're shit!" Afterwards, you can hang up the phone and both you and the "auditionee" can bask in the knowledge that you will never see each other again.
† In Actorspeak, these are called "sides" for no apparent reason other than maybe actors wanted to have some cool lingo of their own that nobody else understands.

One way to save money on your film is in the costume department, as *Class of Nuke 'Em High*'s Jennifer Babtist proudly displays.

When you call them in to read, put them into different groups and combinations to see the different ways they interact. Chemistry is impossible to define and is arguably an even greater quality to capture than individual performances.* And videotape every single thing. Remember that what you're looking for is going to be seen through the camera lens, not with the naked eye.

And speaking of naked, if a part in your script requires a nude scene, you should eventually require the auditioners to disrobe. I have learned the hard way that it's easy for someone to verbally agree to take their clothes off and even easier for them to go back on their word when it's time to bare all. If they're going to do it at all, they will understand when you ask them to do it during the audition process. Anybody who says, "When the time comes, I'll do it . . . but I won't do it until then," is lying. Besides, if you're serious about making your own damn movie, you will eventually lose all your friends and family and the only thing you will have to keep you company is your library of naked audition tapes.

---

* However, under no circumstances should you allow your cast or crew to be chemically altered.

Be careful when you're at this stage of the audition process. If you're a male director, do not audition people by yourself. Ever. Always have a female assistant with you to protect yourself from any charges of sexual harassment, particularly when you're auditioning nude scenes. Otherwise, if you're alone in a room with just the auditioning actor, it's your word against hers. It's way too easy for somebody to say anything they want about what happened in that room and completely fuck up your life forever.*

If you're shooting in New York or especially Los Angeles, you will most assuredly get union actors auditioning for you. This is because the Screen Actors Guild (SAG) couldn't possibly be any easier to get into. Their main requirement seems to be that you have $1,200 for your "initiation fee." Even I'm in SAG and I'm one of the worst actors you'll find. But just because somebody is in the union does not mean they won't work on a nonunion movie. At any given time, only about 1 percent of SAG's active members are actually working, so it's not like they don't have time on their hands, and of the SAG members who *do* have jobs on a union production, the vast majority of them don't get decent parts. They appreciate being allowed to show what they can do on a nonunion gig. Be careful, though, because the union will threaten your actors with stiff penalties and even order them to leave the project if it's discovered that they're working on a nonunion shoot. Unless your actor has a nonunion identical twin, you'll find yourself royally fucked if SAG pulls them off your set.† Once again, bring out the old *Fun With Pseudonyms* handbook and anoint your actors with new handles like Lawanda Huggins, Bob Testes or Kinky Finkelstein (see *Citizen Toxie*).

---

* On the other hand, if you're an actor and find yourself alone in an audition with just one guy, get the fuck out of there. It's bullshit and you're probably in danger.

† Don't think they won't do it, either. The scumbags at SAG even kicked out Aldo Ray (star of George Cukor's *The Marrying Kind*) after he fell on hard times and worked in some nonunion pictures so he could pay the rent.

The main drawback to your production signing with the union (and the big reason we don't) is that SAG imposes all kinds of arcane rules and regulations on productions that will quickly eat through your meager budget. If you have a union actor scheduled to work on Monday and Friday, you've also got to pay them for Tuesday, Wednesday, and Thursday while they're miles away from your set, probably getting assfucked on Fire Island. Most important, I prefer to shoot in sequence. I consider shooting in sequence to be one of the great luxuries of working with a low budget. Low budgets enable you as an artist to exert a greater level of control on your art and, in filmmaking, I believe there is no better way to control your story than to shoot in sequence. This way, you can constantly rejigger your script as you go along, adapting to unforseeable situations and circumstances and working them into your movie.

For instance, if one actor turns out to be a real asshole and another turns out to be much better than you'd anticipated, shooting in sequence enables you to kill off the asshole* and beef up the part of the nonasshole. That's virtually impossible on a SAG movie. You are economically forced to shoot everything you need with that actor in big blocks of time. Since we're constantly rewriting the script, a requirement of the SAG kind would put some pretty big restrictions on our creativity. On *Citizen Toxie*, the idea to once again throw little Melvin out the window at the end and bring the story full circle back to the original *Toxic Avenger* didn't come to me until we were on set and shooting. If we'd shot according to SAG rules, I might have had to shoot the ending first and I never would have discovered the climax we ended up with.

Also, SAG imposes nonsensical rules on its productions like you must provide a meal every six hours and actors must have a minimum

---

* Well, the asshole's character, anyway. You should probably just fire the asshole.

of ten hours between the "wrap"* and the next day's call. If you're running some kind of holiday camp instead of a movie set, by all means follow these rules. But if you're looking to get your movie done on time and on budget, your cast and crew will actually need to work. Besides, whenever actors complain about working thirteen or fourteen hour days, remind them that for most of that time they're sitting around picking their noses and waiting for the crew to set up the shot so they can go out and work for five minutes.

Now if your project is relatively small in scope and you only need a handful of actors, you may actually want to go with the union. If your script is dependent on brilliant performances (i.e., lots of dialogue and emotions more complex than, say, puking), then you will definitely find better actors in SAG (except for me, of course). SAG will work with low-budget independent filmmakers and has specific agreements for low-budget, experimental, and student films. The bad news is that SAG, for all intents and purposes, becomes your partner on the film. They'll take a huge percentage of any money you make and, like any partner, they get the right to audit you whenever they get a tickle in their ass. For productions like ours, which use a shitload of actors, not only is it easier and less expensive to shoot completely nonunion, it gives us more control over the finished product. I truly believe that the great advantage of low-budget filmmaking is the tremendous level of control you have over the movie. The more you can control your art, the better off you are. Ultimately, whether or not you want to work with the union is a decision you'll have to make for yourself.

There will most likely come a time in your casting process where you've narrowed a part down to two or three potential actors. Don't let that bog down the pre-production process. Start rehearsals with the

---

* Wrap = end of the filming day. A gift wrap is the end of a particularly good filming day. A Saran wrap is a filming day that ends with you wanting to put a plastic bag over your head.

cast that you have secured and extend the audition process into rehearsals. On *Citizen Toxie*, we had our Toxic Avenger (Dave Mattey) before we had Sara, his beautiful, blind, blond, bimbo wife. We began rehearsing with three Saras and eventually picked the hilarious, brilliant Heidi Sjursen over the others.* Ultimately, these kind of decisions are based partly on performance, partly on chemistry, and partly on ability to withstand difficult conditions with, if not a smile, at least an absence of bitching.

My one hard rule (which has become flaccid over the years since I often break it) is, has been, and will always be to pick the best human being over the best actor.† When it comes time to make your final decision, you should always pick the individual who would be willing to wade through pig shit and razorblades to complete your film— who knows, you may end up having them do just that for your dramatic "pig shit and razorblades escape" sequence. I'm not here to belittle the "craft" of a serious actor.‡ But finding someone who'll show up on time, hit their cues repeatedly, and is willing to subsist solely on cheese sandwiches and defecate in a paper sack is a far more valuable member of the team than a great actor with a strict vegan diet who requires a trailer or other private spot to "get into character," whatever that means. Remember that these people will be shitting, eating, and maybe sleeping with you nonstop for weeks—their work ethics and attitudes will come into play far more than their ability to act. I cast Vincent D'Onofrio in *The First Turn-On* and when it came time to make *The Toxic Avenger*, I remembered him and cast him in a larger role. But times had changed, and so had his attitude toward

---

* It's also interesting to note that this is a rare case of my choosing an actress with large, melon-heavy breasts over actresses with smaller breasts.

† There may be situations where the best person is also the best actor, but don't bank on this.

‡ Though I guess my putting the word "craft" in quotation marks is kind of there to belittle the craft of a serious actor.

working long hours for very little reward, and I fired him.* After all, the camera is only rolling for a tiny fraction of the time it takes to make a movie.

The really hard part comes once you've found that perfect cast. Now is the time for you to assert yourself as the visionary ringleader, the psychologist, the hypnotist, and the Samurai master of filmmaking. Alfred Hitchcock, a director of some renown, once stated that "actors should be treated like cattle." I followed his advice for a while until I realized that only a few actors enjoy being milked and a good shock from a cattle prod will render your actor unconscious. This eats into your valuable production time.

In other words, it's up to you as the director to figure out how to treat your actors. I can't tell you exactly how to get the performances you need from them. Every director has his, her, or its own method. You'll need to be the visionary so that your actors become willing to go all out and participate in your groundbreaking cinematic tour de force. You'll become the psychologist who has to coddle and "understand" the talent. Your hypnotism skills will come into play when you need to convince the actors that the work is the reward since you're not going to pay them.† The Samurai master will come in handy when you've got to threaten performances out of them with a sharp sword. This is one lesson that will extend to all aspects of producing and directing your film: being able to not only wear many hats, but to be able to switch the hats at a moment's notice. My own directorial technique has always been to either scream at the actor like a madman or cry

---

* I don't remember exactly the circumstances of his being fired but he assured the Troma Team in Park City during the 2000 TromaDance Film Festival that I shit-canned him.

EDITOR'S NOTE: Vincent D'Onofrio later won praise for his work in such films as *Full Metal Jacket*. In this chapter alone, Kaufman has admitted to passing over Madonna and firing Vincent D'Onofrio. Why exactly did we ask him to write this book again?

† The script should be the *only* thing cheaper than paying the cast when it comes to your film. Simply remind the actors that there are many other people who would *pay you* to be in the movie and that they're going to become rich movie stars after this anyway.

Cindy Manion of *The Toxic Avenger* shows exactly what it takes to be a Tromette—mounds and mounds of T-and-A: Talent and Acting!

like a woman, but there may be better ways to elicit a performance.

Casting your movie should be one of the most exciting elements of pre-production. For the first time you will see glimmers of your story coming to life. This is an extremely fertile area for ideas, as new voices can springboard lines, scenes, and even whole characters that are even more interesting than what you've come up with. Listen to these voices. Rewrite constantly and create an ensemble that matches your vision. This isn't about winning popularity contests. It's about the film. Time heals all wounds and, sooner or later, your cast will see that what was perceived as abhorrent, bipolar behavior worthy of a psycho ward was, in fact, a brilliant directorial technique. Make a good movie and all will be forgiven. Make a bad movie and it will never be forgotten.

CHAPTER 5

Pre-Production—The Key to Your Future Therapy

It's a hot Sunday afternoon in Los Angeles, a city I love almost as much as having a cyst removed from my rectal wall. I come out to L.A. fairly often, usually to fellate television executives and video buyers for major retail chains.* I also look in on Troma's West Coast office, a concern that has grown from a tiny one-room office packed full of videos, posters, and sellsheets to an impressive two-story house packed full of videos, posters, and sellsheets in Hollywood behind the American Cinematheque's beautifully restored Egyptian Theatre. Historically, Troma West has been overseen by a variety of talented but mildly disturbed individuals. These days, we employ a record number of employees in Los Angeles: two, including Adam Jahnke, my collaborator on this very book.

Today, I am due to have lunch with John Foster, one of Troma's key financial allies and fund-raisers.† Armed with directions Adam gave me,

---

* EDITOR'S NOTE: When asked about this behavior, Kaufman will attempt to justify it by muttering that this is the only way to convince mainstream companies to stock Troma product. In fact, our private investigators have discovered that Kaufman secretly enjoys doing this and will often schedule trips to Los Angeles even when Troma has no new titles to promote.

† Believe it or not, people are not exactly standing in line to invest in projects that revel in elderly ladies having their heads crushed and tiny-peckered fat guys running naked through Times Square. Because our patrons are few and far between, we do everything we can to hang on to

I arrive at the designated spot, a fancy multistory office building in Westwood, and take the elevator up to where Foster's office is supposed to be. There's an office all right. Just no Foster. It's the offices of the Trial Lawyers Association of Los Angeles. I can feel every eye in the room mentally serving me a subpoena.

I beat an embarrassed retreat to the elevator and dial Adam on my cell phone. Amazingly enough, the reception is clear as a bell.

"Adam, this is Lloyd. I'm at the place you told me to go only there's no John Foster here. Are you sure this is the right place? Did you double-check the address?"

"Yeah, Lloyd. That's weird. Hang on. I'll call Allison (John's assistant) and find out what's going on and call you right back."

This seemed weirder than usual to me but my anger was mitigated by the fact that I had somehow discovered the only elevator in the universe with perfect cellular reception. I stayed in the elevator while I waited to hear from Adam to capitalize on this nexus of cellular technology, trying to smile harmlessly at office workers who must have thought I was some kind of elevator fetishist.

Moments later, the phone rang. "Lloyd, it's Adam. You're in the wrong building. They moved down the street."

"*What*?!!" Suddenly, the fact that I was getting such great reception didn't seem like such a big deal. "What the fuck?! How could that be? So you didn't check the address."

"I asked if they were still on Wilshire and they said they were."

"Oh, for fuck's sake, man! What the fuck! This is fucking bullshit! It's absolute fucking asshole time! Now I wasted eleven dollars on parking in this place, I'm late, and Foster thinks I'm an asshole! This is fucked! Fuck! Now I don't know where the fuck I'm going! Jesus-fucking-Christ on a pogo stick!"

I headed back down to my overpriced rental car and drove down

---

the ones we've got. This includes such unheard-of behavior as treating them with polite respect and arriving on time for meetings.

Wilshire, yelling at Adam the whole time. After a few minutes of brilliantly profane monologue, I realized I hadn't heard his voice for a while and noticed my cell phone has dropped the call. I punched redial and resumed where I left off.

"All right, now what the fuck do I do?"

"Take Wilshire down to Federal."

"There's nothing here. This is bullshit, Adam. There's nothing here but a World Savings Bank."

"That's it. You're there."

"Okay, so I'm here. Where the fuck am I supposed to park?"

"Take a right on Berry. There's a ramp to your right after the stop sign."

"I'm on Berry. There's nothing here. That's exactly where the parking garage is not. This is fucking awful sloppy fucking bullshit."

"I know, Lloyd."

"No, you don't fucking know or you wouldn't have fucking done it! Now I'm late, Foster thinks I'm a fucking asshole who's blown him off, and even if I do make this meeting I have absolutely no fucking idea what the fuck I was supposed to talk to him about anymore! Anyway, I think I'm here now. Okay, thank you, Adam. Thanks."*

I walked into the meeting about half an hour late, dripping with flop sweat and looking like a maniacal asshole that you wouldn't give two bits to for a cup of coffee on the street, much less several hundred thousand dollars to make a movie. The positive side of this incident is that it drilled home for me (and Adam, I hope)† the necessity of being

---

* When you are a low-budget filmmaker, you can't afford to really piss off people who are working for virtually nothing, so you learn to end every conversation by thanking the person you're talking to, even if they just completely fucked you over.

† ADAMS JAHNKE RESPONDS: This entire incident was done intentionally on my part. I'd been working on the book with Lloyd for a few months at this point and it was starting to seem about as interesting as a driver's manual. We needed a little something to spice it up, so I sent Lloyd to the wrong address just to see what would happen. If this plan didn't work, I had a guy standing by ready to try to kill Lloyd next time he came to town. I think I called that plan off . . . pretty sure, anyway.

absolutely anal when it comes to directions and confirmations. If this had been a shoot and I had been driving the lead actor to the set* and gotten that off track, everything would have been fucked. And the time to make sure every single thing is set in stone is pre-production.

The most common misconception in independent filmmaking is that making a movie is a surefire way to fame, fortune, and a lifetime of no-holds-barred, no-questions-asked, guilt-free sex. The second most common misconception is that pre-production is over as soon as your movie is cast. While you might want to hold on to the fame/fortune/sex dream (it's certainly helped keep me going for the past thirty-five years), you'll want to rid yourself of that second fantasy right now.

Pre-production is the low budget filmmaker's best friend and worst enemy. You should use this time to plan every detail of production, from hiring the cast and crew on down to the food and where they'll end up shitting the food. But while you don't want to rush into production too quickly, you also don't want to drag pre-production out so long that the people you're working with lose interest and enthusiasm. It can be extremely difficult to know when to pull the trigger and start production. When I was codirecting with Michael Herz, Michael was expert at knowing when it was time to pull the plug on pre-production. If it weren't for Michael, I'd probably still be prepping for *Waitress!* (1980).

Most of your pre-production time will be spent doing things like writing and refining the script, hiring the crew, and casting the actors. This means that about 75 percent of your pre-production time will be gone before you even realize you're in pre-production. Everything else, including all the picayune little details discussed in this and the next chapter, will be addressed in the last few days before you start shooting.

At first glance, it may seem as though we're spending an inordinate amount of time on pre-production. No doubt some of you reading this

---

* Hell, even if I'd been driving myself to the set, for that matter. There are actually a few people who think the director is essential to have on set during production.

are thinking, "I'm halfway through this fucking thing and he still hasn't shot a single frame! No wonder Kaufman's still just a broken-down low-budget filmmaker while every other person of his generation has gone on to do something substantial with their career. This guy's too fucking chicken-shit to actually go into production on anything!"

While you're right that I'm a complete pussy about making the leap into production, that's not why I'm spending so much time discussing pre-production. It's been my experience talking to other low-budget filmmakers that people don't seem to realize just how important pre-production is. You will be able to save yourself from countless headaches by spending the extra time in pre-production.* I believe that because we spent so much time planning every detail on our productions, movies like *The Toxic Avenger* have more staying power than some of their low-budget contemporaries. And while these chapters may seem somewhat scattershot and disorganized, they're practically a step-by-step recipe compared to what these last days of pre-production will actually be like. Things will come up at the absolute last second and suddenly these things will be the most important jobs in the world.

Without a doubt, this will be the most stressful time as a filmmaker, which puts it high in the running for the most stressful time in your life. It is during these last few days that details will mount up. But, instead of your project being subservient to your will and control, it will feel as if you are a slave to your own creation. You will see this gigantic avalanche of problems and details rumbling toward you and your first inclination will naturally be to run away. After all, you haven't actually shot anything yet. You can still pull the plug on this whole enterprise, return your investors' money and go back to the nice, quiet life you led before you had the insane idea to make this damn movie in the first place.

---

* Don't get me wrong . . . you're still gonna end up with migraines that would cripple a charging rhino. But the extra prep time will reduce the number of headaches from about 10,000 to 5,000.

Do not be discouraged. These feelings are not unique to the first-time filmmaker. I go through this every single time I make a movie. I've written, directed, produced, production managed, and/or wiped asses on about 100 movies, yet pre-production still sends me into a state of withdrawal similar to that which affected Proust and Brian Wilson of the Beach Boys.* So the bad news is if you continue to make your own damn movies, you can look forward to experiencing this almost paralyzing sense of helplessness and insecurity over and over again. But the good news is you *can* get through it. Each problem you encounter has a solution. The one you find may be perfect or it may lead to ten more problems, each of which has its own solution. But you *will* find a solution and you *will* get your movie made. On every single movie I've made, I've run into this same problem where I feel like I don't know what I'm doing. And yet I muddle through and continue to make movie after movie. If a manic-depressive like me can cut through this haze of self-doubt, then surely a well-adjusted individual such as yourself can do the same.

In these final days before production starts, every job is important. And it is equally important that everyone doing her job has a handle on what everyone else is doing. For whatever reason, people become very suspicious and protective of their work on a movie set, especially on big-budget productions. The departments can become separate little fiefdoms resenting one another. I noticed this was a big problem when I worked on movies like *Saturday Night Fever* and *The Final Countdown*. This counterproductive bullshit is a breeding ground for rumor and dissent among the ranks. You'll need to kill it before it takes hold. For this and other reasons, a central production office is an absolute necessity. This can be an actual office, a warehouse, or your garage— just about anywhere as long as you've got a phone and maybe a fax and a computer. On *The Battle of Love's Return* where I did pretty much

* Of course, unlike those guys who were able to actually work while they retreated into their beds, I just want to crawl under the covers and pee all over myself.

everything myself, my "production office" was my mom's house. On *Citizen Toxie*, it was a warehouse and everybody worked together in one big room and slept on the floors. On bigger movies, the production office will be segregated into private offices. On *Saturday Night Fever* and *The Final Countdown*, I convinced the producer to have everyone work together in one big room. Nevertheless, despite my best efforts I still saw whatever sense of camaraderie that might have developed in the team disintegrate into petty rivalries and secrecy.

By including your entire team in every facet of production and not keeping anything from them, you'll create a stronger nucleus that's completely dedicated to your project. If people have questions about your budget (a subject that some filmmakers will guard more securely than their medical history), answer them. On *Citizen Toxie*, a PA asked me how much Hank the Angry Drunken Dwarf was getting paid for his performance and I told him straight out,* even though some filmmakers might have told the kid that it was none of his fucking business and he should go back to emptying the porta-potties like he's supposed to. When investors visit the office, don't be afraid to introduce them to your team. Some filmmakers will worry needlessly that someone else will "steal" their investors away. Don't get in that mode. Remember, it is a team and you are what's holding it together. If you set an example of being open and honest with everyone, hopefully the rest of your team will follow suit.

Once you've selected locations, you'll be heading back to them a number of times during pre-production. First you'll want to bring your entire crew out for a technical tour so your gaffer† can figure out your power situation,‡ your production manager or assistant director

---

* Hank was paid the princely sum of $600 per day for his Oscar-worthy supporting performance as God.

† Gaffer—the person on your crew who repeatedly makes huge mistakes (or gaffes).

‡ Usually your gaffer will be trying to figure out your electrical power situation. However, if you are planning on a run for Senate, he can also figure out your political power situation.

can figure out where to corral the actors between takes, and your DP can figure out where he can sneak off to fuck your leading lady. Later, bring cast and crew out to the location to rehearse. Be sure to video-tape all rehearsals and the technical tour. This will give you a head start on actual production, as well as give you plenty of additional footage to include as a bonus on an eventual DVD.

The job that will eat up a surprisingly huge amount of your time in pre-production (and the job that all others will tend to depend on being done correctly) is scheduling. Movie production is already chaotic enough as it is without a sloppy, half-assed schedule fucking things up even further. The schedule must bring order to the mad-ness of filmmaking. It must be rigid enough that every minute of the day is filled and not a second is wasted. But it must be flexible enough to keep production going even if one of your actors gets sick or a special effect is delayed or a location is wiped out by a tsunami.

You may recall that in the previous chapter I drove home the point that shooting your movie in sequence is one of the greatest luxuries a filmmaker can enjoy. This is true. However, you may not be able to afford any luxuries on your set. On *Citizen Toxie*, I had $450,000 and a 30-day shooting schedule. You might have $45,000 and an 8-day shooting schedule. While we could afford to move back and forth between different locations (shooting in one place one day, another the next, then back to the original place days later), you may be forced by economic necessity to shoot every bit of footage you need in one location in one day, regardless of where it comes in the script. I encourage you to shoot in sequence whenever possible, but you should not do so at the expense of your budget, your schedule or your sanity . . . well, it may be all right to sacrifice your sanity. At this point, it probably won't be much of a sacrifice anyway.

These days, there are computer programs by the truckload designed to make scheduling and budgeting movies simpler. On *Citizen Toxie*, we originally hired a young go-getter to be my AD* and he quickly and efficiently used one of these programs to transform the screenplay into a sleek, computer-analyzed schedule. The young go-getter was fired just as quickly and replaced with Trent Haaga because the sleek, computer-analyzed schedule was an unusable piece of shit. Creating a workable schedule requires an intimate knowledge of the script that a computer will never understand. The computer will break down the script by scenes and locations and tell you that scenes 12–16, 31, and 38–50 are all nighttime exteriors. Therefore, the computer will tell you they should be shot at once. The computer will not tell you these scenes require elaborate special effects, that each needs several hours of prep time, or how many actors you're going to need to control in each scene. You need to figure that out for yourself.

Rest assured that everything will take longer to shoot than you think it does. You can help take some of the pressure off by anticipating what scenes will take the most time and scheduling accordingly. For instance, any scene involving special effects will take more time. Sometimes you'll have a scene that you only get one shot at . . . like a car crash or an explosion or a ritual suicide. Novice filmmakers may think these scenes will take less time. In fact, they take much more.†️ When you only have one chance to get a perfect take, you spend every second up until the camera is rolling to make sure everything is working flawlessly. Likewise, if your movie requires an actor to wear a com-

---

* AD = Anno Domino, or the Year of the Tile Game. It was in the Year of the Tile Game that the domino theory was developed, suggesting that one nation's fall to Communism will cause its neighbors to quickly follow suit. This theory soon gave rise to the shorthand "AD" being used for assistant directors, since an assistant director who is a moron will quickly infest the rest of the crew with his god-given stupidity.

†️ Speaking of things that take more time than you think they will, one of the adages of filmmaking that pop up regularly in how-to books written by people who have never made a movie before in their lives is to avoid working with babies, water, and animals. This is actually 100 percent true, because you will never, ever be able to control these fucking things, no matter how hard you try. I'll return to this subject later on, but pre-production is the time for you to eliminate these elements from your script if at all possible. Of course, if your script is about a monkey that saves an orphaned baby from a sinking ship, you're pretty much fucked.

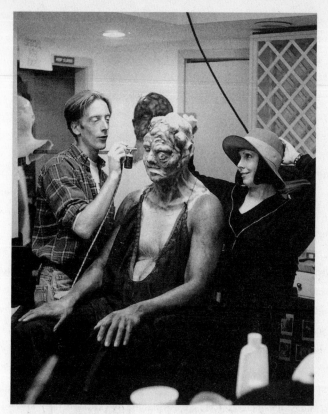

Tim Considine, a veteran Troma special effects artist prepares to use a miniature blowtorch on Dave Mattey's ear as *Annie Hall*'s Diane Keaton visits the set.

plex makeup appliance, you should give your makeup team extra time the first day(s) it's being used. By the end of the shoot, they should be able to slap it together in their sleep but give them time to get to that level of somnambulistic expertise. At first on *Citizen Toxie*, it took our makeup crew about four hours to apply the Toxie or Noxie makeup to Dave Mattey. By the end of the shoot, this crack team of experts had perfected the application to a point where it took five and a half hours.

On the other hand, don't assume that you'll be able to whip through all your dialogue scenes just because you're not setting up extravagant visual effects. Not all dialogue scenes are created equal. Two pages of dialogue between six people will take longer to shoot than two pages between two people, simply because you have to shoot enough coverage* so that you'll have something to edit together.

Basically, scheduling a film requires you to break the script down into individually numbered scenes and create a stripboard. A stripboard is not a 2 × 4 used to aid in the removal of clothing. Rather, it is a frame with each individual scene represented by a removable strip of stiff, multicolored paper. The strips have such key information as scene number, location, characters involved, props needed, and number of pages. Stripboards are useful because you can see the entire script and schedule at a glance and they're a lot easier to rearrange than a spiral notebook with a picture of the Smurfs on the cover.

Production managers will often farm out the task of creating a stripboard to a PA. This is a *huge* mistake. One of the best pieces of advice I ever got was from George Manasse, the production manager on *Joe* (and, even more impressive, producer of the killer worm epic *Squirm*).[†] He told me that the production manager or the AD should always create the stripboard themselves. Whoever does the stripboard will develop an intimate knowledge of the script that no one else on set will have.[‡] I always volunteered to make the stripboard on every movie where I was a production assistant. This gave me a lot of power on set, since I had the answer to virtually any script question the director could dream up.

When you're scheduling your production, you have to decide what the most important elements[§] are in your film. If you're making a horror flick, obviously you'll want your effects scenes to take precedence.

---

* Coverage is simply everything you shoot for a given scene. This includes a master shot, close-ups, reaction shots, and, in my case, usually about three minutes of lens-cap shots.

† Well, one of the best pieces of filmmaking advice anyway. The best piece of advice I ever got was when a rabid gopher turned our backyard into Swiss cheese and my dad told me not to stick my dick in any of the holes.

‡ Except for possibly the writer, though most people are usually totally wasted when they write. In fact, I'm drunk right now.

§ If you're making a circus movie, you'll also face the even more daunting challenge of deciding on the most important elephants.

If you're making a comedy, you'll want to spend more time staging the gags. If you're making a character-driven drama about a Catholic priest's struggle to come to grips with his realization that he's actually a gay Jew, then the numerous therapy scenes will be most important. Whatever the case, make sure your schedule reflects your priorities.

And never assume that your schedule will actually be followed to the letter. There are *so* many things that can go wrong during production that even Nostradamus couldn't predict them all.* Make absolutely sure you have at least one backup plan, so when your key location isn't ready on time or your lead actress suddenly comes down with an explosive case of the squirting ass-goblins, you can at least shoot something. The cliché "time is money" is never more true than when you're on a movie set.†

Flexibility is a key element to creating a workable schedule. If you're working in the time-honored Troma style, your screenplay will no doubt be in a constant state of flux,‡ being rewritten throughout auditions and rehearsals as actors and crew members contribute brilliant ideas that you can steal credit for. At this point, literally anything is possible and you should allow yourself enough latitude to explore these ideas. It's possible that an entirely new scene could be developed in rehearsals and you'll have to work that into your schedule. Even more likely is that existing scenes will get longer or shorter. Just make sure that everybody is kept appraised of the latest changes to the script.

Remember when you're doing rewrites to replace the pages in the original script with pages that are dated and colored differently accord-

---

* It is interesting to note, however, that experts now believe all of Nostradamus's visions do in fact relate to motion picture production in some manner. Apparently he was just like a sixteenth-century gossip columnist.

† In fact, a lot of clichés suddenly seem fresh and original when you're on a movie set, which is why so many movies suck shit.

‡ If you choose to ignore the time-honored Troma style and instead say, "Fuck the flux," you should be aware that you are quoting a line from Troma's 1983 classic *The First Turn-On*, so you still end up owing Troma a debt of gratitude.

Troma spent $25,000 for a day's rental of the Playboy Mansion just to prove to the world that Troma could have as many people standing around doing nothing as those big budget Hollywood movies have. (Doug Sakmann)

ing to each day (pink one day, baby blue the next, goldenrod the next, and so on and so on until your local copy place is rummaging around through their stockroom trying to find bizarre, unpopular colors you haven't used yet). There may well be people on your team who just don't grasp the concept of replacing the pages. One time on *Citizen Toxie*, I presented our second A.D. with new pages for the script. She just looked at them like I'd handed her my Co-Ed To Do List from 1967. Patiently (or as patiently as I get under such circumstances), I explained that these were today's rewrites and they should take the place of the corresponding pages in the script, pointing out to her such details as the date on the page, the page numbers, and the festive coloring. She examined the originals and the new pages with a furrowed brow, then declared that she saw no difference between the two. This turned into an all-out debate on what rewrites are and whether or not the altering of three or four words constituted a full-fledged rewrite. After several minutes, I felt I'd persuaded her (probably by saying something indisputable like, "I'm the fucking director and if I say these are rewrites then they're goddamn rewrites!"). Later on when we came to film the scene in question, it turned out that I hadn't been nearly as successful as I'd thought, since nobody had the new pages.

Finally (as far as scheduling goes), you should always try to schedule your first day of shooting at a location where everyone's already been. Whether that's your production office or where you held the auditions or the local jail, make sure that you start things on semi-familiar territory. Your first couple days of production are already going to be unbearably stressful. You do not need to compound the situation by making your entire company trek out to the boondocks and try to find some obscure place that your team has only seen once or twice before. You're already about to embark into uncharted territory. Let them have some kind of familiar landmark, however feeble it may seem.

CHAPTER 6

Covering Your Ass

(Both Metaphorically and Literally)

A well-functioning production team will develop into a single giant organism working toward a single goal. You work together, you think together, you eat together, and you rest together. So it should come as no surprise that a creature of this enormity will have a gigantic ass sticking out behind it. As with any target of this magnitude, you'll want to spend a shitload of time protecting your collective ass. You will be shocked and amazed at the power and variety of anal probes people will be able to find to stick up your ass before, during, and after filming. Use pre-production to build a sturdy protective shield around your ass. You won't be able to deflect everything aimed at your posterior, but you can at least grease yourself up enough that some of them will slide in a little easier. Who knows? You might even enjoy some of 'em.*

This phase of pre-production isn't just about solving the problems you're confronted with right now. It's about anticipating future problems and either making sure they don't happen or pre-solving them so when they do happen you're ready. If you're making a gritty urban drama and you lose a screw without which the camera won't function,

---

* EDITOR'S NOTE: What the hell is Kaufman talking about here? Note to self to check on Kaufman's marital status and the roots of Troma's gay/lesbian fan base.

it's a pain in the ass but you can pretty easily replace it. If you're making something like *Evil Dead*, filming in an abandoned cabin in the middle of nowhere and that screw disappears, you're fucked.

As I indicated before, one of the most important things to straighten out in pre-production is making damn sure that your team knows how to get to wherever you're filming. Start somewhere familiar but when you do move away from your base of operations, make absolutely, positively 100 percent sure that you have clear, foolproof, *confirmed* driving directions that even Joey the Retarded Production Assistant can figure out.* The image of my driving around Los Angeles like an asshole trying to find John Foster's office (recounted in gut-wrenching detail in the previous chapter) should demonstrate the validity of this point. Bad directions will fuck up your entire schedule. Wrong directions, like Adam idiotically gave me that awful, awful day in L.A., will destroy you, miring your entire production in a swamp of incompetence, laziness, and probably a near-suicidal level of manic depression. Adam probably has no idea of how close he came that day to making me blow my fucking brains out and ruining everything that Troma has come to stand for over the past thirty years.†

Not only is it necessary for you to have crystal-clear maps and directions for your team, you should also be familiar with the entire area in which you're shooting. There's every possibility that you will run out of something important on set, so you should know the locations of nearby grocery stores, hardware stores, gas stations, and sex shops.

Shooting the scene in *Terror Firmer* wherein fat, wee-dicked Yaniv Sharon runs naked through the streets with his head wrapped in gauze, we all remembered exactly why it's so important to familiarize yourself

---

* EDITOR'S NOTE: Before Joey sues St. Martin's for slander, it should be pointed out that Joey is not in fact retarded. This is another example of Kaufman's brilliant handling of the art of human relations, which has resulted in Troma having a higher rate of employee and volunteer turnover than a medical testing facility. To see more of Kaufman's shrill directorial style, watch the documentary *Farts of Darkness* on the second disc of the *Terror Firmer* DVD.

† ADAM JAHNKE RESPONDS: Jesus, Lloyd . . . let it go, will ya?

with the area where you're shooting. For some bizarre reason, the crew decided that continuity was unimportant for this sequence and had forgotten to bring Yaniv's head-cast appliance along. Making one of those strong directorial choices that Troma's movies are famous for, I decided that the audience might indeed notice if Yaniv's head was entirely wrapped up in plaster and bandages one second and as exposed as the rest of him the next, and decreed an emergency gauze run be made. Unfortunately, we were shooting in unexplored territory: Brooklyn. Nobody had the first clue if Brooklynites even used gauze, much less where they went to buy some. So one of our PAs went off on a mad search for gauze. This blind search led him directly into a car accident, knocking the van the PA was driving on its side and sending the van's contents (including Chinese food for seventy-five people) flying everywhere. It's possible the other driver was drunk. It's possible the PA imagined he was Hemingway in the ambulance corps during World War I. Whatever the reason, I think that had we been even slightly organized, and the PA had known where the fuck he was going in the first place, the accident might have been averted.

The PA escaped that accident unharmed (except for the fact that to this day he reeks of garlic chicken). But we are certainly aware of how lucky we were for him to escape injury. When you're familiarizing yourself with the area, you also need to know where the nearest hospital is, just in case (god forbid) anybody should get hurt. If this sounds like needless worrying, remember that you're responsible for all of these people. It's okay if they think you're an asshole. It's less okay if they think you're a murderer. Safety is not a function of budget, as evidenced by the decapitation of Vic Morrow and two Vietnamese kids on the set of Spielberg's megabudgeted *Twilight Zone: The Movie*. On our movies, we immediately post the three rules of production in our production office: 1) Safety to humans; 2) Safety to other people's property; 3) Make a good movie. Then as soon as the art director is hired, his or her first job is to create nice looking, professional versions of these signs. The idea being that our people will take these lessons more seriously if they see we've put some time and effort into creating the signs, instead of just Scotch taping a bunch of construction paper and magic marker signs all over the place.

Coincidence or not (and I happen to vote for not), one of the only real accidents we suffered on *Citizen Toxie* occurred on a set that did not have those signs posted. We were filming a car crashing through an artificial wall. As we were getting ready to go, the stunt coordinator showed us the "line of safety" and said that everyone had to stay back behind this line. We looked at the line, looked at the wall we'd be demolishing with the car, and said, "Fuck that shit!" Stunt performers know their business and firmly believe in safety, but I'd been around enough out-of-control cars to know that it's pretty damned difficult to predict with any degree of certainty where they're going to stop. We moved the crew back even further away from the "safety zone" that the stunt man had designated. But there's always at least one thrill-seeker that wants to be as close to the action as possible. Sure enough, a still photographer crept back up to the "line of safety" and perched himself upon a ladder to get pictures of the stunt.

I called "Action!" and the car came crashing through the wall.* Just as I'd feared, the car went well beyond the point it was supposed to stop at, past the "line of safety" and smack into the ladder. The ladder came down and so did the photographer. Fortunately, he must have landed on his head because he escaped without injury. Here again, we lucked out. And I do believe that if the Rules of Production signs had been posted here like they were everywhere else, we wouldn't have been so quick to let photoboy climb into harm's way.†

---

* Incidentally, the car we used for this piece of action was my own personal car that I'd rented during our stay in Poughkeepsie. If you get the optional insurance with a rental car, I recommend using it for any stunt work short of setting it on fire or beating the shit out of it with a baseball bat.

† We will see photoboy again a little later on, at which point I bet you'll agree with my feeling that this guy may have been the stupidest asshole to ever work for Troma. I realize he has a lot of competition for that title, but it's true.

Ron Jeremy, as the mayor of Tromaville in *Citizen Toxie*, shows how it blows to be a Catholic priest. (Doug Sakmann)

On Troma productions, we're supposed to fill out Location Fact Sheets for every single location we're using.* Besides including the whereabouts of nearby stores and hospitals, the fact sheets tell cast and crew who has the keys to the location, where toilets and changing rooms are, how long we have a given location . . . things of that nature. These will save you from having to tell people where to go tinkle twenty times an hour.

Also, for each location indicated in the script, we find two separate locations and draw up contracts for both the preferred location and the backup. This way, if you arrive to shoot on your scheduled day and the location owner has suddenly found Jesus and refuses to let you and your heathen crew film a single frame of your disgusting movie at his place, you aren't completely fucked over. You should have a Plan B for everything, from locations and schedules to actors and props. If you're lucky, you won't end up using any of your backup plans. But if you're that lucky, you should forget about filmmaking and hit the blackjack tables.

---

*We're *supposed* to do a lot of things that would make production easier, but often the lazy fucks don't do it and our lives are made just a little bit more hellish.

REGARDING BACKUP PLANS—WHEREIN LLOYD REJECTS A PERFECTLY GOOD BACKUP PLAN ONLY TO, IN THE END, USE IT TO GREAT SUCCESS or THE MIDGET STORY

Trent Haaga

Okay, so Lloyd has and will pound into your heads that you should *always* have a backup plan for any occurrence on set. This is true in most every case for Lloyd. But there are some instances where the backup plans just won't do . . .

One evening after a long day of shooting *Citizen Toxie*, Lloyd called me and Patrick Cassidy out to the parking lot of the school in which we were shooting.

"All right. We need to talk."

"Okay, Lloyd."

"We're shooting the goddamn fetus fistfight in a week, right?"

I didn't need to check the schedule. I made the damn thing, so I knew it by heart.

"Yeah, Lloyd."

"So . . . where are our fucking *feti?*"

There's a crucial scene in the film where two fetuses, one good and one evil, fight for domination of Sarah's—the Toxic Avenger's wife—womb. We had built a huge womb out of chicken wire, plastic sheeting, and foam rubber and now we just needed two fetuses.

"Well, Lloyd, Patrick and I have been working on this and we think that we could put out some flyers around town and we could probably get a couple of eight-year-old kids to be the fetuses—"

"Goddammit, Trent. This is total *asshole* time."

"Huh?"

"I said you are indulging in asshole time. Eight-year-old kids don't look like feti, for Christ's sake! Feti are malformed! Feti are out of proportion! Feti have big heads and tiny hands! *Midgets* look like feti, goddammit!" Actually, midgets are perfectly proportioned. Dwarves, however, are recognizable for their oversized heads and stumpy limbs. I didn't bother to correct Lloyd. After all of his years working with "little people" (as they prefer to be called), Lloyd still considers anyone shorter than himself to be a midget. From time to time, he will also refer to everyone on the production staff as a "mental midget" during production . . . which, quite frankly, next to Lloyd's incredible intellect and cyborg-like brain, they may well be.

"Lloyd, we're in Poughkeepise, New York. If you really want midgets we've got to go to the city, pick some up, have their heads cast by special effects for their fetus masks, drive them back to the city, pick them up again next week for the shoot, and drive them back again. And midgets aren't cheap, Lloyd. We've discussed this—"

"The audiences expect *realism*, Trent! Nobody's going to believe that the two feti are fighting in the womb if we don't get the *midgets! And cost is no matter!*" I was witnessing history. This was perhaps the only time in history that Lloyd had uttered that sentence. I only wish he had said it regarding the film's screenplay. "We need midgets for this scene! If you don't get me two midgets by the day after tomorrow there's *no picture*, you got that? I'll pull the plug right then and there!"

Despite Lloyd's insistence that we figure out ways to shoot without other seemingly "necessary" items like toilet paper ("use dirt") or actors ("we'll fix it in post with a little dubbing"), I believed that we truly needed the midgets in order to finish the picture. So Patrick and I went to work desperately trying to find two willing little people.*

Two days later, we had two small men sitting in our makeup chair. Lloyd was very happy to meet them and was his usual charming, gregarious self as he regaled the diminutive talent with tales of how exciting making a Troma movie is. With the heads cast and the little guys safely back in New York City, I walked up to Lloyd with a smug smile of satisfaction.

"Well, Lloyd, we got the midgets!"

"Great. Where's the fucking green car for the car chase? If we don't get a green car, *we don't have a fucking movie!*"

Yeah, we needed to find a car that matched the *Sgt. Kabukiman NYPD* car flip footage from 1989.† But that was another concern entirely.

"Patrick and I'll get right on that, Lloyd. But first I need you to sign this purchase order so that we can pay the midgets."

I gave Lloyd the purchase order. His pen hovered over it and his brow furrowed.

"Holy shit, Trent."

"What?"

---

* LLOYD KAUFMAN RESPONDS: The Troma Team and I happily admit to a bizarre midget fetish, with little people in prominent roles in everything from *Stuck On You* and *The Toxic Avenger* to Troma movies I didn't direct, like *Bloodsucking Freaks* and *Sizzle Beach U.S.A.* Troma would never have established such a long and distinguished history with dwarfs, midgets, and half-pints if they had been expensive and, in fact, we never had a problem securing their services for very little money until Mini-Me came along in *Austin Powers*. Since then, the price of height-challenged actors has skyrocketed. So be prepared . . . the weirdest things can become popular fads overnight and something you budgeted a couple hundred dollars for might all of a sudden set you back several grand.

† See Chapter 9 for this and other brilliant ideas on saving money creating stunts and special effects.

"These midgets want $1,000 apiece for a day's work?"

"Um . . . yeah. We tried to talk em down, but they weren't having it. This is a discounted rate already."

"Jesus, Trent."

"Lloyd, you said that money was no object . . ."

"Well, yeah, but I didn't mean . . . what was that you were saying about getting a couple of eight-year-olds?"

We jettisoned the midgets even though without them *we had no movie* and ended up replacing them with two eight-year-old kids who cost us nothing. And the fetus fight scene is still the best intra-uterine fistfight committed to film despite the fact that our fetuses didn't have short, stubby fingers. Some things are more important than others on a film set and money is perhaps the most important thing of all.

During this time when you need to be overly cautious and must think and rethink every detail from every conceivable angle, you will be happy as a lark to have a production manager or a line producer.* You are going to have your hands full with a million things, from the script to rehearsals to meeting with your DP and designers, so it is extremely likely you will forget some minor but vital detail. And even if you do remember everything, you can't be everywhere at once. At times like this, you'll want to have a line producer or someone scrambling around taking care of some of this shit.

A lot of the Covering Your Ass work is legal paperwork. If you're

---

* Before you get too excited about how easy your life will be with a production manager, you should know that the Audubon Society recently classified the lark as one of the most depressed and angry North American birds. So while you may well be happy as a lark, it's still not all gonna be sunshine, lollipops, and skip to my lou.

anything like me, it's something you won't understand or particularly care about. Of course, ignoring it completely is an excellent way to get yourself sued. So while you may be an inherently trusting person, you should still have everybody in the production sign contracts and, in the case of anybody who appears on camera, release forms. Contracts can be long, involved, mind-numbing affairs amounting to numerous pages filled with legal jargon in tiny print. They don't necessarily have to be. Troma usually has everyone sign a fairly basic contract that essentially says that the writer/actor/grip/fluffer is working for whatever the agreed-upon dollar figure is (if any) and that every single thing they do for the next six weeks (or however long it is) is in service to our production and belongs to Troma in perpetuity, in sickness and in health, for as long as we both shall live. In legalese, these are known as work-for-hire contracts. In lay terms, it's known as legalized slavery.

As a perfect example of ass-covering, I am *not* including a sample Troma contract in this book for you to learn from. I mean, what would happen if some serial killer decided to slaughter a bunch of people under the guise of making a movie and the police go through his paperwork and see that all his contracts were cribbed from this book? I'd be looking at lawsuits from here to Timbuktu. If you're really interested in seeing a Troma contract, send proof of purchase of this book along with a sworn statement that you are not now nor have you ever been a serial killer to lloyd@troma.com and I'll e-mail one to you.

You may also hear concerns from location owners, stuntmen, and/or actors involved in special effects sequences about insurance. Now if you're making a DV feature for a couple thousand (or even hundred) dollars with a cast and crew of less than ten people, odds are pretty good that you're not going to bother with insurance. However, in most states you need a certificate of insurance in order to get permits. Insurance is one of those complicated areas that if I tried to address it here, you would quickly become bored and, even worse, make a lot of mistakes because I'd probably end up giving you completely wrong information. Suffice it to say that you should be aware of the possibility that you may need a certificate of insurance for your production. If you think there's the slightest possibility you might need one, you should investigate it with someone a lot smarter than I.

The one piece of advice I can offer is do not go to somebody who claims to be a specialist in movie insurance. Most motion picture insurance policies are written by one or two companies, so the movie broker will put in a huge markup because this is where they get all their business. Instead, go to your or your parents' or your grandparents' insurance broker, the dorky guy in the ill-fitting suit with the fifteen-year-old copies of *Life* magazine in his waiting room who deals with homeowners insurance. Ask Poindexter for help in securing a motion picture insurance policy. It's easily taken care of and they won't rip you off as badly because their business comes from a multitude of areas. And, as I've said before, the same holds true for lawyers. Entertainment law is no more complex than any other field. If anything, it's simpler because the entertainment industry is run by morons who couldn't hack it in any real profession. When Troma was starting out, Michael Herz dealt with most of our legal stuff himself and anything that he couldn't handle, my father could. So don't deal with "entertainment" lawyers. Any minority shareholder derivative class action lawyer as per Section 16-B of the Securities and Exchange Commission Act of 1932 will do.*

* EDITOR'S NOTE: Though you wouldn't think it to look at his offspring, Kaufman's father was such a lawyer. Until 1993, he supervised most of Troma's legal strategy. Surprisingly, Kaufman and Herz have not continued to employ him after death.

HOW TO SEE THE INSIDE OF A COURTROOM

In today's sue-happy society, you should be aware that even the most innocent, off-handed comment can be grounds for a lawsuit centered around emotional distress, sexual harassment, and any of the thirty-one assorted flavors of slander that comprise the American judicial ice cream parlor. Does this mean you should automatically censor yourself for fear of pissing off some litigious production assistant? Fuck, no. But you should be aware that making a movie is practically tantamount to putting a big neon sign around your neck that reads SUE ME. People assume that filmmakers are money trees waiting to be shaken. This may well be true in Hollywood but in the world of guerilla independent filmmaking, nothing could be farther from the truth.

When we made *Waitress!* back in 1981, we shot a scene involving a horse. This horse had been on *Saturday Night Live,** performing in a TV studio in front of a live audience, and was ancient as hell. He was basically glue on four shaky legs. Our scene required one of our actresses to lead the horse around. We had the horse's trainer, a production assistant assigned to follow the horse and make sure it didn't kick anybody,† and two more PAs on horseshit cleanup detail. Besides all these guys, we had seven cops on set. It was a bright, sunny day at lunchtime on Park Avenue and Fortieth street in New York, one of the busiest intersections in town. We did the scene without incident but a couple days later, we received a letter from an attorney repre-

---

* The horse actually had a more impressive résumé than some of the human cast of *Waitress.*
† The ass-guard was an NYU film student, so he was highly qualified to supervise a horse's ass.

senting a woman who claimed the horse kicked her as she passed by. There were tons of people on set that day, yet she couldn't produce a single witness to back up her story. There was no record of her visiting a hospital afterwards. But she was still able to drag me into court for two weeks, where she dragged her leg around like Igor in *Frankenstein* and accused us of being careless incompetents. The insurance company ended up settling the case with her, despite the fact that there was videotape of her dancing at a nightclub while the case was going on.

On *Squeeze Play*, we shot a scene with hundreds of extras. Out of this teeming multitude, one guy did not sign a release form and somehow this one guy managed to infiltrate every single shot. When the scene was cut together, it was like this guy was the Flash, the way he appeared all over the place. Because he didn't sign a release, he sued us and shook us down for a few hundred bucks, easily making him the most expensive actor-person we ever engaged.

Besides imaginary accidents and paperwork errors, you also need to be careful what you say in your movie. Public figures are notoriously protective of how their names are used, even when the context is clearly a joke. Fortunately, movies are clearly fiction, so you can feel free to have your characters make as many jokes about Richard Gere's sexuality as you like. It's for reasons like this that most movies end with the ass-covering disclaimer: "This is a work of fiction. Any resemblance to persons living or dead is purely coincidental." When you're writing a nonfiction book for a major publisher, on the other hand, a pack of wild lawyers goes over every syllable with a microscope, making sure there's nothing even remotely libelous in there. Prior to the publication of my first book, *All I Need To Know About Filmmaking I Learned From The Toxic Avenger*, the crack legal team at Penguin

Putnam issued a five-page memo outlining items that they felt needed to be altered in order to cover their collective ass.

That's why we have tried extremely hard on this book to walk the straight and narrow and only tell stories that can be documented with hard, cold facts. Like the time Woody Allen and I were hanging around a public swimming pool waiting for a class of junior high school students to **CENSORED***

In addition to watching what you say, you also need to be very careful whom you say it to. Case in point: Miss India Allen, *Playboy* Playmate of the Year in 1988 and producer of popular skin flicks *The Chosen One* starring Carmen Electra and *The Rowdy Girls* starring Shannon Tweed and Julie Strain. Not long ago, we had India produce two feature-length DV movies starring Julie Strain. Unfortunately, we had a dispute and sued her over the projects after production wrapped. How large a dispute wasn't entirely clear until we received legal notice that India was counter-suing us. The complaints: 1) Breach of contract; 2) Slander per se; 3) Sexual harassment; 4) Trade slander; 5) Intentional infliction of emotional distress. You can imagine the fun times at the Kaufman household when I brought home the sexual harassment charge, which stated that I "engaged in employment discrimination consisting of making repeated and unwelcome demands for sexual favors" and that following her exit from Tromaville, India was "informed and believes and thereon alleges that she was discharged because of her refusal to engage in a sexual relationship with Cross-Defendant."† Not

---

* Editor's Note: Just kidding Woody.
† TRENT HAAGA AND ADAM JAHNKE RESPOND: Wait a minute . . . you mean, we could have *refused* to engage in a sexual relationship with Lloyd? Goddammit!

long after, we received an amended document from the lawyers. My name had been whited-out of the Sexual Harassment charge and in its place was Michael Herz (though it was spelled "Micheal").

On the Slander per se charge, it was asserted that "Kaufman charged Cross-Complainant (India) with stealing and other illegal business activities and also disparaged Cross-Complainant's abilities and skills as a film producer." If I sued somebody every time they disparaged my abilities and skills as a film director, I'd never leave the courthouse.

Without a doubt, though, my favorite charges were for trade libel and intentional infliction of emotional distress. I like it so much, allow me to quote extensively from the Fourth Cause of Action:

> On or about June, 2000, Cross-Defendants published a letter which stated that Cross-Complainant was a "thieving cunt" and otherwise disparaged Cross-Complainant's abilities and work as a film producer. The entire letter is false as it pertains to Cross-Complainant. This letter is libelous on its face. It clearly exposes Cross-Complainant to hatred, contempt, ridicule, and obloquy because it accuses Cross-Complainant of being a dishonest and inferior professional in the film industry. The letter was seen and read by numerous executives in the film industry in Los Angeles, California. As a proximate result of the above-described publication, Cross-Complainant has suffered loss of her reputation, shame, mortification, and hurt feelings all to her general damage.

So what lessons can the first-time filmmaker learn from all this? First, if you're not acting as your own producer (and you probably should be), keep a very close watch on whoever's doing it. Don't just dole out large sums of cash to people and expect that they will be good and true with it. Second, and perhaps more important, people can sue your ass over just about anything. Over hurt feelings, over misunderstandings, over shit that never even happened except in their own brains. They can go back and amend their complaints over and over again. As of this writing, this case still hasn't reached a conclusion, so who knows what'll happen. Being in the right is not always enough in the eyes of the law. At times, the system works and the law protects the innocent and punishes the guilty. Other times, the law is a thieving cunt.

The good news in all this is that we were able to some extent to rescue the Julie Strain DV features from movie purgatory. We shot some additional scenes with people like Trey Parker and combined the two films into one *Twilight Zone*-esque movie. The finished product will be called *Tales From The Crapper*.

If you're filming on city, state, or federal property, then the final elements in your Paper Triumvirate are filming permits. A lot of guerrilla filmmakers will think that applying for a permit means you're sucking up to The Man, playing directly into their hands and becoming just another cog in the machine. Fine and good but all the punk attitude and rebellious posing in the world isn't going to help you much when you get shut down. There is nothing more embarrassing than to be filming a routine scene, without any naked fat guys, explosive diarrhea, and/or full-on head-crushings in it at all, and have the police shut you down just because you don't have a permit. Taking a little time in pre-production to get your permit may save you entire days of work later on.

It is always advisable to be completely honest and upfront about what you're going to be filming, especially when dealing with location owners and permit applications. In my experience filming in New York and California, if you organize things properly, you can get away with shooting just about anything your perverted little heart desires. Most of the problems I've had with permits have come as a result of our production staff's laziness. While we were shooting the now infamous (and much referenced in this book) "Non-Seeing Naked Fat Guy With Diminutive Penis Runs Through Times Square" sequence in *Terror Firmer*, we did in fact have our permit revoked. This was because instead of it saying on our permit that we were shooting a non-seeing naked fat guy with diminutive penis running through Times Square, our permit described the scene as simply "Man walks through Times Square." I firmly believe that if the production staff had taken the time in pre-production to meet with the police and describe the scene, we could have worked out a system where Yaniv Sharon (our brave actor) had run from blanket to blanket. As it worked out, the cops thought we were yanking them around, so they yanked back and forbade us from shooting at any exterior location in New York City for the rest of the day. We quickly improvised a Plan B and high-tailed it to the roof of the Troma Building. We dressed the roof to look like a city street (unfortunately, we were unable to hoist any taxicabs up with us) and continued shooting. While we filmed up on the roof, the Art Department, hung over and resentful of the fact that they were being forced to work in the middle of the week, prepped an interior cover set for us to continue on the next day.

With your ass sufficiently covered in paperwork,* you can continue worrying about the million and one things you're going to need to bring into the field. I always tell people that preparing for production is exactly like a field general preparing for war. I get a lot of appreciative nods of understanding when I use this metaphor but I realize that

* Hopefully quilted paperwork for extra softness.

none of the young people I've told this to have any idea what it's like to go to war.* So imagine some other major project that you've been involved in, like moving across country. You know those little Movers' Guides you get at the post office with the change of address cards? They have little checklists in them that tell you every last thing you need to do: use all perishable food items, disconnect your telephone service, reconnect your telephone service, wipe your ass in a backward motion, etc. Well, you need to picture the rest of pre-production like that checklist. You have to think from every angle and imagine every single last item you're going to need on location. I assure you, you will not remember everything. But if you remember most of it, you'll be in a much better position to improvise something on the spot for the prop, equipment, costume piece, or toiletry you forgot about.

Hopefully by now you've had at least one serious conversation with your DP and have figured out little details like what format you're going to shoot on. What you choose to shoot on will probably be based 99 percent on economic factors and 1 percent on aesthetic factors, but each format has its pros and cons. Obviously it's much, much cheaper to shoot on video than on film.† DV tapes are loads cheaper than film stock, you don't have any lab fees or processing delays, and the camera is much lighter and more mobile. You'll also need more lights if you use film instead of video and the more lights you have, the more amperage you'll need. But investors may be more attracted to a project shot on 16 or 35 mm film. So while it may be more expensive, you'll probably already have more money to play around with. Also, many people, including me, believe film is capable of a lot more

---

* Hell, neither do I for that matter. I went to Chad rather than go to Vietnam (see *All I Need To Know About Filmmaking I Learned From The Toxic Avenger* from Penguin Putnam for all the gruesome details). And in the unlikely event I had gone to war, there's no fucking way I would have made general. I would have been stuck at private for my entire tour of duty, crying like a prepubescent girl the entire time.

† Though there can be some hidden costs in video, depending on where you want your movie to end up. If you envision a theatrical run, you'll have to transfer it to a print sooner or later (though a growing number of theaters and film festivals can now project video).

Moments after Noxie (Dave Mattey) unleashed the "bubble" of the century fart at the Playboy Mansion grotto during *Citizen Toxie*. (Doug Sakmann)

subtleties than video. I know, I know ... a few chapters back Trent devoted a whole sidebar to his opinion that you should shoot on digital video. And while I respect Trent, I don't think his figures are quite correct. He claims his $35,000 DV feature has been sold to Blockbusters around the world, but frankly, I've never seen it there. Personally, I prefer film to video.* Most DV movies suck shit. Sure, there are rare exceptions like Mike Figgis's *Timecode*, but by and large they all look shoddy and amateurish. Of course, if all you're worried about are aesthetics, you're probably reading *Film Sense* by Eisenstein or something instead of this book.†

---

* TRENT HAAGA RESPONDS: Of course you do, Lloyd. You've been working with it for over thirty years and soon you'll be dead, so who gives a shit what you prefer? Believe me, shooting on DV will save you time, money, and frustration.
† Editor's Note: Kaufman actually has been a pioneer in the non-film revolution; *Red Neck Zombies* (1985) was the first movie shot entirely on video to be distributed world-wide. Also he recently issued the Dogpile 95 Doctrine of digital moving making (www.dogpile95.com). Troma also was the first studio to embrace DVD, as evidenced by Kaufman's huge collection of porn.

Whether you're shooting on video or film, you will need lights at some point. If you're lucky, your DP has his own package of lights or free access to some and is on top of the situation. Otherwise, you'll have to rent something basic like a Lowell DP Kit.* Strangely enough, it's pretty easy to find places that rent things like this. Just about any large- to medium-sized town will have somebody prepared for Elks Club dinners, strip-mall grand openings, and independent film productions. It should be reasonably inexpensive, just make sure your camera team is involved.

The most commonly forgotten item on any film shoot[†] is a bounce card. What's humiliating about forgetting this is that a bounce card could not be any more basic. It's just a big white stiff card used to reflect sunlight onto the actors when you're shooting exteriors. At Troma, we have a shitload of posters mounted on white foam-core board that we use to promote the movies at places like Cannes. So we usually use the back of one of these as a bounce card, so at least we get some use out of the piece of shit movie that tanked.

When you're out getting tape or film stock, you should be aware of the shooting ratio. Don't think that because you're making a ninety-minute movie, you need to purchase ninety minutes worth of tape. The shooting ratio is the number of takes you will shoot to the number of takes you can actually use. So a ratio of 4:1 means for every four takes, one will be usable. If you're shooting on tape, it's pretty easy to figure out your shooting ratio and calculate how many tapes you'll need. If you're shooting on film, you're going to have to do some math, so good luck.[‡] The typical Troma shooting ratio is 25:1, also known on set as "Shoot 'em all and let God sort 'em out." This shooting ratio is virtually

---

* A Lowell DP Kit consists of four lights and light stands.
[†] Well . . . any Troma film shoot, anyway. The most commonly forgotten item on big Hollywood productions is the screenplay.
[‡] Eleven minutes of 16mm film is 400 feet. Eleven minutes of 35mm film is 1,000 feet. So, if $x = \sqrt{3}$ and $y \approx -82$, then the amount of 16mm film you will need to shoot a twenty minute film is π.

the only luxury we enjoy at Troma. By burning a lot of film, we get plenty of different takes and angles to choose from in post-production. When we have stunts or special effects, we're able to cover them with multiple cameras and select the best-looking angles later on.

Pre-production will also demonstrate the absolute necessity of automotive transport. The very first question you should ask any of your unpaid production assistants is, "Do you have your own car?" If the answer is no, they are a liability, a deep, festering malignant tumor in the heart of your production and they must be cut loose and removed immediately. During these last days before production, you're going to have people driving all over hell and gone picking up shit like costumes, makeup pieces, props, and equipment. You're also going to need multiple cars throughout production, in case someone or something needs to be picked up or dropped off. You simply can't have a production run smoothly without multiple vehicles.

Going hand in hand with having members of your crew running all over the place is the absolute necessity of proper communication.

The Three Stooges of Tromaville: Moe, Larry, and Trent. (Doug Sakmann)

When I started out, you either had walkie-talkies or carrier pigeons or you had each crew member lashed to another through an elaborate series of ropes. Today we still occasionally tie crew members up, but cell phones have made communication infinitely easier. Walkie-talkies are still used to communicate on set but in pre-production, when everyone's running around trying to get things done, cell phones are indispensable. Back in the days when cell phones were only used by the FBI and weighed about ten pounds, we used pay phones extensively and told our PAs to carry a roll of quarters with them everywhere. But using pay phones tends to piss off your friendly neighborhood crack dealer, so it's much safer these days to use cell phones. Some of our PAs continue to have rolls of quarters sewn into the front of their pants, but I don't think they're using them to make calls.

You're also going to need to prepare for what people are going to be eating on set. While it's true that the movie business is the only industry in the world that is actually expected to feed its workers, this certainly beats the alternative of leaving a couple dozen or more flaky "artistic" types to their own devices for an hour while they try to go get something to eat. If you let these people go, you are guaranteed to not see them again for well over the allotted time and your schedule will be shot to shit. Therefore, it is much more cost-effective to bring sustenance to them. If you want to be a nice guy, you can get them nutritious and delicious hot meals like Chinese take-out or pizza. But at Troma, what we optimistically refer to as "craft services" is usually a table full of day-old bagels, goldfish crackers, and water. You can make a deal with a bakery to get day-old bagels that otherwise will be tossed away but are still perfectly delicious. Sometimes you can even get them free. As for the water, if you fill up Evian bottles with tap water, your team will think you're a hero.* We put our budget (meager though it may be) on screen, not in our cast

---

* Similarly, you can refill those little but costly whiskey bottles from a hotel mini-bar with piss to avoid getting charged. This tip doesn't really have anything to do with filmmaking, but it's good to know. This is why you should always sniff the contents of any liquor bottle you get from a hotel mini-bar.

We used Andrea Yates's pre-partem depression in the famous fetus fight in *Citizen Toxie*. (Doug Sakmann)

and crew's stomachs. There will be plenty of time after the movie is shot for everybody to go out and eat a good meal on their own dime.

So you've got all your paperwork in order, your crew is standing by with all the tape stock and equipment they need, and you've got an eager cast ready to go. You've got food, toilets, water, first-aid kits, walkie-talkies and/or cell phones, and an armada (or at least a number) of gassed-up cars and trucks.* Your script is getting better every day, everybody on your production team is enthusiastic and excited to get going, and you still have a gut-churning sense of panic and inadequacy and are prepared to call the whole damn thing off at a moment's notice. Perfect. Everything is exactly where it should be. Now you're ready to really fuck up.

---

* You should assign a PA to keep your vehicles full of gas. If someone needs to make an emergency run in the middle of production, it becomes an emergency crawl if they have to stop and get gas before they do what they were supposed to do in the first place.

CHAPTER 7

Locations—Shooting in Society Without Completely Pissing Off the Locals

One good way to tell whether or not you're a died-in-the-wool, no-hope-for-saving independent filmmaker is if your first reaction on seeing a new and interesting place for the first time is not, "What splendid architecture" or, "What a majestic view" but, "This would make a fucking great location." The first time I'm in someone's house or apartment, I'm not looking at the furniture or whatever's objets d'art they have lying around. I'm looking at their hardwood floors, thinking, "This would be a great place to do a dolly shot. We wouldn't need to put down tracks." At cocktail parties, I try to sneak off to the fuse box to see if we could tap into their power without blowing out a line. When I'm groveling for money in some posh corporate suite, just before I perform fellatio I think about how great the view from up here on the thirtieth floor would look on camera. Location scouting is one of the most important things to be done on any movie. Perhaps the only task more important is location management (that is, managing to hang on to the fucking great location you've scouted). But first, you need to find a place. We can worry about the zillion ways you can lose the location later.

As I said before, three rules of production are posted on every surface of a Troma set, visible to one and all. These rules are:

1. Safety to humans.
2. Safety to other people's property.
3. Make a good movie. (*note much smaller type*).

Location shooting deals with all of these rules. You're in a new, uncontrolled environment so there's a much better chance that people will be hurt. But you have an even greater chance of wrecking someone's house, store, restaurant, or bordello. Filmmaking is destructive and it's simply a fact that you will wear out your welcome. But there are ways you can shoot your movie, not break anything (including any of Troma's Three Rules of Production), and get out before you are irreversibly hated by your hosts.

By far the best way of staying on your location owner's good side is simply by being completely honest and upfront with him about what's going to be happening in their place. If you want to stage a crucifixion on somebody's front lawn, it'll be much smoother for everyone if you tell whoever owns the place that you want to nail a buck-naked Jew to a burning cross before you do it. This is much easier than the alternative of having the location owner rushing up to you while you're raising the cross and you telling him off-handedly, "Oh by the by, we're gonna be crucifying today. Would you mind parking on the street?"

Besides being completely honest with them about what you're going to film, you also have to make it crystal clear what's involved in the filmmaking process. Inviting a film crew into your house for the day essentially means that whoever lives in that house is gonna have to make themselves scarce. Tell them that there will be a few dozen asses shitting in their toilets, that you're going to need to set up an area for people to eat, that people will be roaming all over their house and that the family can't just sit in the living room watching cartoons while you film around them. Sure, you have your location owners sign a location release contract before you start but those are virtually useless. If the owner doesn't like what's happening, there's really nothing you can do to stop him from kicking you out.

When we made *Stuck On You* in 1982, we learned how hiding details from location owners can come back to bite you in the ass. We were shooting for a day in someone's house and the family hadn't been properly informed about just how large this operation was going to be. So our first problem was trying to keep Mr. and Mrs. Average American out of our hair while we tried to make a movie. An even bigger problem was that nobody had bothered to tell them what we'd be shooting. The scene in question was the one that puts the "stuck" in *Stuck On You*, where experiments in the art of body painting result in two naked, copulating consenting adults gluing themselves together. Usually, if you tell someone that you're going to be filming a scene like that in their home, their reaction is one of barely contained glee. After all, who doesn't want young, attractive naked strangers in their house? But when you don't tell someone that you're going to be filming such a scene, you can find yourself running into unforeseen obstacles. Like we did, when we got down to filming the naked beast with two backs right around the same time as the children arrived home from school. Needless to say, this did not go over well with the parents, who summarily ejected us from their home and told us never to come back. We had most of what we needed, thank Buddha, so we were able to finish the scene elsewhere and avoided having to change the title of the movie to *Stuck On You But Only Metaphorically Because the Location Manager Was a Fuckup*.

Despite the headaches and inconvenience of actually having to tell people the truth, location shooting will, without question, help you immeasurably in your goal to make a good movie. For one thing, with a great location you can get a set that looks better and more natural than the highest-paid art director in Hollywood could ever hope to build. If some major studio wants to film a scene in a small town bar, they'll build the thing themselves and decorate it according to what they think a blue-collar dive bar should look like. Never mind the fact that these guys pull down six or seven figures a year and probably haven't set foot outside of Los Angeles in a decade. If an independent filmmaker wants a bar, he just needs to go find one.* Any real location, whether it's a bar or a bakery or a public bath house will have accrued years of details that no set designer can replicate. Even if the camera doesn't catch each and every one specifically, the accumulated weight of these details will be captured on screen. The right location can give your movie a very high production value for little or no money.

On *Cry Uncle*, a movie on which I was production manager, we were in search of a headquarters for the character of the billionaire. One day, we read an article in the *New York Post* about a bankrupt cruise ship that was docked illegally and was about to get a parking ticket. Its crew had abandoned her and the ship's owner was understandably desperate. John Avildsen, the director, dispatched us to get that ship for our billionaire. We called up the New York City Office of Motion Pictures and T.V.† and they helped us find the owner of the boat. The script was retooled to work in the ship and a movie with a budget of $185,000 ended up with an enormous location that, under any other circumstances, would have cost a small fortune.

Besides the economic consideration, good locations can also serve a necessary aesthetic purpose. In my own case, Troma makes movies with a lot of special effects and fantastic elements (or, as our detractors call it, "impossible bullshit"). Things like people mutating into hideously deformed creatures of superhuman size and strength after being doused in a vat of toxic waste instead of dying a painful and horrible death. For that reason, we like to shoot on real locations as much as possible. By using real-life environments instead of constructed sets which still look fake, no matter how well-made or how

---

* And it's usually not very difficult at all for an independent filmmaker to find a bar. It's more difficult for him to find his way out of the bar.
† The NYC Office of Motion Pictures and T.V. is there to give permits, info, etc. to people who film in N.Y.C.

much money is thrown at them, we keep one foot in reality. That way, the impossible bullshit starts to seem plausible and we can get away with a lot more.

For instance, in *Terror Firmer* we had a scene that required 500-pound Troma ensemble actor Joe Fleishaker to be ground up and eaten by an escalator in an office building. Finding an escalator in New York City is not a problem. Because they're all in public places, finding one you can film on is. To our rescue came Jerry Rudes, director of the Avignon Film Festival (which had hosted *Tromeo & Juliet*) and my literary agent. Thanks to Jerry's connections with the Alliance Française, he was able to convince the owner of the building that houses the Alliance's headquarters in New York to permit us to film their escalator. Here is a common trap that first-time filmmakers fall into. You must get the location *owner* to sign a release. Not the custodian, not the assistant manager, not a clerk, and not the piss-scented wino lying in the parking lot. If any of these people tell you it's okay to film somewhere, odds are good that they're going to be in Tijuana on the day you asked to film and the owner's going to be there with a pit bull and a baseball bat saying, "Get off'n my land."

Anyway, thanks to Jerry, we'd secured our perfect escalator. However, a few small obstacles remained before we could turn Joe into frappé. For one thing, the escalator has yet to be built that could make a dent in Joe but, since we've never let a little thing like the laws of physics stand in the way of a good bloodletting, that was a minor concern. A far more pressing issue was the impossibility of hosing down the beautifully decorated lobby of New York's premiere French cultural center with several gallons of fake blood and potentially sparking an international incident. At the very least, we'd be setting Franco-American relations back several hundred years. And, far more important, we needed to shoot a scene in the Alliance's screening room two days later. We couldn't afford to piss them off. So we shot everything in that building that we possibly could, including Joe's arrival at the building, his heart-stopping plunge down the actual escalator itself,* and the aftermath of his gory demise. For the bloody effect, we moved to the Troma office where we built a small set that was supposed to be an exact replica of the top of the escalator. In fact, it resembled nothing so much as a giant can of tuna fish on its side, sitting next to a couple of stairs. Nevertheless, the end result always gets a great reaction from audiences who, for at least a couple minutes, believe that this morbidly obese man could be completely consumed and liquefied by an ordinary escalator going about one mile per hour and with less than an inch of space separating the steps and the floor.

Also, if used properly, the right location should actually become a character in the movie. In fact, it might turn into your favorite character since it won't have any lines to fuck up, demand lunch breaks or worry about motivation. The bar we used in *Squeeze Play*, a lovely place called Cus' From Ho, eventually became a character in its own right, symbolizing the male domination of the females and providing an appropriate setting for the women to turn the tables on the men. With everything from the look and feel of your movie to your budget riding on the right location, you should definitely expend the time and energy to find the perfect place, instead of forging ahead and shooting your climactic courtroom scene in your neighbors' wood-paneled rumpus room.

Location scouting should really start at the script stage. The old adage, "Write what you know," doesn't just refer to characters, plot, and dialogue but also to locations. If your dad or grandparents or diseased cousin Clem owns a farm somewhere, come up with a scene to utilize that. If you know somebody who owns or manages an amusement park and will allow you to shoot there after hours (for free), try

---

* Accomplished by Joe's eerie twin-like stunt double, a black man less than half his size and weight. *See also* Chapter 9: Stunts and Special Effects—How to Simulate a Violent Death and Stay Out of Jail.

to work in a scene that features the amusement park. Even the most rudimentary inventory of friends and family will yield potential access to a surprisingly wide range of locations.

Unfortunately, not every location need is going to be fulfilled by Uncle Pete's barber shop or the fortuitous illegal docking of a luxury yacht. The script for *Citizen Toxie* called for a major fight scene to take place in a hospital. This seemed like a brilliant idea while we were writing it but, when we began to look for a place to film, we were shocked to discover that most hospitals don't fancy having thirty guys slaughtered by the Toxic Avenger in their hallways. In the end, we found ourselves presented with the option of filming in an abandoned mental hospital. Now sooner or later, every independent filmmaker acquires a working knowledge of mental hospitals, including addresses, procedures, meal times, and which pills you should swallow and which you should hide under your tongue. However, we realize that the first-time filmmaker probably hasn't had that experience yet. But that doesn't mean you have to give up your dreams of filming in the crazy house.

The first step for any independent filmmaker should be their state or local film commission. These boards exist for the sole purpose of encouraging the film industry in their state or community and are more than happy to give you as much help as possible free of charge. For those of you who are rigorously following my 817-point step-by-step guide to becoming a filmmaker, Step #54A is to marry your state film commissioner.* However, if you don't want to get that involved, I'm quite sure whoever is appointed to that position in your state will be happy to help you out with little more than a polite inquiry.†

Our quest for a hospital began at the New York State Film Com-

---

* Editor's Note: Kaufman is married to the beautiful, brilliant, and blue-blooded New York State "Film Commissioner" Pat Kaufman, who, when asked what it was about Lloyd that inspired her to marry him thirty years ago, confided recently "I thought he was rich."

† Although a bottle of wine or bouquet of flowers are always appreciated. In fact, if you'd like to send some to me, deliveries are accepted at the Troma building weekdays during regular business hours.

mission, which provided us with a complete list of hospitals in the state. For a short time, we toyed with the idea of filming in a hospital that was still in use. However, it was soon pointed out that our lights and equipment would cause a power drain on the hospital, endangering people on life support. While I do expect filmmakers to die for their art, I don't expect total strangers to do so against their will. But fortunately, back in the '80s, budget cuts enacted by the Reagan administration shut down a lot of state mental hospitals, freeing up plenty of locations that sit abandoned to this day, not to mention sending thousands of mentally unstable individuals into the streets to fend for themselves.*

Each hospital on the list the Film Commission gave us had a contact name and phone number. It then boiled down to getting in touch with these people, driving out, and touring as many locations as we could. After we'd narrowed our choices, the decision came down to the same thing that, sooner or later, every decision on a movie set comes down to: money.†

Now it's important to understand that if there is *any* way possible to avoid paying for a location, then that is the avenue you should take. Unfortunately, when you're dealing with a state-run institution like a hospital, there's no real way to avoid it. The state has dealt with film crews before and they know what the going rate is. It is infinitely easier to deal with individuals than institutions when you're trying to secure a location. With an individual you can dazzle them with the glamour of moviemaking. As Michael Herz always says (or, at least, would always say if I hadn't sworn to him on a stack of Tijuana Bibles that I wouldn't mention him in this book), everyone has two careers: their own and the movie business. Everybody wants to be a movie star so, if push comes to shove, promise them a role in your movie. On *Citizen*

---

* Not to mention to find gainful employment as unpaid actor-persons (aka extras) on low-budget independent films.

† For that matter, that's what every decision in life boils down to, from what car should I drive to should I go for full-service or just hand-release?

Toxie, we found a great junkyard owned by a very nice old lady. We asked for permission to film in her junkyard and, in return, promised her a part in the film. In the end, we got a great location and a brilliant performance for free. You can see the little old lady in the final film being hit by a car driven by Evil Kabukiman. Of course, while we were trying to secure the junkyard location we didn't tell her that she would end up being having her head crushed by the tires of a car and pissing and shitting all over herself as she dies. This is not lying. This is dispensing information on a need-to-know basis.

When you're dealing with individuals, particularly individuals away from movie capitals like L.A., it's very, very easy to get a great location for little or no money. Simply be honest, treat them and their property with respect, and be completely upfront with them about how their property will be used. I was in charge of locations on *Saturday Night Fever* and had to go door-to-door in Brooklyn, meeting and greeting families as though I were running for city council. We got the house that John Travolta's character's family lives in for very little money simply by treating the family that lived there with respect. Travolta was a big TV star on *Welcome Back, Kotter*, so I had him spend some time with the families. We got the neighbors to cooperate this way, too, getting them to keep their lights on at night and allowing us to mount these huge lights on their roofs. You probably won't have John Travolta in your movie* but you should act like you do. Keep a suit in your car for when you go to meet the owners of prospective locations. Don't be afraid to act like a bigger shot than you really are. Diplomacy, courtesy, and respect will go a lot further than money in almost every situation. *The Toxic Avenger Part II* was filming in Japan at the same time as the big-budget Ridley Scott movie *Black Rain*. Our crew was mostly Japanese, we used translators to speak to the people in charge in their own language, and we got permission to film in some of Japan's oldest, most sacred shrines. Meanwhile, the arrogant Hollywood big boys

---

* On second thought, after movies like *Battlefield Earth* and *Lucky Numbers*, you might.

swaggered in, acted like they owned the country, and got no cooperation whatsoever. They eventually packed up and finished their movie
on sets in Hollywood. We got complete cooperation, just by turning
Japanese for a little while.

Our hospital situation, on the other hand, required us to lay out
some cash. In the end, we arranged to pay $1,200 per week and sched-
uled one week of shooting. Considering that this sum bought us
access to many acres of land and a hospital with hundreds of rooms, a
theater, a church, a commissary, offices, and a huge kitchen, this was
money well spent. Now for a major Hollywood studio production,
$1,200 per week is less than nothing.* If one of the major studios
wanted this location (assuming they didn't just build a hospital themselves), they'd pay whatever the state asked, book it for a month, spend
three weeks repainting, rewiring, trucking in beds, hospital equipment,
sparkling water, gourmet cuisine, and drugs, they'd become board cer-
tified to operate as an actual hospital, shoot for five days and go home.
On a Troma production, $1,200 is an astronomical sum. We could rip
off a couple dozen arms and legs for $1,200. So if we invest it in a
location, we make damn sure to try to get more than our money's
worth, with a partial refund if possible. Since it's a nonunion shoot,
you can work your crew twenty-four hours a day and shoot two weeks
worth of footage for the price of one. Even better, if you really haul
ass and get everything wrapped in less time than you anticipated, try to
get a refund on those unused days.†

While you're looking for the perfect location, your mind will be
focused on the big picture and how this place will fit into your grand
artistic vision. With your head off creating extravagant visions of cin-

---

* To put this in perspective, I seem to remember several years ago CAA agent Marty Baum
informed me that in addition to the millions she gets for her shitty acting, Sandra Bullock's
contract stipulated a hair budget of $700,000. Of course, it's worth every penny because Ms.
Bollocks's hair extensions for *Miss Congeniality* were weaved follicle by follicle from the butt-fur
of an African spider monkey.
† Of course, whenever possible it's always best to pay for a location only after you're finished
using it. This provides the owner with a great incentive to not kick you out.

Kaufman and Herz travelled 15,000 miles to Japan in order to brilliantly avoid filming the beautiful temple; and instead filmed typical "severed head falling to earth against sky" which they could have done in New Jersey. Naturally, this scene was deleted from *The Toxic Avenger II*.
(Tim Considine)

ematic history in the making, you will forget about the little things, the details, the everyday rudimentary necessities that every one of us takes for granted. Here are a few of the biggest details that you will probably forget about:

1. **Toilets**—Considering just how far most filmmakers have their heads up their asses, it's really quite remarkable how little they think about toilets. For four days at the mental hospital, we had one Porta-Jon (which was never cleaned) to handle the waste of eighty-five people. Allow me to give you a sense of how much material passes from the bowels and bladders of eighty-five people in ninety-six hours. On the first day, the Porta-Jon could be used normally. On the second day, you noticed that there was very little delay between the time your ass released a turd and it hit the pile below. By the third day, you would stand up and there was more shit on your ass than had come out of it. By day four, the shit had somehow managed to reach higher than the toilet seat. It peeked out of the bowl like a newly formed volcano. If the Porta-Jon had been on an island in the South Seas, natives would have formed an altar around the bowl, worshipping Mount Crappa Loa. On *Tromeo & Juliet* we shot in an abandoned building in New York City without *any* Porta-Jons. People were reduced to defecating into paper bags and tossing them out the window. While this was almost certainly a life-altering experience for them, it was one they may well have been able to go without. The ship we used in *Cry Uncle* had hundreds of toilets. Not a one of them worked. Cast and crew formed something of a toilet relay, going from toilet to toilet in search of one that had not been befouled. So always remember: clean, working toilets make people happy.

2. **Electricity**—Does your location have any? If you're shooting in an abandoned mental hospital, or any abandoned structure, it might not. Bring your gaffer* out to the location as soon as possible. If the location has electricity at all, find out if she or

---

* Gaffer: a person who hauls salmon out of the water with an iron hook attached to a long rod.

he will be able to tie into it. If you're shooting in a building that's a century-and-a-half old, you might not be able to. Find out where the fuse box is. Figure out if you're going to need your own generator. On *Citizen Toxie*, we lucked out and our hospital did have electricity. According to the independent filmmaking law of averages, this stroke of good fortune meant we had twenty-five major fuck-ups, near-catastrophes, and outright disasters waiting for us.

3. **Water**—This is easy to overlook but the insidious thing about water is that you will always need it. You will need more of it than you think and you will need it in more situations than you will ever begin to guess ahead of time. Our hospital did not have running water. The problem here is that we were shooting a huge massacre scene where Toxie messily kills a large group of neo-Nazis. We doused the actor-persons and the hall with gallons and gallons of fake blood. We shot the scene and it looked great but at the end of the day we had all these people covered head-to-toe in sticky, uncomfortable red goo with nowhere for them to wash it off. For that matter, we couldn't properly clean the hallway itself. We did what we could but eventually faced up to the facts: that floor would now and forever have a reddish tint. In addition, you can rest assured that no matter how many signs you post or how loudly and often you announce it to the crew, someone will not get the message that there is no running water. We did everything but individually tattoo a message on each and every person on set that we had no running water and the indoor toilets were not to be used. This did not prevent one anonymous asshole from taking a fragrant and mighty dump in a bone-dry toilet in a room adjacent to where we were shooting. As horrible as that was, nobody could really blame me. Have I mentioned that, while on location, toilets should be clean and plentiful?

4. **Convenience**—Where exactly is your perfect location in relation to where everybody else is? If you have to drive two hours just to get there, you have to realize that's four hours out of your day right there that you're not shooting. Be prepared to live on or near your location for a while. If you have to put your crew up in a motel, don't believe the thing on the door that says "room capacity." Believe me, that's just there as a conversation starter. You can get a couple dozen people into a room designed to sleep four. If you're really lucky, members of your crew will get intimate and an illegitimate child will be born from these conditions. When this happens, it's usually pretty easy to convince the parents to name the tyke after your movie.* The aroma du Troma has resulted in a number of happy unions, including the wedding of Jennifer Babtist and Robert Prichard after the production of *The Toxic Avenger* and a brief but torrid affair between myself and a puffer fish after *Sgt. Kabukiman NYPD*. Ron Fazio, who played Toxie in *The Toxic Avenger III: The Last Temptation of Toxie*, recently reminded me that the art department on that film practically turned our motel in Peekskill into the Marquis De Sade's playground. They brought in leather swings, restraints, and all manner of bondage gear. I shared a room with Jimmy London, the DP on that picture, and we woke up in the middle of one night to terrifying howls and screams coming from the room directly next door. Once we realized it was just our crew "bonding," we slept soundly.

---

* *See also* Chapter 11: Marketing, Publicity, and Distribution—Whoring Yourself Out for Your Art Yet Again.

THE TROMA HISTORICAL RECREATION SOCIETY PROUDLY PRESENTS *DACHAU IN POUGHKEEPSIE*

Trent Haaga (on accommodations)

Citizen Toxie is a case study on inconvenience as far as transportation and housing and bathing goes. Since the film was to take place in the idyllic town of Tromaville, New Jersey, we had to find a place outside of New York City to shoot. This was no problem as New York is full of towns outside of the city. It was, however, a problem because our cast and crew were all from the city. Thanks to the New York State Film Commission, we found a town that was willing to let us take over their streets—Poughkeepsie. Now we had to deal with the real logistical issues of getting our crew up there (about two hours outside of NYC), housing them, and feeding them.

The first order was transportation. We had to rent vehicles for our equipment. No problem. We had a massive crew, however. The average Joe from New York City—particularly average Joes who were destitute enough to work on a Troma film for about $10/day—doesn't own a car. We had to rent about fifteen passenger vans in order to transport the cast and crew to Poughkeepsie and then to the daily locations. This became a problem when we would need to make runs to the city for equipment or to turn in the film for processing. Suddenly we had ten to fourteen extra bodies to transport with no vehicle. We managed by cramming whatever vehicles we had left way beyond capacity. One night we were shooting in an abandoned mental hospital about forty-five minutes away from Poughkeepsie. Fellow line producer Patrick Cassidy and I had been securing our equipment and doing cleanup, etc. We locked the doors and were ready to go home when we realized that everyone had left already. The assistant director and the line producer, two of the most crucial and important members of the team, had been abandoned on the grounds of a very spooky sanitarium. This might not have happened if we had had a few more vehicles at our disposal. Or if we didn't assign the driving to only the most useless and ignorant PAs. Or if the vehicles weren't so crammed full of people that accurate head counts were pretty much impossible. We ended up having to ride to a diner in the back of a pickup truck and call someone to drive all the way back from New York City to pick us up.

Housing was perhaps the most inconvenient and horrific aspect of staying in Poughkeepsie. Lloyd says that you can ignore the "maximum capacity" signs in hotels. So why didn't we get hotels for the crew in Poughkeepsie? Lloyd got a hotel. The DP got a hotel. After threatening to walk off the set, the costume designer got a raise and a hotel room. The rest of us—about forty cast and crew members—ended up staying at an empty warehouse that used to be a furniture factory or something. We rented the entire space for a month. We bought forty inflatable air mattresses. We moved the crew in. It was horrible. Being away from home was bad enough, but the living conditions were worse than an army barracks. People of all sexes, shapes, sizes, and bodily odors clumped together on the cold concrete floor trying to stay warm—there was no heat. Everyone used the same two showers and toilets. No one was assigned to clean said showers and toilets. In addition to there being no heat, there was no hot water. The place had been empty for years and the cold water that remained in the water tank stank like sulfur. After a long, hard day of shooting, your only option was to take an ice-cold shower that smelled like rotten eggs. Many of us—myself included—gave up on even attempting to stay clean. I probably took three showers in thirty-two days. I changed my clothes as many times. A few crew members who had access to vehicles would do late-night trips to a campground where, as long as the park rangers didn't bust you, you could take a nice hot, non-smelly shower.

Moving your cast and crew to a foreign place where it's impossible to get home without quitting the film and hitchhiking back was probably a wise move on Lloyd's part. America could have declared war and we wouldn't have known about it. Our families could have died and we wouldn't have found out until the film was shot. We had no choice but to live, breathe, eat, and shit *Citizen Toxie*. And what did Lloyd care? He merely had to show up in the morning, work with us during the day, and go back to his hotel room with its shower and fluffy, fluffy bed.* On any other set, a cast and crew that has to live where they're shooting gets a per diem, some daily amount of money that they can use to buy their dinners, since they aren't provided on set.†

---

* Editor's Note: Lloyd is fifty-six years old, feeble, and deserves his $17.00/night, flea-bag hotel room. Also, he farts enough to stampede a herd of Walrus's; so the crew would have been happy to pay for Lloyd's "flea-bag" hotel rather than live with him communally! He has also been known to try to enter the sleeping bags of young, male NYU student PA's while they are sleeping (says sources who wish to remain anonymous)—further reason for Lloyd not sleeping where the crew sleeps.

†LLOYD KAUFMAN RESPONDS: Per diems are sometimes not a bad idea, if you have a crew that is responsible and trustworthy enough to allow off the set for any length of time. On bigger film sets, I've seen crews hold the gourmet food they've been served in utter disdain. When we stopped serving food and started giving them a $7 per diem, they would eat the most stomach-cramping junk food they could lay their hands on. Presumably, they spent $2 on food and pocketed the extra five. If it's cheaper and more efficient for you to do this, do it by all means. Since you can never be sure that the crew will actually return in a timely manner after you let them scour the city for food, it's often wiser to provide them with food and just deal with the whining and complaining that will inevitably follow.

This can get expensive and it's why most people don't like to shoot too far away from home. If you shoot near home, you don't have to pay for lodging and per diems. You also apparently don't have to pay for these if you're Troma. I ended up spending a great portion of my daily wages on beef jerky and Ding-Dong dinners, as did the rest of the cast and crew.

The long and the short of it is: stay near home and you won't have to deal with these issues. Your other option is to create a brand-name recognition with your product for twenty-five years until you develop a Jim Jones-type cult following. Then get a group of these extremely dedicated or idiotic (or both) zealots to forego all creature comforts in order to make your vision a reality all the while telling them that this is *exactly* how you're supposed to make a movie.

One of the great advantages a low-budget movie has over its multimillion-dollar Hollywood doppelganger is the ability to move quickly. If you're out in the field and you discover a great location that you can use immediately, do it. Right there and then. The low-budget filmmaker must be able to think on her feet. Trying to get a major studio production to act spontaneously is like trying to turn an aircraft carrier at sea. The low-budget filmmaker can see something she likes, work it into the script, rehearse it, shoot it and move on while the big-budget crew is still forming a committee to discuss the possibility of organizing a scheduling meeting. *Citizen Toxie* features a major fight scene in Mad Cowboy's butcher shop between Toxie and the evil versions of Kabukiman and Mad Cowboy. As originally written, this scene was to begin outside and then move into the butcher shop, which was a set we'd built. Once we got to the mental hospital, we discovered an amazing-looking industrial kitchen, much more impressive than any set we could hope to build. Of course, it didn't exactly look

Mad Cowboy's udderly masterful performance made *Citizen Toxie* a very moo-ving picture. (Doug Sakmann)

like a butcher shop so it couldn't completely take the place of the set. We ended up adding the kitchen as a link between the outside world and the set. Adding the kitchen provided the entire scene with that sense of reality I alluded to earlier. And this was a location that we'd just stumbled upon. We weren't looking for an industrial kitchen but once we had one, we knew we had to use it.*

For every location that luck or circumstance just happens to send your way, you can be sure that another will be taken from you. The *Citizen Toxie* crew discovered a beautiful 150-year-old mansion on the grounds of one of the other hospitals we'd toured and we immediately made plans to use it as the abode of the evil Noxious Offender. It was

---

* That kitchen also housed these huge soup vats, one of which had become the final resting place of three mummified mice. This inspired us to fill the vat with body parts and dump live rats on top of them. We borrowed the rats from a nearby pet store, dying their fur with black Streak n' Tips hair spray to make them look more like . . . rats.

a gorgeous house, built in the late 1800s, that had fallen into a little bit of disrepair but, for our purposes, was perfect. The paint was peeling and big chunks of it were lying on the floor but that's to be expected in a house that old. We moved the crew in and almost immediately para-noia ran through the ranks about the dangers of lead paint poisoning. In particular, there was one fucking kid who somehow managed to find the time to go to the library and do research on lead paint while the rest of us were trying to make a movie. He returned from his stud-ies with reams of photocopies on the dangers of lead paint poisoning. Sure, every bit of research he'd done related to industrial dangers of exploding or imploding a building but by then it was too late. Paranoia had taken hold and logic took a holiday.

At a certain point in time, this entire incident would have been over before it started. Back when we made the original *Toxic Avenger*, we shot for some time in an abandoned hospital in Jersey City. In one of the rooms, Barry Shapiro, our art director, constructed Toxie's shack. To cover the linoleum on the floor, Barry ground up a bunch of old ceiling tiles that had fallen out and scattered them around. Here, there was a real possibility that we were inhaling asbestos particles every time we took a step. But the only person who asked for a surgical mask was laughed at and considered a wuss by every single member of the crew and he ended up not using it. In this case, we were totally focused on making the film. Now however, times have changed and it doesn't take much for your crew's attention span to go wandering off to the land of make-believe.

In an attempt to appease the crew, our line producers Trent Haaga and Patrick Cassidy bought kits to test the lead levels in the house. It turned out the undercoat tested positive for lead but the paint on the surface was perfectly safe. Of course, all the paranoid crew heard from that report was "tested positive for lead." So Trent called the EPA to find out if the house was safe.

"Well, how much paint are you removing?" asked the EPA spokesperson.

"None."

"Oh. Well, are you knocking a wall down or something?"

"No. We're not touching the goddamn walls. We're occupying a house for a day that tested positive for a lead base. We will be standing and walking on big hunks of flaked-off paint."

The EPA guy laughed in his ear and probably wished Trent had come out to his office in person so he could laugh directly in his face. "You've got absolutely nothing to worry about. You can only get lead paint poisoning from a huge, sudden influx of airborne particles or if you're living in the house for a long, long time and breaking the paint down. If you're really worried about it, you need to have a local building inspector come out and give the place a once-over but that's going to cost you."

The crew still wasn't about to take Trent's word, even if it had the authority of the EPA behind it, so he called up a building inspector. He heard the same thing from him. There was absolutely no danger.

"Okay," Trent continued. "Then can you give me a signed paper certifying that this building is safe to shoot in?"

The inspector refused to go that far. "Sounds to me like you've got a bunch of sue-happy pussies working for you. If I put my name on something then ten, twenty years down the line, they can come back and hold me accountable. The only way I'll sign something for you is if you give every member of your crew a blood test before and after so they can't come back on me and sue me later over some bullshit. I can tell you off the record you've got absolutely nothing to worry about. But I can't sign anything for you."

In the end, the sue-happy pussies won the day and we were forced to jettison the location. What lessons can the low-budget filmmaker learn from our experiences here?

1. People fear the unknown. On location, you have to take control immediately, cover every single aspect of the space, from aesthetics to practicalities to health and safety, and communicate the fact that you have it covered.

2. Never risk everything on a single location. You can lose it at

any time for any reason. If we'd needed that mansion for more than a day, we'd have been completely and hopelessly fucked. As it was, we were merely fucked.

3. Know the difference between someone's genuine safety concern and someone who is just looking for any excuse to slow down production. The ringleader of the Lead Paint Losers was fired after this incident but he came sobbing to me, begging for another chance. I stupidly gave him one. Remember the photographer I mentioned in Chapter 6 that climbed up onto the ladder that got hit by the car, despite all our warnings to get the fuck out of the way? Same guy. This guy didn't care about safety. He was just a negative, whiny, spoiled little suck-tit whose mind was everywhere except on the movie. If you have somebody like this, get rid of him immediately before he kills somebody.

While it's difficult to fight against imagined dangers, it's a lot harder when you're confronted with real ones. On-set accidents can usually be avoided if your crew is capable of exercising a little common sense, like not sticking their tongues into electrical sockets and not demonstrating their clog-dancing skills on disintegrating floors. You shouldn't count on anybody exercising anything even remotely like common sense, though, so make sure your AD lectures one and all on whatever pitfalls may surround your location, whether it's an unsafe building, a nearby pack of man-eating squirrels, or just plain old household safety tips. For instance, no one should ever run on set. Ever. There's simply no excuse for it. Nothing is so goddamn important that it can't wait an extra ten seconds to be walked to. If someone is tired or careless or nervous and they start running on set, they're going to trip on one of the 1,001 cables lying everywhere and violate Troma's First Rule of Production: Safety to Humans.

Sometimes, however, you won't know about the potential danger until you start filming. In fact, sometimes your filming might spark dan-

After actor Barry Brisco walked off the set of *The Toxic Avenger*, instead of recasting the role of Pompey, Lloyd decided to clone him. The result was the horrible three-headed, four-legged monstrosity called Briscor! He is currently an executive at Miramax. (Tim Considine)

ger. For instance, one of the more . . . shall we say, controversial scenes in *Citizen Toxie* is inspired by the Texas murder of a black man by being tied up and dragged behind a pickup truck. Now in the context of the movie, this all makes sense and our black man lives on as a disembodied head in a bucket, becoming a friend to Toxie and a hero in his own right. But while we were filming, all the residents of Poughkeepsie saw was a black guy getting dragged behind a truck . . . over and over and over again. Sure they understood we were making a movie, but exactly what kind of movie we were making was anybody's guess.*

---

* By the way, it's a credit to the good citizens of Poughkeepsie that they reacted to this unexplained scene with shock and horror. Usually I'd be extremely proud of them but since they were fucking with my movie, I wanted them all to shut up and mind their own goddamn business.

As the day wore on and we shot take after take of this poor black guy slowly being dismembered, it came to everyone's attention that we were drawing a substantial crowd. This is not unusual in and of itself. But this crowd seemed to have a lot more hostility than usual, with lots of angry glares and ominous whispering amongst them. This probably would have been okay, but for the fact that we still had to shoot the punchline to the whole sequence that night, in which our truck drivers got their comeuppance at a Ku Klux Klan rally. As we started to set up the Klan sequence, our black actor came over and said, "I'm getting the fuck out of here before we're all killed." Sure enough, the angry crowd had not dispersed. If anything, it was larger and the appearance of Klan outfits and a soon-to-be-burning cross seemed to be more than they were prepared to take in their little town.

It's not often that a filmmaker will have to choose between completing a sequence or facing down an angry mob armed with torches and pitchforks. If this happens to you, I recommend following our lead. Discretion is indeed the better part of valor. Envisioning headlines that read "Race Riot in Poughkeepsie," we decided that we'd better pack it in and call it a day.* We cut work short that day and sneaked back later like the weaselly little pussies we obviously are and completed the sequence with burning crosses and a full-scale lynching while the concerned citizens of upstate New York slept, secure in the knowledge they'd prevented a faux Klan rally from being held in their city.

* You must understand that, except for Toxie, the Troma Team is not made up of the most physically imposing motherfuckers in the world. If your crew is comprised of pro wrestlers or Hell's Angels or something, you might opt to face down the angry crowd. That still probably isn't a great idea. Remember, they are the hosts, you are the guests. It's never a good idea to cultivate a Sharks/Jets type relationship between your team and the locals.

THERE'S NO SUCH THING AS BAD PUBLICITY . . . UNLESS YOU'RE FILMING AN AFRICAN-AMERICAN BEING DRAGGED TO HIS DEATH BEHIND A PICKUP TRUCK
Trent Haaga

While there were no newspaper headlines that read "Race Riot in Poughkeepsie," Troma's presence in this peaceful little burg *did* end up in ten points on the front page of the *Poughkeepsie Journal* (or whatever the hell the local rag was called). Particularly after the dragging/lynching scene was shot.

Let's go back to the beginning . . .

Jerrod Alterman, our locations manager, had found a sweet little town that seemed to contain all of the locations in our script. It was two hours away from home, but we had to start shooting in about two weeks and were running out of options. After a quick trip up there with Jerrod, we decided that Poughkeepsie was as good as we were going to get, so I made an appointment with the mayor of Poughkeepsie. Two days later, I stood in the mayor's office with the mayor, the chief of police, the fire chief, the town council and their legal aides, and a few janitors who stopped to find out what all the hullabaloo was about. Armed with a fancy business suit and some thrown together "press kits" (which consisted of *Toxic Crusaders* ad slicks and copies of the *Toxic Avenger* comic book), I had to convince those in charge that shooting *Citizen Toxie* would be "good for the economic development of Poughkeepsie" and that this film would "put Poughkeepsie on the Hollywood map." All I needed in exchange was the absolute and total green light to do whatever we needed to do in Poughkeepsie to get the film done. This included, but was not limited to: the use of some Poughkeepsie police cars, being able to block off some streets for a car chase, being able to detonate explosives, and general use of any and all public places without having to pay for permits. I don't know how I did it exactly, but I was able to convince them that allowing Troma to take over their town for a month would be good for them. There were a few concerns, however:

"What is this film going to be rated?"

"Well, Ms. Mayor. I won't lie to you. These films go straight to video and need to compete right next to big Hollywood (I dropped the word "Hollywood" as often as possible) pictures, so we have to put in elements that the bigger-budgeted films don't. There is nudity in our films, and violence. But it's tastefully done nudity and what little violence there is is cartoonish and all in the name of good, clean fun."

"We can't allow public nudity or scenes of a graphic nature filmed publicly."

"I understand, Ms. Mayor. You have my word."

Three weeks later, we had four topless women—one of them an actual street whore—begging the Toxic Avenger for a heroin fix on one of Poughkeepsie's main thoroughfares. Small children stopped and pointed at the whore's nipples, "Look, Mommy! What's she doing?" We had public nudity, public simulated ass-raping, public drunkenness, public simulated drug abuse. The town began to grumble.

Then came the infamous "dragging" day, which happened to take place in an area of town inhabited by a predominantly African-American populace. During the town's harvest festival. Right next to the public parking area.

The following day, one of the PAs came to me on set (we happened to be shooting a scene at the production offices) and told me that there was a phone call for me. I went into the office and answered the call. It was a reporter from the Poughkeepsie paper.

"A lot of residents of Poughkeepsie were shocked and disturbed by what you guys were filming yesterday, Mr. Haaga. We've been getting a lot of calls about it. Would you care to comment?"

"Not really. I mean, what's there to comment about? We're making a movie."

"Well, sir, you can choose not to make any comment. But we're going to run a story anyway, so you might as well try to explain yourselves."

"Explain ourselves? About what? We're making a movie. I don't understand."

"You were dragging a black man behind a pickup truck."

"He was a stuntman."

"Several people were witness to this event, Mr. Haaga. They were not amused. Just the opposite, in fact. People are angry. What sort of a film is this? You're making light of a very serious incident."

"What makes you think we're 'making light' of it? You're taking the sequence completely out of context."

"This is why we're attempting to get your side of the story, Mr. Haaga."

"Okay, look. The Toxic Avenger is a *superhero*. Superheroes fight bad guys. Bad guys do terrible things to innocent people. A good guy needs bad guys to fight. Besides, this part of the script is based on actual events. Horrible actual events. The world can be a terrible place. Humans can be evil. We do things like this all the time. Denying it isn't going to do anybody any good at all. Hey, if it's any consolation, the guy lives . . . even though he's just a bodiless head . . . and ends up becoming the Toxic Avenger's sidekick. I don't understand why everyone's getting all excited about this. It's only a movie! Doesn't the paper have any real tragedy to shine the light of truth upon?"

With that, the conversation was over. I went back onto set and told Lloyd what had happened.

"Goddammit, Trent. You shouldn't have said a damn thing to the paper. We don't have to answer to them. They'll twist your words around, the media. Just you watch."

The next morning it was the lead story in the paper, rife with shock and outrage. Below the headline, in bold 18 point lettering:

EXPLAIN OURSELVES? ABOUT WHAT? WE DO THINGS LIKE THIS ALL THE TIME. I DON'T UNDERSTAND WHY EVERYONE'S GETTING ALL EXCITED ABOUT THIS.

—Trent Haaga, Producer

This was the beginning of an onslaught of commentary pieces and angry letters in the local paper. The townsfolk were up in arms and blamed the city officials for not reading the script before saying yes to us. Little did they know that wouldn't have mattered—we already had a "clean" version of the script available to any official who asked to see it. All references to nudity, sex, drug abuse, excessive violence, and all the curse words had been removed from this version of the script. It was about forty-five pages long. You may want to have a "clean" version of your script for these same reasons.

Luckily we were almost done with shooting when the hoopla began. At the peak of the town's anger, we quietly packed up our shit and left Poughkeepsie, never to return. Initially, the town wanted us to come back and have the world premiere at one of the local theaters. It was one of the conditions of being able to shoot in Poughkeepise. We didn't end up doing the premiere there. No cast or crew member has ever gone back, as far as I know. It's probably a wise move. I'm sure the lynch mobs are still waiting for us.

The moral of the story? As far as locations go, try to find someplace that hasn't been tainted by another film company. You'll get a lot more cooperation from the locals. By the time they've changed their minds about the whole thing, you'll be long gone.

Any film shoot will run into minor problems and setbacks that you cannot foresee or avoid. Sometimes the fact that you are shooting on location will exacerbate a minor problem into a major catastrophe. Another major location we used on *Citizen Toxie* was a school for the opening massacre sequence at the Tromaville School for the Very Special. Like hospitals, schools are virtually impossible to replicate and it always looks much better if you just use the real thing. Unlike hospitals, however, schools aren't open for business twenty-four hours a day, so it's easier to find one that will allow you free reign as long as they're not trying to educate our nation's future at the same time. This meant that our time at the school was limited to a holiday weekend. We absolutely, positively had to shoot every frame we needed in the school during that weekend or lose the thing entirely. We had to follow the school schedule religiously.

Probably the single worst thing that could happen while you're in production is to have 85 percent of your cast and crew drop dead from a flesh-eating virus. Fortunately, the odds of that happening are fairly remote. The second worst thing would be to have your one and only camera break down in the middle of an extremely tight schedule. And that is exactly what happened at the school. Since we were shooting in Poughkeepsie, this meant a two-hour drive back to New York City, an undetermined amount of time for the camera to be repaired, and two hours to drive back. By the time all that happened, we'd have been surrounded by kids learning their ABCs and pledging allegiance to the Toxic Avenger. The good news was that we did have a backup camera. The bad news was that this camera was not equipped with sync sound and we had dialogue scenes a'plenty to shoot. In the end, we really had no choice at all. We shot the rest of the day MOS* and had to bring super-Tromette and independent film goddess Debbie Rochon back in post-production to rerecord all her lines.

When you're working under a strict schedule and a low budget, often the mantra "fix it in post" will be the only thing between you and hari-kari. Now of course, not everything can be fixed in post. If half your footage is out of focus, there's probably not much you're gonna be able to do to fix it.† But if it comes down to a choice between abandoning a day's work or shooting something with less than optimal equipment, you should always try to make the backup plan work, no matter how unlikely a solution it may seem at the time.

For all the problems and headaches it will cause you, shooting on location is still one of the best ways for a low-budget film to disguise its low budget. Remember, if your script takes place in a small apartment, filming in your dorm room does not mean you're filming on

---

* MOS = Murder Or Suicide . . . these are the two things you will feel like doing when a vital piece of equipment breaks down. We also shot without sound for the rest of day, which coincidentally is also referred to as shooting MOS.

† I suppose you could try to add some narration to justify your boneheaded stupidity as an artistic choice. Plenty of modern artists have performed similar tricks. Of course, most of them died as broke alcoholics and/or junkies, so you might want to choose whose footsteps you follow carefully.

Killed by himself . . . the man Toxie is strangling is none other than Mitch Cohen, who played the original Toxic Avenger.

location. A movie shot entirely within those confines will quickly become tiresome and your audience will think you were too lazy to broaden your scope. Filming on location will mean a lot more planning and forethought on your part, but you can make it work. If nothing else, Troma movies are proof positive that location filming is possible on a meager budget. After all, if we can slaughter an ass-load of retarded kids in a real school, stage a bloodbath with a hideously deformed creature of superhuman size and strength battling troops of neo-Nazis in a real hospital, drag a black guy behind a real pickup truck, and get a naked fat guy to run blind through the real Times Square,* then pretty much the sky's the limit. All it takes is time, persistence, respect, organization, and a clean bucket to crap in.

---

* Admittedly, the infantile size of Yaniv's penis may have helped with this scene, since unless you looked really closely, it appeared as though he was wearing a flesh-colored body suit.

CHAPTER 8

Welcome to Your Nightmare

The First 24 Hours of Production

So this is what it's all been leading up to: your first day as a bona fide, honest-to-goddamn motion picture director. Inheritor of a lineage that includes such giants as John Ford and Samuel Fuller . . . not to mention pretentious, substance-free, self-satisfied pablum producers like Penny Marshall and Lawrence Kasdan. Up till now, you've probably felt like a writer, a casting director, a production manager, a producer, a flim-flam artist . . . lots of things but not really like a director. Don't worry. You'll feel it in your gut your first day on set the first time you call "Action!" Be sure to have plenty of Bromo Seltzer on hand.*

The first day of production is like the first day of school, only with less gunplay. With everyone working together so intensely, you'll be surprised at how quickly the group dynamic forms. If you haven't already established yourself as being firmly in control of this project, you'd better damn well do it now. It's also in these first few days that

---

* Bromo Seltzer has 1,001 uses on a Troma set. As discussed in *All I Need To Know About Filmmaking I Learned From The Toxic Avenger*, it can be used to create beautiful foaming-mouth effects. It can also be used as a female douche, a flea and tick shampoo, a high colonic irrigation fluid . . . oh, and apparently some people use it to aid in the relief of upset stomach. Whatever.

you will be able to see which of the people you hired are even better than you could have dared hope and which of them are lazy, incompetent bastards. *On Terror Firmer*, for instance, all the people who quit did so after four days. From that point on, we had a stable team that stuck it out to the very end.*

Just because you've warned everyone in advance that you're embarking on a risky and uncomfortable venture and everyone's said, "Yeah, we understand it's going to suck, we want to do it anyway," don't think that you've got yourself a group of troupers that'll see you through thick and thin. The first day of shooting *Troma's War*, there was an assistant cameraman who started complaining the second he got on set. Before we started, we'd told him over and over again that conditions were going to be subhuman and we had a miniscule budget, every penny of which would be put into the film and not into providing creature comforts. The guy knew full well what he was getting into, but that didn't stop him from making life on the set a living hell for all of us. He went around saying we were all idiots, the whole shoot was fucked, and nothing was working the way it was supposed to. This may have been true, but he wasn't telling us anything we didn't already know. This kept going until we broke for the first meal of the first day. The cameraman was standing in the chow line looking at what was provided and said the food looked like shit. Phil Rivo was the production assistant who was in charge of catering and he heard this remark. Phil countered with something like, "How do you know? Does your mother cook shit for you?" This pushed the cameraman over the edge and he hauled off and punched Phil. Obviously we fired the guy immediately, but we probably should have fired him before it got to that point. Although it was pretty damn cool to see Rivo get clocked.

One school of thought when you're making your shooting schedule

---

* But on *Citizen Toxie*, people quit all the time, including a mass walk-out after about three weeks of shooting. This happened immediately after the crew's first day off, so I learned my lesson. Obviously I never should have given them a day off in the first place because this gave them all time to remember there was a world outside Tromaville.

will tell you to make the first day a light one. Personally, I think the first day should be extremely heavy. Schedule something difficult, like a stunt you want to get out of the way. This way, you toss the team into the freezing cold water and see immediately who sinks or swims. Often we'll schedule a shooting day into pre-production where we take the cast, crew and equipment out for a test run to make sure that everybody's working in concert. When you do this, you're able to see what goes right and what goes wrong and correct your mistakes so when you get to the first day of actual production, you can jump right into the thick of things. At the beginning of production, everyone's energy is high and they're itching to get going. Take advantage of that and schedule a difficult, complicated day that requires everyone's full concentration.

Trent Haaga here. Sorry to interrupt Lloyd's gestapo-like insistence on making your crew work like Alaskan sled dogs in the Iditarod on the very first day, but I thought you should probably be aware of the following. On the first day of shoot-ing Tromeo & Juliet, *Lloyd scheduled an extremely involved street fight scene that used pretty much the whole damn cast. Apparently thinking he was the Evel Knievel of filmmakers and needed an extra distraction to make things even more difficult, he also invited a news crew from CNN down to the set. Because Lloyd is such a firm believer in pre-production and rehearsals, he had, of course, rehearsed the scene over and over again. But some details tend to be overlooked in the rehearsal process and one such detail that went unnoticed was that actress Tiffany Shepis would be wearing spike heels in the scene. She hadn't worn them during rehearsals. So when the time came to shoot the scene, no one took into account the extra inches and Tiffany accidentally kicked Stephen Blackehart* in the head. Knocked him out cold. They had to call an ambulance in for him. And, of course, CNN got the whole goddamn fiasco on tape. So you might want to bear that in*

---

* One of the stars of *Tromeo & Juliet* and *Rockabilly Vampire* and, according to the Internet Movie Database, Marlon Brando's son. Not the son who allegedly killed his sister's boyfriend but still, clearly not a family you want to fuck with.

mind when you're trying to decide whether to make your first day a heavy one or a light one.

Okay, I admit I forgot about that little incident. Nevertheless, I'd still argue that a heavy day is better than a light one, simply because your team will be fresher and more alert. If Stevie had been kicked in the head later in production when he was exhausted and weak, maybe he wouldn't have recovered as quickly . . . maybe he would have died a slow and agonizing death.

The only good reason to make your first day a light one is so that you can stay on schedule, because most of your first day is going to get eaten up by all sorts of auxiliary bullshit that doesn't really have anything to do with filmmaking. All your equipment will be packed up and it will take time for this crap to get unloaded. You're going to have to set up a generator or tie into the existing electrical power supply. You're going to have to set up a wardrobe area and a makeup area. You're going to have to rummage through a couple dozen boxes to figure out where the hell your PAs hid the toilet paper.* And you will have to set up your craft services table with whatever scraps of food and water you're providing.

The craft services table might seem like an indulgence but it is extremely important to set it up right away. I guarantee there will be at least one shaky-limbed junkie on your team who is pathologically unable to function as a human being until they get a cup of coffee. In fact, probably the most often asked question on the morning of the first day is, "Where's the coffee?" The irony of this is that nobody on a movie set ever drinks the coffee at craft services. First of all, coffee is only slightly less expensive than heroin, so all you're going to be able to

---

* PA = Pennsylvania or Pencil Vanya, as in Anton Chekhov's play *Uncle Vanya*. In the play, Vanya labors arduously for many years with little reward or recognition. The Pencil Vanya is someone who does this kind of backbreaking work until they get completely worn down. This is why a production assistant is referred to as a PA.

afford is twenty-year-old generic-brand crystals. Then invariably the PA who is put in charge of craft services is some nineteen-year-old kid who drinks nothing but Mountain Dew and doesn't have the first fucking clue how to make a pot of coffee. So what you end up with is a pot of repulsive brew with an oil-slick rainbow floating atop it that tastes like black lung phlegm. But on the first day, nobody knows this yet, so the mere presence of the coffee will be enough to inspire the caffeine addicts on your crew. They will learn soon enough to buy their own damn cup of java on their way to the set.

After the coffee situation is taken care of, the most commonly asked question will become, "When's lunch?" Scheduling meals is another pointless arena that unions insist on imposing picky little rules. On a union set, you must schedule the first hot meal after six hours of work and a second hot meal after twelve hours. If you're not working under the union label, then you can feel free to play fast and loose with these rules. One day on *Citizen Toxie*, we worked ten hours (from 6 A.M. to 4 P.M.) before we broke for lunch. That may have been a little extreme, but it was necessary for the day's work. On your first day, try to schedule a break after six hours or so and try to adhere to that schedule as closely as possible. After all, you don't want to work these people to death in the first twenty-four hours. Expect lunch to take about ninety minutes. Even if you've scheduled it to take no more than half an hour, it will still be ninety minutes before everyone's eaten, digested, farted, and got their energy back.*

What we experienced on the first day of production on *Terror Firmer* was typical of what you can expect to encounter on your first

---

* Usually, I don't eat lunch at all. While everybody else is stuffing their faces, I sit where everybody can see me and make notes and plan the next set-up. After about twenty minutes of this, the DP and I start working. When the rest of the crew sees what's going on, the more conscientous among them filter over and start working too. This is an excellent way to passive-aggressively keep breaks short and work moving forward. There's plenty of other mindgames you can use to fuck with your crew, but this is one of the more constructive.

day. We shot in a derelict freight terminal in Greenpoint, Brooklyn. Once upon a time, it was the largest such facility on the East Coast but time had marched right over it and now it stood abandoned. Nevertheless, it was still full of shit like large bales of rotting textiles. Parts of it were literally falling to pieces. Because the location was owned by one of our investors, we were able to film there for next to nothing. Unfortunately, it has since been developed, thus robbing low-budget cinema of a prime waterfront location.

For a 35mm movie with a budget of less than $400,000, *Terror Firmer* was an extraordinarily complex shoot, with an extremely large cast and numerous action and special effects sequences. But we didn't shoot any of that on the first day. The first day we had no crowds, no explosions, no violence (staged or otherwise), and no big makeup effects. Instead, we started with sex, which is nearly as strenuous.

While I usually shoot in sequence, the one exception to this rule is that I try to shoot sex scenes early on. These are always the most uncomfortable scenes for the actors, so I want to get them out of the way immediately. If you shoot these scenes later in production, your actors will approach that date like they're on the Battan Death March. With the sex scenes out of the way right away, they'll be able to concentrate on more important things, secure in the knowledge that they won't have to take their clothes off again unless they really, really want to. So for the first two days of *Terror Firmer*, we'd scheduled a pair of sex scenes. The first day was between Toxie (played by Roy David) and his beautiful blond blind bimbo bombshell wife Sara (played by Carla Pivonski) that was to be a scene in *Terror Firmer*'s movie within a movie. This, of course, was supposed to be a closed set but because there was the promise of nudity, most of Brooklyn turned up to ogle. This real-life event was echoed in the script for the second day's sex scene between our leads, Alyce LaTourelle and Trent Haaga. These two lucky bastards would also be doing a sex scene for the movie within the movie, with the entire fictional crew standing around getting a great big eyeful.*

Day one began quietly enough. We all met at the shipyard around 6 A.M. and began to establish work areas. When you're using a sprawling location like a freight terminal that has all sorts of nooks and areas for idle cast and crew to go exploring, it's vital to set up a holding area for your actors. Having gathered everyone there, I had the AD deliver a speech about the location. Since this was an abandoned series of buildings, there were very real dangers and we didn't want anybody to go wandering off and end up crashing through a weak floor and plummeting two stories, ending up with a steel pipe lodged through their chest. Despite these warnings, people started to splinter off almost immediately.

You can tell pretty quickly who is going to work and who is going to fuck around on set. The bigger your crew is, the more people you're going to have dicking around, chatting, flirting, and generally behaving like they're hanging out in the high school courtyard between classes. In principle, these fucker-offers should be fired immediately. But if you take the time to do that, you're taking time away from getting your movie shot and you're running the risk of delaying things further by having to find replacements. It generally isn't worth firing people over mere laziness. To get fired from a low-budget movie set, you must display an amazing degree of gross incompetence that would put you into remedial classes in the real world. This idiocy must waste money, damage property, ruin a major shot, or come close to injuring somebody pretty important, like your lead actor or primary investor.

At some point during your first day, you're going to stop unloading equipment, lecturing your crew, and fielding complaints about the cof-

---

* As you've probably noticed by now, Trent had to put up with a lot of shit before he was allowed to cowrite this book. I emphatically deny the charges that I required Adam Jahnke to participate in any humiliating sex scenes before we signed him. Not for a movie, anyway.

fee and start thinking about actually shooting some film. The two hardest shots of the day to get off the ground are the very first shot and the first shot after lunch. The very first shot is tough because you've got to focus everyone's attention and start the engine rolling. The post-lunch shot is just as difficult because, unless you're feeding everybody sugar packets and Jolt cola, eating makes people tired. It doesn't matter how little tryptophane you've got in the lunch meat, people will feel satisfied and sleepy. Now you've got to get the whole enterprise running again and this is never as easy as it seems. In worst case scenarios, a blast of ice-cold water from a high-pressure fire hose usually wakes people up.

If you don't have a fire hose handy, sugar can be just as good, especially if your crew is primarily made up of young people exhilarated by the idea of working on a movie. It'll take a little time (hopefully not too much) for people to realize that hard work is actually required on set, so you may run into the problem of having your crew staying out

Lloyd Kaufman's failed milk ad campaign. "If you don't got milk, your bones will break!"

all night then coming to work the next day and being completely useless by noon. Or, if you're really fortunate, some of your crew might
be working so hard they actually forget to eat. This happened with
Trent when he was AD on *Citizen Toxie*. I noticed that Trent would
start the day full of energy and enthusiasm, but would become one of
the walking dead within a few hours. Rather than risk losing a key
member of the production team, I started to come to the set with my
pockets full of Snickers bars. Whenever I saw Trent's eyes start to sink
back into their sockets and his voice drop down to a low mumble, I'd
call him over for a private meeting and feed him a Snickers. Within half
an hour, Trent would be bouncing off the walls, which is exactly what
we needed.* Not only did I get my AD back in action, I discovered
that if I ever got sick of the movie industry I could always get a job at
Sea World as a dolphin trainer.

THE MYTH OF EATING PROPERLY
Trent Haaga

It's true that I was so busy on the set of *Citizen Toxie* that I often
forgot to eat. But there were times that I was hungry. Then I saw
what the soup kitchen caterer had brought and would promptly
lose my appetite.

Any nutritionist will tell you that if you're going to be working
a group of people sixteen hours a day for a month, then you
should provide healthy foods if you expect them to be on top of
their game. On Hollywood pictures, the amount and variety of
food is unfathomable. The crew are fed well and fed often. Their
daily craft services bills alone would finance Troma's *Superstarlet
A.D.* (directed by John Michael McCarthy) in its entirety. But these

---

* For more details on the tortures of the damned that Trent endured, see the documentary on
the making of *Citizen Toxie, Apocalypse Soon,* on the *Citizen Toxie* DVD.

are people who are making films for a living, not because they're dedicated to making cinematic art. Fat Hollywood grips will quit the films they're working on if the food isn't up to par because, quite frankly, they could be working as mailmen or house builders. They only take the Hollywood jobs because the pay is great and the meals are paid for. On a low-budget film, the cast and crew are there to make a film. That's the bottom line. In reality, getting a slightly more adept and tasty catering service with a better menu selection wouldn't have killed Lloyd. But we were in Poughkeepsie to make a movie, not to eat gourmet meals. This is why the food was often congealed and cold by the time we actually got to it. I remember the day we waited ten hours before breaking for lunch on *Citizen Toxie*. Hour six passed without event. By hour eight, the principal crew was beginning to get testy. By principal crew, I mean the handful of us that actually worked all day—the DP, the assistant cameraman, the sound guy, the actors, Lloyd, and myself. The rest of the crew was able to find some shade, rest, and craft services while the rest of us shot. At hour nine, Brendan Flynt, the DP, was threatening to walk away from the camera. Our food— naturally it would be cold-cut sandwiches and not something hot when we're in a shadeless field in ninety degree weather—had been fermenting in the sun for hours. I pulled Lloyd aside and told him that the crew was going to rebel if we didn't break for lunch.

"Just a few more shots, Trent. Don't worry about Flynt. He won't ditch us. Keep shooting. It's gonna be dark in three hours anyway."

We kept shooting. Ten hours after our 6:00 A.M. call time, Brendan and the rest of the crew were becoming downright surly. Or they would have been if they had the strength. I finally put my foot down. Ten hours without a break was approaching abuse as far as I was concerned. I once again pulled Lloyd to the side.

"This is it, Lloyd. Ten hours of shooting without a break? I'm calling lunch right now. This is ridiculous. I'm calling lunch right now."

Lloyd looked at me with utter disdain, "Oh, I see. You're *competent* and *compassionate*." The italics denote withering sarcasm, if you were wondering.

I broke the crew for a truly rancid lunch of warm meat cutlets and soggy bread. I, naturally, didn't eat. I spent the lunch break looking for some sort of physical proof that Lloyd wasn't really some sort of evil filmmaking android. Because, once again, Lloyd didn't eat a bite.

There were many days that I didn't eat lunch due to stress or because the food was completely unpalatable. But another reason that I didn't eat was because Lloyd *never, ever, ever* ate on set. Sure I was tired and hungry. But I'd be goddamned if I let some fifty-four-year-old out-do me in the realm of spartan lifestyle while making a film. If Lloyd wanted to eschew food and talk about the next setup while the rest of the crew ate, I was right there with him. I have known Lloyd for many years now and have only seen him eat a handful of salted nuts from a jar on his desk. I have never seen him eat on set. He drinks about 300 cups of coffee a day, but never eats. How could a man live on no food? How could Lloyd run circles around a crew of kids half his age and never eat? It was confirming my suspicion that Lloyd wasn't human. He had to be an alien or robot—pythons only have to eat once every month or so . . . maybe Lloyd was a genetic experiment. This question kept me up at night (maybe that was malnutrition, stress, and the fact that I was sleeping on a concrete floor). Regardless, I was in awe of Lloyd's superhuman strength and endurance.

It was about halfway through the shoot that Brendan Flynt approached me one morning. He had been overcome with hunger the night before. It being late, he had gotten out of bed and gone to the only twenty-four-hour diner near his hotel.

"You should've seen it, Trent. Lloyd was sitting in a corner booth all by himself. He was reading the paper and didn't even see me. I couldn't believe it, Trent. The entire table was covered with plates. He had biscuits and gravy on one plate, steak and fries on another, and a *whole pecan pie* on another. He was drinking a pot of coffee, a bottle of wine, and a carafe of orange juice all at the same time. I've never seen that much food on a single person's table. Even the 500-pound Joe Fleishaker's! It was amazing, Trent. Lloyd put down every bite. He didn't even stop to breathe."

So that was Lloyd's secret. I had been starving myself to get into a pissing contest with a man who had the metabolism of a dromedary.

It doesn't cost too much to come up with good food for your crew. And a well-fed (or at least decently fed) crew works better, longer, and faster than an undernourished crew. Do yourself a favor and splurge a little bit to provide at least this small nicety to the folks who are helping you create your vision.

Craft services trucks and tables can be seen on large film sets from several miles away. They dole out snacks and drinks all day long for the cast and crew. On Troma films, craft services consists of a few brown bags with generic potato chip crumbs in them and several two-liter bottles of "No Frills" brand soda in a cooler half full of brown, lukewarm water. While it may behoove you to have some sort of liquid refreshment on-hand, craft services is an excuse for valuable crew members to disappear every once in a while. Craft services on a low-budget film ends up becoming more expensive than feeding your crew one fine meal per day. If you purchase a couple of cases of soda a day, you'll be out twenty bucks and will have to clean up all of the half and three quarters-filled soda cans at the end of the day. Your crew should be so dedicated to the job at hand that they don't even need craft services. Save your money for lunch.

When you're setting up the first scene to be shot, it is extremely helpful if you as the director can first look at the scene through your editor's eyes.* Hitchcock was an expert at knowing exactly how a given scene was going to be cut. This enabled him to shoot only what was necessary and run a tight, efficient production. Of course, not everybody is Hitchcock and almost nobody is Hitchcock on his first film. This being the case, it is certainly better to shoot more than you need than not enough. Try to envision all the different ways you might be able to cut the scene and walk through it with your DP†, figuring out in advance where the camera should be placed.‡

On Day One, you absolutely, positively cannot allow people to talk back to you. This undermines the entire crew's confidence in your ability as a director. On the first day of shooting *Tromeo & Juliet*, Brendan Flynt mouthed off repeatedly in front of the entire crew. Finally, I took him aside and said, "Look, you can't talk to me like that. For better or

---

* This does not imply that you should gouge out your editor's eyes and bring them to the set. There will be plenty of time for that in post-production.

† DP=Deep Pee, Woodward and Bernstein's other, and far less useful, informant during the Watergate scandal.

‡ Theoretically, you've already done this several times . . . during location tours, in storyboards, during the videotaped rehearsals, and in the night tremors you're probably enduring every evening. It's still a very good idea to walk through it again on set before the lights are set and block it like you're doing it for the very first time. The reality of production may give you new ideas that are better than what you'd planned on doing.

worse, I'm the director and all these people have to listen to me. If I'm doing something stupid, take me aside and tell me that's the stupidest fucking shot you've ever heard of in your life. Take me aside and tell me that we can't do a dolly shot on this sandy beach because we don't have any tracks. But don't do it in front of everyone." And from that time on, Brendan and I enjoyed a harmonious working relationship, one in which he calls me a total fucking moron in complete privacy.

Once you and the DP have reached some kind of consensus, bring the actors in for a rehearsal. Do this before they scurry off to wardrobe and makeup so they have something to think about while they're getting ready other than the Polish sausage they sucked down the night before. Once you've rehearsed and everybody knows what he's doing, send the actors off to get beautified while the DP sets up the lighting. Both the actors and the DP will want to spend much more time doing this than is practical or necessary. The actors will never think they look good enough and the DP will never think the shot looks good enough. Crack the whip on them though and keep things moving as smoothly and coordinated as humanly possible.

Since we were shooting a sex scene, you'd think that it would take no time at all for the actors to go through wardrobe and makeup since for all intents and purposes, there really was no wardrobe. But in fact, if a gyno is required to be nude in a scene, it will take her even longer to get ready. Since she doesn't have any clothes to fuss with, she'll obsess over her hair, her makeup, her lighting, everything and anything. This despite the proven fact that most men who see a naked woman don't give a shit about her hair, they're just happy to see a pair of tits. Try to explain this to your actress, however, and you'll more than likely end up with her knee smashing into your balls. It's not a bad idea in these circumstances to give your actress a tiny bit of extra time to prepare herself.

When you're shooting a fuck scene . . . I mean a tender, romantic love scene, it's a good idea to give the actors time during pre-production to block the scene themselves. This gives them time to get to know each other and results in a scene that's a hell of a lot more natural than having you bark at them to move his left elbow counterclockwise around her right areola. After they've blocked the scene, you can simply pick the angles that will work best. I did this with Will Keenan (Tromeo) and Jane Jensen (Juliet) during *Tromeo & Juliet*. I wanted them to develop a very intense relationship and indeed they did. But they decided that they shouldn't actually have off-screen intercourse until after the movie. I don't remember whether they ever did but this gave their on-screen scenes together terrific sexual tension and was something a sex-crazed pervert like me would never have thought of in a zillion years.

Something else you will notice very quickly in these first days of production is the complete lack of respect given to the sound guy. Now it's practically a given that the sound guy is always the weirdest freak on the set. Sound guys have to contort their bodies into uncomfortable positions so they stay out of the shot. They're always wearing headphones so you're never sure if the guy's listening to you, eavesdropping on a conversation in the next room, or listening to the playback of a dying cat he recorded the night before. So if the sound guy is treated like he's the geek in a traveling circus, that's not too big a surprise. They're almost as creepy as those Internet webmaster nerds. What I'm talking about is the lack of respect given his job. Say you're setting up a shot in a closet. You spend an hour placing your actor (or actors if you're shooting something really kinky in there), getting your camera in place, framing the shot, and beautifully lighting everything. At long last, everything looks perfect. Now where are you gonna put the boom mike?

Don't treat sound as an afterthought. I can't tell you how many low-budget movies have been ruined by piss-poor sound.* Figure out where you're going to place the mike *while* you're setting up the shot, not after it's all ready to go. Too many times people will excuse bad

---

* It's not that I don't want to tell you, it's just that it hadn't occurred to me until this very second, so I haven't exactly been keeping score. Trust me, it's a lot.

sound by repeating the "fix it in post" chant. While you can sweeten your sound to some (usually very minor) extent in post-production, you can't work magic with what you don't have. On the movie *Joe** (which I was shit-boy . . . I mean a production assistant on in 1970), editor George Norris was extremely proud of the fact that because Michael Scott Goldenbaum's direct location sound was so good, none of the movie had to be looped.† On the other hand, when we produced *Troma's Edge TV* in 2000 for Channel 4 in the UK, we had outstanding recordings of Los Angeles dogs, earthquakes, airplanes, sirens, cars, wind . . . pretty much everything except the actors' dialogue. This happened because I allowed myself to be convinced by so-called "experts" that recording sound for video was different than recording sound for film. It isn't. You still need to have the Mike pointed at and held somewhat close to your actors' mouths so it'll pick up the sounds that are coming out of them. Good sound is especially important on a low-budget movie. Not long ago, I saw an episode of that amazingly shitty HBO show *Project Greenlight*, the show where the pretty-boy actors decided to throw a million bones at some fat, self-absorbed, whiny fuck-face to make the most maudlin, god-awful boring piece-of-shit movie in creation. On the episode I saw, Chunky pissed and moaned about how important it was for him to get this location by a railroad trestle. Ultimately, the spineless producers caved and Fatboy got his perfect location. Surprise, surprise, they couldn't record a single line of dialogue because there was train traffic going by every two seconds. This is sheer, unadulterated stupidity.

* *Joe* was a $150,000-budgeted movie directed by John G. Avildsen and featured the film debuts of Susan Sarandon and Peter Boyle. The script by Norman Wexler was nominated for an Oscar. In fact, every single person involved with *Joe* went on to amazing success except for me.
† Looping is the process of re-recording dialogue in post-production. The probable source of this term is actress Lupe Velez, better known as the Mexican Spitfire, who killed herself in 1944 when she realized she'd never be remembered for her movies so she might as well be remembered for her death. She planned an elaborate, elegant suicide but ended up dead with her head in the toilet. So "looping" is when you plan something to be really great (like your sound or your career) but it gets so fucked up that you have to go back and fix it (by re-recording sound or killing yourself in an embarrassing way).

SOUND: THE ONE THING YOU ARE
MOST LIKELY TO FUCK UP
Andrew Rye

Andrew Rye was sound mixer on two independent films that feature Lloyd Kaufman's acting abilities: The Tunnel, *directed by Ramzi Abed, and* Prison-A-Go-Go *directed by Barak Epstein.*

Sound is what it is, and for the most part, cannot be manipulated on set like lighting or f-stops. It is the sound man's responsibility to eliminate or deafen unwanted noise at its source, because manipulating sound with your equipment only hides it. So if the camera's magazine is making too much racket, don't try to hide it by playing around with the mixer because it will still be there. Instead, wrap the shit out of that mag and cover your own ass! Modern technology is extremely advanced, but it is not to the point where it can warp reality. For instance, no matter how good the sound may be on *The Tunnel* and *Prison-A-Go-Go*, there was absolutely no way that I was ever going to be able to manipulate it enough so that it seemed like Lloyd was giving a halfway decent performance in either film.

Sitting in on an editing session is extremely helpful for a sound mixer because it allows the sound guy to realize what sounds he needs to record on location to make post-production much easier and better sounding, like room tone and wild lines. The most important aspect of a sound man are his ears.* An

* LLOYD KAUFMAN RESPONDS: I always felt a sound man's most important equipment was in his pants, but I guess I'm thinking of a different definition of the word "sound."

experienced sound mixer is not measured by his knowledge of equipment or lingo, but how well he listens and identifies sound. The best sound mixers can differentiate between the most subtle changes in background noise ratio, so be sure to take good care of your ears!

Once everyone's ready to shoot (or more likely, once you've looked at your watch for the hundredth time, started to panic, and have decreed that it's time for everybody to stop fucking around and get something on film or else this fucking movie will never get done), it's time for your AD to swing into action. A good AD should be the drill sergeant on set, keeping everyone focused and busy and listening to what you have to say. When it's time to go, your AD needs to make everybody shut the fuck up. Your AD needs to know where everybody is at all times and be able to get all necessary personnel on set at a moment's notice. A good AD cannot worry about being liked. They've got to take and dish out a lot of shit for the betterment of the project.

On *Citizen Toxie*, we had a day where we shot a large crowd outside the Tromaville School for the Very Special. Showing big crowds of people on film is a great, easy way to get high production value on a meager budget. To get people to show up, we just had to put up the "Be A Movie Star" signs that I discussed in Chapter 4. We got several hundred people to turn out, but we knew that very few, if any of them would be willing or able to stay for the entire day. So we scheduled them in shifts throughout the day, with waves of 50–100 people coming in at different times so we always had a decent sized crowd of onlookers.

One of the AD's jobs whenever there's a scene like this is to control the actor-persons.* Anybody who's ever been in a crowd of more than

---

* Or extras, if you're a heartless cad who doesn't value their contribution, or background artists if you're a pretentious snob who wants everyone involved in your project to feel like Matisse.

twenty people knows that this is a fuck of a lot harder than it looks, and it looks nearly impossible. Furthermore, the AD has to do so without being in the least bit condescending or rude. On a Troma set, every position is equally important. The production assistants are not there to carry the actor's suitcase for him. Everyone from the director to the actor-person who comes in for half a day is there with one goal: To make the movie, and to get that done, every job is vital.

In this case, we had a fairly large number of people who showed up that day as if it were a tailgating party, clutching 7-Eleven Big Gulp cups full of liquor. Armed only with a bullhorn, Trent faced down the crowd, giving them directions like "Look scared" or "It's Toxie! Look excited!" As the crowd edged closer to becoming a mob, they started shouting back to Trent, "Fuck you, faggot!" A lesser AD would have grown belligerent or hostile, but Trent realized that he'd only incite the crowd further by doing that. Instead, Trent merely shouted, "Yeah, fuck me but look scared while you're doing it!" By absorbing and shrugging off the unruly crowd's abuse, Trent was able to save the day and get the phone numbers of a couple excited dominatrixes in the process.

Besides throwing your AD to the wolves, there's some easy ways you can ensure that your actor-persons are cooperative and feel involved. One is just by spending some time with them. On major Hollywood productions, the actor-persons often never even see the actual director of the movie unless they bring binoculars. I make a point of hanging out with them when the camera crew is setting up the shot. I have a pretty good short-term memory,* so I try to learn as many of their names as I can. You never know . . . you may find some hidden gems amongst your actor-persons. Troma's 500-pound action superstar Joe Fleishaker began his career as an actor-person on *Troma's War*. And on the day Dave Mattey was late to the set of *Citizen Toxie* (discussed by Trent in Chapter 3), we pulled a guy (a black guy, actually,

---

* My long-term memory is shot to shit, though. While working on this book, I kept having to ask myself why I'm writing all this into the screenplay of *The First Turn-On*.

who looked nothing like Dave) out of the ranks of the actor-persons, put an old stunt mask from *The Toxic Avenger Part III* on him and went on shooting. I believe Dave had a Joycean epiphany that day when he realized that he was really just a big guy in a mask and if he kept giving me attitude, there were plenty of other big guys in masks around. On a low-budget movie, you can't afford to be held hostage by anyone or anything. The guy we pulled out of the crowd that day went on to play Toxie again in the Macy's Thanksgiving Day Parade. Mattey was supposed to do that too but quit the day before Thanksgiving. It actually costs money* to be allowed to march in the parade, so I assume Mattey felt he was really fucking us by waiting until the last minute before quitting. He didn't. We just called up our standby Toxie from before and enjoyed a wonderful Thanksgiving Day.

The sex scenes we were shooting on the first days of *Terror Firmer* were more complicated than your usual, run-of-the-mill fuck shots. Not because we were trying to be "artistic" like the French and get our actors to actually engage in intercourse, but because the plot of *Terror Firmer* revolved around the making of a low-budget film. Since the scenes were part of a movie within a movie, we had a lot of other actors involved other than the two who were getting naked. Odds are probably pretty good that your sex scenes won't include crowds of onlookers. But if they do, you should do as we did and break the scene into its component parts. We filmed the actual sex stuff in the morning with the two actors, then scheduled the rest of the cast for after lunch. Not out of respect for our actors' privacy, but so we wouldn't have to feed a bunch of extra people that day.

I should mention here that I do *not* recommend that you film a scene with thirty-plus extras in a hazardous location on your very first day as a filmmaker. My first day as director on the set of *The Girl Who Returned*† (1968) was vastly different from my first day on the set of

* Which is donated to a Children's hospital, I believe.
† See Kaufman's first book *Everything I Need to Know About Filmmaking I Learned from the Toxic Avenger* for an in-depth description of this monstrosity of a feature-length movie.

Terror Firmer (1998). Sure, there's some constants, like the need to make shit up on the spot when your carefully planned shot doesn't pan out like you'd expected or feeling like you're strapped naked to the engine of an out-of-control locomotive careening down a steep mountain. But don't think that just because you've read a few books and seen a shitload of movies, you're automatically ready to jump into the deep end of the pool. Even little twelve-year-old Stevie Spielberg didn't make a pretentious Super-8 flick about a bunch of naked Jewish chicks getting gassed right away.* Filmmaking is a skill honed through experience and everything you shoot adds to that experience. If you do have a scene with several dozen actor-persons in a building that ought to be condemned, for fuck's sake schedule it later in production. Start small and work your way up to it. You'll be glad you did.

Your first day or two on the set will really test your skill as a multitasker. You may think you were multitasking like a son of a bitch during pre-production, but that was a cakewalk compared to what you're going to be faced with now. In pre-production, if somebody interrupts while you're in the middle of something else and you never get back to what you were doing in the first place, it's not the end of the world. On set, everything that requires your attention must be brought to completion. If something goes undone, you'll pay for it sooner or later. I recommend practicing multitasking at home as much as possible by doing several completely unrelated things simultaneously. Personally, I enjoy jerking off while rewriting screenplays and talking on the phone to my dentist's receptionist. Not to practice multitasking, of course, it's just something I enjoy.

---

* Though I've heard rumors that he did film his sister in the shower when he was a kid, so obviously he was already sowing the seeds for his later work.
EDITOR'S NOTE: Kaufman, do I really even have to tell you to get rid of this statement? This is totally untrue.

ALL I NEED TO KNOW ABOUT FILMMAKING I LEARNED FROM *THE TOXIC AVENGER*, QUITE LITERALLY

Doug Sakmann

Doug Sakmann is Head of Production for Troma Entertainment, a title that carries about as much weight and status in Hollywood as Hall Monitor or Fish Gutter. Here, Doug describes his experiences as Troma's fall guy.

I first joined the Troma team as an actor-person on *Citizen Toxie: The Toxic Avenger Part IV*. My role was that of a "Special Student." In other words, I play a retard in the opening scene. Lloyd told us that even though we only had small roles, we should still put some thinking into it and bring what we could to our characters. So as my fellow students and I sat in the classroom waiting for the shot, I saved all the spit in my mouth until I had a mouthful. When Lloyd called action, I spit and slobbered all over myself and the actor-persons around me. When the shot was done, Lloyd said, "Whose idea was the Bromo Seltzer? That's brilliant!" With a mouth full of spit, I said it was my own saliva. The rest of the cast and crew thought it was disgusting, but Lloyd thought it was genius. To this day, I think Lloyd hired me because he was impressed by my ability to store spit in my mouth.

I had such a great experience getting involved with all aspects of production of the classroom scene, that I decided I would put all my free time into helping out with the film. I worked as much as I could on the rest of the month-long shoot, putting my heart and soul into everything I did, be it foaming at the mouth or pouring blood over naked bodies at the Playboy Mansion. I learned all kinds of things, just by experiencing them firsthand. Lloyd took notice of this and when the film wrapped, he gave me credit as "Associate Producer" of *Citizen Toxie*, and offered me a job. Here I was, 19 years old, fresh out of high school with no formal film training, and he was offering me a major position in his nearly thirty-year-old film company. Needless to say, I took the job and here I am almost three years later, head of production for Troma.

Besides all the basic duties associated with this title (like unclogging the toilet, a job that will be much easier once Lloyd and Michael Herz buy me that plunger they've been promising), I have headed the Troma Team at Cannes and TromaDance for the past three years now, as well as co-produced and co-directed Troma's Edge TV for Channel 4 in the UK (I've also banged a lot of hot Tromettes to boot). Being in Tromaville for three years now, I have gained so much invaluable experience with all aspects of the filmmaking business (and with women). Thanks to Lloyd and Michael, I understand how the industry actually works (again, I have also learned how women work. At least more than I knew before). I can honestly say that if not for Troma, I probably would have never stood a chance in the film industry (also, I would be reading this book instead of writing for it).

Troma has been called the hazing of the film industry, and whoever said that was absolutely correct. Once you've worked for Troma and survived, you can take *anything* that Hollywood can throw at you. I know, because thanks to Troma, I have seen it all, and then some.

Probably the single most important thing to do on your first day is to stick to your schedule. If you fall behind immediately, you can rest assured that you have set precedent for the rest of the shoot. You have already fallen irreparably off track. Even worse, you have undermined your team's confidence in you as a leader. Sometimes the need to stay on schedule will require you to sacrifice your vision to some cold, hard practicalities. The first time you're faced with this choice will be the hardest. It'll be like *Sophie's Choice*, except instead of being forced to sacrifice one your children to the gas chamber, you're going to be forced to give up the beautiful, gifted child that means more to you than life itself, and replace her with an albino mongoloid with a cleft palate and vestigial tail. If you're serious about getting your damn movie made, you should always go for what's possible over what you'd ideally like to see. We're not all Kubrick and we can't all afford to shoot eighty-seven takes of a guy picking up the phone. However, you should also allow for the possibility that your beautiful, gifted child isn't as beautiful as you think she is and the retarded albino might not be as hideous.

It's really *very* seldom that everything gels in filmmaking exactly the way you want it to. Sometimes it's better. Sometimes it's not quite as good. That's simply the nature of the craft you've chosen to pursue. Filmmaking is a collaborative effort full of compromise. If you're a perfectionist married to your artistic vision, maybe you should be a painter or a writer instead.* Being a filmmaker means striking a balance in your excitement to disappointment ratio. If you find yourself being constantly disappointed, either you've chosen a project that's

---

* Though if you're going to be a writer, maybe you should do a novel instead of a nonfiction book about filmmaking with multiple collaborators.

ADAM JAHNKE RESPONDS: Fuck that. If you're working with somebody as malleable as Kaufman, you can get away with whatever bullshit you want.

LLOYD KAUFMAN RESPONDS: Not true! I vetoed the "Adam Jahnke, Long-Donged Love God" chapter, didn't I?

TRENT HAAGA RESPONDS: Are we still working on the book? I thought we'd moved on to *Saving Private Toxie: The Toxic Avenger Part 5*.

EDITOR'S NOTE: When we received this manuscript, the margins were full of this sort of bickering, mostly written in crayon, feces, and jelly.

When potential investors suggested that Lloyd shove the screenplay of *Terror Firmer* up his ass, they never expected him to really do it.

way too ambitious for what you have to work with or you're turning into a doormat and you're losing control of the project. Don't sacrifice everything just because your crew tells you it's hard. But if you're getting completely bogged down because you can't find a way to get a shot where the camera glides up six flights of stairs, over to an open window, and hurtles back down to the ground below, it's time to come up with another idea.

Your work isn't done once you've wrapped for the day. If you're shooting on video, you'll be heading home to review the day's footage and figure out where you stand. Cut the movie in your head while you're doing this, take notes to help you and the editor when you're in post. After you've done this (or if you're shooting on film and it's your first day so you haven't got any dailies back from the lab to review yet), it's time to prep for the next day. This probably means you're going to get about two hours of sleep at most. Don't worry about that. You can sleep when you're dead. Some of the most creative and intelligent people in history functioned on very little sleep, including Albert Einstein,

Thomas Edison, Winston Churchill, and Jack the Ripper.* Any sleep you do get will be consumed with thoughts of the movie anyway, so it's not going to be the most deep and restful slumber you've ever had.

Now that you know roughly what to expect from your first day on the set, mark this page and go on with the rest of the book. Then, once you've started production and have come home from your first day on set, come back and read the rest of the chapter. Good luck, have fun, and we'll see you back here then.

Congratulations and welcome to the club! You are now a gen-yoo-wine, dyed in the wool filmmaker, part of a secret society that pulls the strings of cultural and political thought around the world. The secret handshake is performed by placing your right hand down the front of your pants and thrusting your index and ring fingers through your open fly. The responding filmmaker will then open your fingers into a V shape with his or her left hand while saying, "Orson died for our sins." The next time you see Steven Spielberg or Jean-Luc Godard or any other filmmaker in the supermarket checkout line, don't be afraid to go right on up to them and introduce yourself with the secret handshake. They'll be able to tell you where and when local chapter meetings are held in your town. If you live in New York, I look forward to seeing you at the next meeting!

---

* Granted, Einstein slept about ten hours a night but Einstein was a shitty filmmaker.

CHAPTER 9

Stunts and Special Effects— How to Simulate a Violent Death and Stay Out of Jail

In early September 2001 as we were getting our shit together to write this chapter on creating world-class special effects on a miniscule budget, terrorists seized control of a handful of airplanes and rammed them into the World Trade Center and the Pentagon. Perhaps you heard something about this. Suddenly, special effects were being looked at in a different way. On September 10, Hollywood thought nothing about using computer effects to simulate the destruction of national monuments. Hell, audiences were actually encouraged to applaud the obliteration of the White House in 20th Century Fox's zillion-dollar crapfest *Independence Day*. On September 12, they thought nothing again and used the same technology to erase the World Trade Center from the Manhattan skyline. Why? Well, the party line was that the studios did not want to appear "insensitive" or "exploitative" at this time of national crisis. How exactly a glimpse of the Twin Towers during an episode of *Friends* could be defined as exploitation was not really clear, but who ever understands why Hollywood does anything.

Even if we'd wanted to go back through the voluminous Troma library and erase every shot of the World Trade Center, there's no way we could afford to.* So while the major studios were trying to hide the past through computer programs and by burying movies and TV episodes with potentially touchy topics like airport security or tourism in Manhattan, we were being asked about our future. Overnight, the number-one question I got asked in interviews changed from "What the hell were you thinking?" to "Will the events of 9/11 change the way you make movies?" The answer to that one is a qualified *yes*. Any artist, whether a filmmaker or a poet or somebody who paints with their genitals, reacts to the things that are going on in their life and an event of this magnitude affects every one of us. The artist's job, really, is to interpret these reactions and reflect them in her work. Does that mean Troma is going to stop filming people getting their dicks sliced off or their heads destroyed between a pair of mighty tits?† Hell, no! And neither should you, if that's where your muse takes you.

While not every film has special effects or stunts, the odds are pretty good that if you're reading this book, the movie you want to make probably has one or more of the elements that you love in Troma movies. Things that make life worthwhile like cannibals, zombies, decapitations, head-crushings, projectile vomiting, defenestration, disembowelment, and/or a variety of lethal weapons including but by no means limited to guns, knives, crossbows, chain saws, and out-of-control motor vehicles. At first glance, it may seem cheaper to simply perform these acts of mayhem for real, but then all your money

---

* Unless we just took a black Sharpie to the prints themselves and manually scribbled out the towers. As a matter of fact, the very first shot of *Citizen Toxie* is the skyline of New York with the World Trade Center standing proudly. In this case, we could have easily snipped the shot out without even breaking a fingernail, but instead we left it in. When the movie came out, only about a month after September 11th, audiences applauded the appearance of the towers. Around the same time the movie was premiering, editors at Sony were tripping over each other trying to airbrush out any glimpse of the WTC from trailers and posters of *Spider-Man*. This decision seems unlikely to win any kudos from audiences, so perhaps the Sony executives can simulate the sound of applause by slapping big wads of money against their legs.

† For a demonstration of this latter effect starring *Teenage Mutant Ninja Turtles* co-creator Kevin Eastman and independent film goddess Julie Strain, see the Tromadu sequence in *Citizen Toxie*.

The only time the crew smiled during production of *Terror Firmer* was when they blew up the Lloyd Kaufman effigy. The applause lasted for three days.

goes to defense attorneys instead of on-screen where it belongs. And while you can certainly create decent looking special effects on a limited budget, you can't do it for free.

Well, actually, there are some things you can do for free. If you know that a building in your town is going to be demolished (preferably by implosion), you can go film that and work it into your script. On *Class of Nuke 'Em High* (1986), my sister Susan* learned about a building in Jersey City that was due to be demolished. We wanted the school in our movie to explode too, so we hightailed it over to Jersey City to capture the moment of destruction. The doomed building looked absolutely nothing like our school, but we framed a very tight shot and got the implosion on film. If you watch the movie on DVD and freeze-frame through the explosion, you can see the buildings don't match, but when viewed at normal speed, it looks just fine.

Similarly, if you're lucky enough to be on the scene when an elderly

* Producer of the Troma classic *I Was A Teenage TV Terrorist.*

woman gets mashed into a purplish mass of goo by a convoy of eighteen-wheelers, you can try to film that. Of course, working this kind of thing into your picture depends entirely on timing, your own creativity, and your willingness to risk the fiery pits of hell for exploiting a tragedy. Don't worry too much about that last one. If you end up burning for eternity, at least you'll have plenty of company from multimedia news conglomerates. Rupert Murdoch's newspapers didn't hesitate to print graphic close-up photos of people plunging to their death from the upper floors of the Trade Center, complete with inset POV (point-of-view) photos showing what the jumpers would have seen on the way down. And pretty much all of the networks used footage of the 9/11 catastrophe in commercials for their news programs. So if the great devil-worshipping conglomerates can exploit this kind of thing for their own gain, why can't the independent? But I digress . . .

Another free special effect that you can slap together on the spot is the Miracle of the Upside Down Camera. Say you want a shot of a guy's head getting stomped on from the point of view of the victim. If you just go ahead and shoot somebody's foot coming down at the lens, you're more than likely going to end up with a broken camera, not to mention a cameraman with a bunch of glass, film, and metal embedded in his brain. So instead, you shoot the action in reverse. If you're shooting on celluloid, your cameraman needs to hold the camera upside down, effectively turning the tail of the film into the head and vice versa. If you're shooting on video, it's even easier because you don't have to go through all that. You can hold the camera right side up and reverse the action in post without any muss or fuss. You then have your cameraman lie down with the upside down camera (or right side up video camera) and your actor places his foot within a centimeter or so of the lens. All he has to do then is raise his foot. When you run the footage in reverse, it looks like the foot is crashing down on the camera. To see this effect done incorrectly, watch *The Battle of Love's Return* (1971). We used it for a scene where I was supposed to be hit by a car. Because I didn't know what I was doing, I made it a lot more complicated than I should have. I started on the ground, jumped up on the hood of the car, slid off the car as it pulled away in reverse, and walked across the street backwards. It looks pitiful because unless your actor is on leave from Cirque du Soleil, there's no way he can do that much activity in reverse. Multiple shots are needed. If I'd had the camera in the car and started with my face pressed against the glass, then jumped off and walked backwards, it would have looked fine.

Because special effects can be costly and dangerous, before you go crazy writing a bunch of gunfights and spontaneous combustion scenes into your script, entertain the idea that you might not need them. Believe it or not, there are many excellent films that do not feature a single castration.* The first movies I made didn't have any of that shit in them. Before *The Toxic Avenger*, the most complicated special effect I attempted was showing a guy catch a softball in his ass in *Squeeze Play* (1976).† Guns, weapons, stunts, and pyrotechnics will eat through your budget pretty quickly, so if you can avoid using them, maybe you should.

I'm not necessarily suggesting that you should abandon your script for *Rampage of the Gun Maniacs* and make *My Dinner With Andre II* instead.‡ I'm simply saying you should weigh the importance of these scenes in your film and try to find safe, creative, and inexpensive ways to do them. For instance, if you're using guns in your movie, it's never a good idea to have real guns on set. Especially when there are toy guns on the market that are so realistic looking that cops will shoot you dead if they see you waving one around on a crowded street.§ Filmmak-

---

* Although I have to admit I always thought *The Graduate* would have been much improved if it had ended with a big castration scene. Instead of just interrupting the wedding, Dustin Hoffman should have sliced the dick off the guy Katharine Ross was about to marry and use the severed penis to lock the doors of the church instead of the cross. Now *that's* filmmaking!
† An effect that was achieved, I might add, through the Miracle of the Upside Down Camera.
‡ EDITOR'S NOTE: Kaufman was production manager on *My Dinner With Andre*, where he lobbied Louis Malle, Wallace Shawn, and Andre Gregory to conclude the film with a castration scene.
§ If you can't find those kinds of realistic toy guns, buy some of those pink or yellow water pistols and paint them black.

ing depends on the art of illusion and you can create a perfectly believable gunfight with toy guns, post-production sound effects, and judicious editing. You don't necessarily have to actually show your gun being fired. If you do, just have your actor mime the action of the gun and add white frames in post-production to create the illusion of flashes coming out of the gun. You can also make it look like your plastic gun is really firing by adding digital effects in post-production. I come from a generation that thinks computers still run on punch cards and occupy entire basements, so I haven't exactly embraced digital effects yet. But some pretty amazing things are now possible thanks to computers and the cost of these programs are dropping every day.

Besides being a hazard to every single person on your set, real guns will cost you some major dough.* Unless you live in Montana and can just go borrow a bunch of automatic weapons from the militia next door, gun rentals are extremely expensive. On *Troma's War*, we only ever had two or three working guns going at a time. You can make the most of your limited weaponry by filming the action with multiple cameras. On *War*, we used three cameras for gunfire. The first camera was a wide shot, the second was a close-up of the tip of the gun filmed at ninety-eight frames per second,† and a third camera filming a close-up of the entire gun. We were able to use the close-up footage all over the place. All we had to do was shoot a close-up of the actor's face while he was firing the gun, then intercut it with the already shot close-ups.

The reason gun rentals are so pricey is because not only are you renting the guns themselves, you have to engage a weapons expert to

---

* So will squibs, which are the tiny little explosive charges that you attach to actors to simulate being hit by a bullet. Squibs will set you back $50 a pop. I've tried to replicate the squib effect using squab, which is much cheaper but most actors don't enjoy having a bunch of tiny little birds attached to their bodies. On *Troma's War*, we had squibs everywhere and the MPAA made us cut them all out to secure an R rating. At the same time, the squib-happy *Die Hard* came out and entertained children everywhere with its R rating. So before you squib up your movie, remember that our experience has been that the MPAA treats independent violence a lot differently than studio violence.

† This eats up a hell of a lot of film but it makes it possible for you to see the bullets coming out of the barrel and it looks really, really cool.

supervise the handling of the guns. If you pay careful attention to the Diaper Mafia sequence in *Citizen Toxie*, you'll notice there are only two guns. In the script, there were guns everywhere but they all got cut when we found out how much the damn things were going to cost. The cost escalated even more when our expert told us we also had to hire his assistant. So now we were paying for guns, two people (by the hour), and feeding them to boot.

The day we were using the guns, a PA was sent to pick up the expert and his entourage at his place. As it turned out, the "assistant" was the guy's thirteen-year-old daughter and he had absolutely no interest in even being on the set, much less in doing any assisting. Even better, the guns that I selected for us were these gigantic fucking anti-aircraft weapons. There was no way to squeeze the expert, his antagonistic off-spring, the guns, the ammo, and the driver into the PA's Geo, making it necessary for us to make multiple trips and delay filming just a little bit more.

Once everything was assembled at the school location, the expert took Trent aside for a crash course in handling a gun.* Even after a Snickers energy boost, Trent could barely lift the thing, much less strut around confidently with it like it was an organic part of his body. Still, he soldiered on, no doubt out of concern that a lack of manliness on his part would result in his losing the coveted role of Tex Diaper.†

One shot required Trent to mow down an entire row of retarded . . . um . . . I mean differently-abled students. Nothing partic-ularly difficult about this, except that even when you're using blanks, a small hard wad of paper gets fired out of the barrel of the gun. If we were filming this outside with a good distance between gunner and

---

* Trent was not required to pack heat as part of his duties as AD. In addition to writing the script and assistant directing, Trent was cast as the leader of the Diaper Mafia in *Citizen Toxie*. A good way to make your AD really earn the respect of the crew is to dress him in a diaper, bib, bonnet, and pacifier for the first several days of production.

† TRENT HAAGA RESPONDS: This is partly true, but not because I really wanted the part. I just wanted to keep everything on schedule and I knew my credibility as an AD yelling at actors would be out the fucking window if I couldn't even do one scene.

gunnee, this wouldn't have been such a problem. But we were filming inside, in a small classroom, with just a few feet separating the gun and the victims. Our expert's solution to this was to instruct the actor-persons to keep their eyes on the gun and pretend to be hit and fall before the gun got to them. This looked pretty stupid but it was infinitely preferable to staging a mass reenactment of the death of Brandon Lee on the set of *The Crow*. One actor-person reported feeling one of these wads whiz past his ear and, sure enough, we saw them afterwards embedded into the wall. The guy was amazingly good-natured about it, not at all bitter about the fact that he came within a hair's breadth of being an unwilling method actor.*

The other problem with the gun in this scene was that it ejected scalding hot shell casings after they were fired. Michael Buddinger, who played Tito the Retarded Rebel, was crouched on the ground at Trent's feet while Trent was firing the gun. He ended up being showered by hot metal. Fortunately, he wasn't burned badly enough to require hospitalization, but he made it clear that it still hurt like a son of a bitch.

If the injuries and threats of injuries to our cast, who didn't know the first fucking thing about firearms, isn't enough to convince you of the danger of working with live weapons, take into consideration our so-called "expert." While he was demonstrating the gun to Trent, he sliced his hand wide open. After the gun was fired and we were handing it back to him, he burned his other hand. And while he was unloading the gun, he accidentally fired it. Rest assured that none of these mishaps inspired confidence in either our expert or our own physical safety.

Guns are relatively easy to work around and fake so you don't have to burden yourself with the real deal, but what about other stunts? As with everything else, safety should be your paramount concern (or maybe even your MGM concern), and if safety comes at a price then so be it. If you want to set somebody on fire in your movie, you simply

---

* Again, see the *Apocalypse Soon* documentary on the *Citizen Toxie* DVD for all the action.

have to hire a professional stuntperson and they ain't cheap. Both *Terror Firmer* and *Citizen Toxie* had a lot of stunts and every single one of them was a big disappointment. If a stunt turns out poorly, not only does it hurt your movie, it hurts the morale of the crew. The crew looks forward to days when big stunts or effects are scheduled. They're like little rewards for everybody on set. After all, these scenes are part of the reason why most people want to work in film in the first place. How many times do you get to see somebody completely immolated in the real world without going to jail?

We wanted to set people ablaze on both *Terror Firmer* and *Citizen Toxie*.* On *Terror Firmer*, the microscopic flames came about six inches off the guy's arms and back for about half a minute until he dropped and rolled and he was extinguished.† After this ridiculous spectacle, we improvised Plan B. Fortunately, we had a big blowtorch on set that we were using to create a lethal fart. We took the Fartmaker 2000 and created a wall of flame and positioned Will safely behind it where he was in no danger of catching fire or even breaking a sweat. Using a very long lens,‡ we filmed Will writhing in agony behind the wall of flame. We kept this going for awhile and as I was looking through the camera, I felt we had at least a few seconds of usable footage from that. Still, it wasn't enough to create a believable effect. So we pulled Plan C out of our asses and dressed a mannequin in the same costume and set it on fire. In the finished film, we used a few seconds of Will behind the fire, a few seconds of the stuntman and everything else was the other burning dummy. We could have had a better, cheaper effect if we'd just set a GI Joe on fire.

On the other hand, the full body burn on *Citizen Toxie* was irre-

---

* Of course I mean we wanted to show characters in the film on fire. It goes without saying that I've wanted to set certain crew members on fire on practically every movie I've made.

† The stuntman standing in for Will Keenan was the same afroed black guy who stood in for Joe Fleishaker elsewhere in the movie. See the *Terror Firmer* DVD documentary, *Farts of Darkness*.

‡ Long lenses like 75 mm or 120 mm compress fields giving the illusion that foreground (fire) and background (actor) are together.

deemably pathetic. It looked pretty damn underwhelming while we were shooting it, but we didn't realize how sad it really was until we watched the video playback. On film, you couldn't even see the flames at all. We had a very clear shot of a guy staggering around covered head to toe in protective gel, but that wasn't exactly the effect we were going for. Trent and Patrick Cassidy approached the stuntman (who was acting as if he'd just been racing back and forth into a burning old folks home, rescuing goldfish and parakeets) and said, "Jeez, y'know, that was pretty weak. I think we're going to have to do it again."

"Well, I dunno," he gasped between hits of oxygen and gulps of water. "I mean, you asked for a full body burn and that's what I did."

"Yeah, technically, I suppose so. But the flames don't even appear on film. You can't see anything. We'd have seen more flames if you'd just held a Zippo lighter in each hand."

"Hmmm. Well, all right. But I'm gonna have to get paid for another burn."

And right there is the inherent danger in working with professional stuntmen. They've got you over a barrel and they know it. You obviously want desperately to have this stunt in your movie or you wouldn't have bothered to hire the guy in the first place. So if you want to get it done, you've only got one option. In this instance, since we didn't have the Fartmaker 2000 at our disposal, we did the only thing we could do. We cut the stunt out of the movie. That showed the greedy stuntman who's boss.

Invariably, the best special effects are the simplest. *Terror Firmer*, for instance, features a head being crushed under a stampede of people fleeing a talk show. This may well be the shittiest effect of all time but it works. It gets the reaction we want from the audience, just by putting a wig on a melon filled with blood and hamburger. We've been crushing heads for almost twenty years now, using basically the exact same technique. A lot of people don't believe that's really how we achieve that effect, dismissing it as being so hokey and cheap that it couldn't possibly work. Believe me, it always does. As long as you shoot and edit the effect with a reasonable amount of creativity, you can create amazing illusions. In *Terror Firmer*, we were trying intentionally to call attention to some of the Troma trademarks like melonhead crushings and the familiar car flip footage we've used on virtually every movie since *Sgt. Kabukiman NYPD*, so we liked the fact that the wig fell off and it was damn obvious that we were seeing a melon being trampled. But when we've used the effect on other movies, like *The Toxic Avenger* and *Citizen Toxie*, we took a little more care setting up the effect and it works great. The idea behind any visual effect, or indeed behind filming any scene, is to create an emotional response in the audience. We get a bigger response by using a 99¢ melon than if we crushed an expensive, lifelike fake head cast from the actor's own melon.

You can also pull off more elaborate effects very cheaply with camera trickery. On *Citizen Toxie*, we blew up the Tromaville School for the Very Special. Even if we had the cooperation of the school we were using to actually destroy their building, we would never have been able to afford that much explosive. So Brendan Flynt, the DP, took a still photograph of the building, trimmed it so that all we had was the building without any background and pasted it onto a piece of wood. This was mounted several hundred feet in the foreground of the shot, so when you looked through the camera the photograph lined up perfectly with the building itself. In other words, Brendan created something like a very cheap matte.* We rigged the photo with a bunch of firecrackers and doused the whole thing in gasoline, then stood back and watched the sparks fly. While the photo was going up in smoke, we also had people running around in the foreground as if they were fleeing the conflagration. The whole effect cost about $10. Then,

---

* Strictly speaking, a matte is a painting or photograph used in the background of live action footage. On major studio productions, mattes are often used to create imaginary landscapes like fairy kingdoms, cities of the future, unspoiled Amazon rain forests, and safe, clean New York City streets.

along with the footage of the exploding picture, we blew smoke, flame, and debris out the door of the building itself. This is where we ended up having to spend some money, because the pyrotechnics crew got a little carried away with the smoke and stained the roof just inside the door completely black. There was no way we were going to be able to clean it properly, so we had to pay for smoke damage to the school. Even with this minor error, the effect still cost a fraction of what a major studio would have paid. A major studio would have blown the building up for real or built a miniature version of the school and blown it up, all for something that lasts less than fifteen seconds on screen. Our way was just as effective, much safer, and infinitely less expensive. Also, audiences love this effect, often applauding the scene in screenings I've attended.

Without a doubt, the best effects on a low-budget set are achieved simply with a bunch of fake blood, some tubes, and a Hudson sprayer.* In *Citizen Toxie*'s hospital massacre, people are slaughtered left and right, mainly just by running a tube up the actor, having them hold it somewhere like against their neck with their hand and spraying blood all over creation while the actor screams and thrashes. This simple effect is just as effective in its way as Toxie's elaborate three-hour makeup job. And the reason is simply that the audience doesn't notice the effect. It's not one of those effects that throws the audience out of the picture and makes them wonder how we did that or how much it cost. It just does the job. So whenever you're in doubt about an effect, squirt blood like a motherfucker and make your actors flail around like they're having the worst epileptic fit of all time.

When you're setting up something like this, you'll discover that

---

* For those of you whose green thumbs are a result of something other than gardening, a Hudson sprayer is a portable, hand-pump device usually used for pesticides. Filling a fire extinguisher with fake blood is also great, though they might be a little more expensive than Hudson sprayers. We used a fire extinguisher in the opening scene of *Terror Firmer*, for the scene with the guy's leg getting pulled off.

Production of *Citizen Toxie* was so grueling the drug-addled
cast quickly ran out of inconspicuous veins.

special effects guys are almost as bad as DPs when it comes to setting up a shot. If the DP is only interested in making your film look
good and doesn't really care about the story, the effects guys would
just as soon forget about the rest of the movie entirely. Some effects
guys do not give shit one about your movie. All they're interested in
is the one thirty-second bit they're working on so they can put it on
their demo reel. So they'll want to have all the time in the world to
set up and make themselves look good. Don't let them trick you into
thinking things are more complicated than they really are. If they
tell you they need two hours to set something up, give them one. If

they ask for an exorbitant amount of money, give 'em half of whatever they ask for. Most makeup effects guys got obsessed with this crap when they were teenagers creating monsters and gore in their parents' garage, so they know how to pull this shit off for next to nothing. Remind them of the good ol' days when they did it out of some perverse love. Over the years, Troma has been incredibly lucky with makeup and effects people, from Jennifer Aspinall on the original *Toxic Avenger*, Tim Considine on *Terror Firmer* and *Citizen Toxie*, and Robert Hall on *Citizen Toxie* and *Troma's Edge TV*. We've been able to attract some of the best makeup effects artists in the business to work for a fraction of their usual cost simply because they're fans . . . genuine artists.

Sometimes somebody will think they're being clever and thrifty by going to the butcher shop and getting a bunch of pig intestines and guts to use in the effect. For fuck's sake, don't let that happen. I mean, Jesus Christ, you didn't hire a bunch of backwoods, inbred waterhead

A typical craft service meal on *Citizen Toxie*. (Doug Sakmann)

fucks to make your movie.* You're working professionally, so you should act like professionals. The intestines you get from the butcher shop are rotten and smelly and covered with bacteria. You've probably already got enough health hazards in your toilet area. You don't need to import new ones. It's just as good and just as cheap to make intestines out of liquid latex. Any moron can do it. They're just intestines . . . big long tubes. Roll 'em out, slather 'em with fake blood and you're good to go. This is exactly what we used on *The Toxic Avenger Part III* when Toxie skipped rope with a bad guy's intestines. On the other hand, real animal parts were used on *Terror Firmer* for the scene where my character is blown up. Needless to say, everyone connected with the movie gleefully anticipated the day when I would be killed as messily as possible. It may well have been the most cathartic moment I've ever witnessed on a film set. In retrospect, however, it was probably a huge mistake to explode actual animal guts and have them come raining down on cast and crew. The set stank for the rest of the day and I understand we had the largest outbreak of foot-and-mouth disease amongst a film crew since Oliver Stone made *JFK*.†

When you're shooting a blood effect, the best thing to keep in mind is just keep rolling the camera. If it seems over the top to the naked eye, then keep going. Scale the plateau and jump off the other side. It always looks different on film than it does in real life, so the more blood you can pump, the better. We always run into actors who are worried about getting blood on their clothes, even in the rare instances when we've provided a costume and they're not even wearing their own clothes. It's just a force of habit for people to try to keep shit off their clothes. Break them of that habit right away. People who are

---

* If you live in the Appalachian Mountains, perhaps you did and if so, I'm sure they're fine, hard-working individuals. Please do not take offense at that remark and bring your brood to the Troma Building with pitchforks and scatterguns.

EDITOR'S NOTE: Mr. Kaufman's opinions on the mountain folk of Appalachia are entirely his own and in no way reflect the opinions of St. Martin's Press. St. Martin's loves and admires all rustics and their kin.

† My mistake. *JFK* had the largest outbreak of foot-*in*-mouth disease. Sorry about that.

really getting their arm ripped off do not aim the stump away from their flannel shirt so they can look neat and clean for the coroner.* By the same token, your PA might be reticent to spray as much blood as you want because he doesn't want to have to clean it up. Well, you know what? It's already a mess. You fucked it up the second you started spraying blood around, so you'd might just as well go whole hog and really hose down the place.

Furthermore, don't let anybody talk you into showing blood drip or ooze out of a wound. Sure in some cases it might be slightly more realistic but you ain't exactly making *Shoah* here. Cinematically, a spray is always preferable to a drip. And this is true whether you're shooting a western or a horror flick or a porno movie. Of course, when you're spraying fluids everywhere, you should be very careful to protect your equipment. If you've got blood and shit flying all over the place, it would be very, very bad for any to get into your camera. Cover everything expensive and irreplaceable with sheets of plastic.†

You should also make sure to sit down with the actors involved in these effects and let them know just how unpleasant it's going to be. Even the most gung-ho actor will lose his enthusiasm for being killed after spending forty-five minutes sitting in a puddle of congealed fake blood, particularly if you're shooting outdoors in the middle of summer and you've unwittingly turned your actor into bee and ant bait. Keep in mind that the basis of all Troma fake blood is Karo syrup and when you hose somebody down with syrup it's like opening the world's biggest picnic basket for every insect within five square miles. Makeup effects really fucking suck for the actor who's stuck in the middle of them. I had

---

* Of course, if you can turn it into a character thing and make it funny that this asshole stockbroker just had a limb torn off and is more worried about keeping his Armani suit clean, go for it.

† Garbage bags will also work if your equipment doesn't necessarily have to be able to see what's going on. For instance, your sound equipment probably doesn't have to be exposed. Your camera lens probably should.

to have my head cast* for *Terror Firmer* and even though I knew in advance that it was going to be god-fucking-awful, it was infinitely more claustrophobic and disturbing than I'd assumed it would be.† Unfortunately, there really isn't dick you can do about this except keep things moving on set and warn your actors over and over and over that they are about to be more uncomfortable than they've ever been in their lives.

While shooting effects sequences are relatively simple (just position the camera, or if you're lucky enough to have more than one, cameras where they're going to see as much blood as possible and let 'er rip), shooting fight scenes are more complex. These involve choreography, timing, and safety. It's really easy for actors to get carried away in fight scenes; during one on *Tromeo & Juliet*, Valentine Miele hauled off and clocked Sean Gunn.‡ Of course we left it in and the deafening "crack" sound Val's fist made as it struck Sean's schozzle! This genuine punch is quite compelling, but I'd have preferred if it hadn't happened at all.

Fight scenes are another area where if you have the ability to shoot with multiple cameras, you should. Keep one camera wide and use another to pick out individual pieces of the fight. It's quick and effective to use handheld cameras during fight scenes to lend the action a nervous energy and intensity. You should also try to break the scene down into individual punches. Get plenty of close-ups of punches being thrown toward the camera and whenever someone's supposed to be hit in the

---

* A head cast is the process of creating a fake head from a plaster impression of the actor's real head. To do this, you have to completely encase the poor bastard in plaster, depriving him or her of sight and hearing, and forcing them to breathe through a straw stuck up the nose.

† In fact, having my head cast was the inspiration for Yaniv Sharon's naked run through New York in *Terror Firmer*. I was wearing a suit and tie that they made me take off, allegedly so the plaster wouldn't ruin my clothes. So I was sitting there in my underwear with my head completely encased in this horrible, incapacitating gunk. As always when I'm left alone with my own thoughts, my mind turned to the worst possible scenarios. What if a fire broke out? I realized that anybody could come along and do anything and I would be totally helpless. At the time, I thought a gorgeous gyno-American might actually have come up and given me a blow job but later I realized that it was just a stray cat that fell asleep in my lap.

‡ Whether this was due to the fact that the actors were tired and getting sloppy, or because there was already bad blood between them and Val had a convenient excuse to deck Sean, is open to debate.

head, have water or fake blood spray out of their mouth. Not only does this look good on film, you can torture crew members you dislike by instructing your actor to aim their spit in a certain direction.

Every filmmaker has a different attitude toward production and you won't really discover yours until you get in there and do it. Hitchcock thought production was a chore, a necessary but annoying step between the planning of the film and putting it all together in post. Other directors see it as one of the most rewarding and creative aspects of filmmaking. The only thing you can say with any degree of certainty about production is that it will be unpredictable. You can learn from (or at least be amused by) our mistakes but the problems we faced aren't going to be the same as the problems you face. You can make it easier on yourself by spending plenty of time in pre-production and by being a creative thinker. Adapt, adopt, and improve as they said at the Round Table.* Stay alert and your production should go as smoothly as possible.

Can you spot the "real" dummy in this photo from *Terror Firmer*?

* Of course, this motto was usually invoked when they were making their own mead and drunkenly gang-raping the serving wenches, but it's still a damn good motto.

TROMA'S E-Z BAKE SPECIAL EFFECTS RECIPES
FOR BOYS AND GIRLS

In my first book, *All I Need To Know About Filmmaking I Learned From the Toxic Avenger*, I filled a lot of space . . . I mean, discoursed with keen insight and perception on the topic of how to create your own special effects. We didn't really want to cover a lot of the same ground as the first book, but we do still have a minimum word count to live up to, so to save you some time on set, here are a few common, easy to create special effects that you can cook up in your spare time.

Now, we realize that there's every possibility in the world that your brilliant movie won't have a single special effect in it. That's okay. You can still learn a thing or two from this. In the words of Louis Pasteur, "There is an easy solution to every problem." When we do special effects in our films, we don't spend hundreds of thousands of dollars doing digital effects that dazzle the audience with bullshit. We spend (at most) dozens of dollars creating actual, tangible, on-set effects. Think about it. When you go see *The Lord of the Rings*, are you honestly so taken in by the computer work that you actually think what you're looking at is real? Of course not. If you're absorbed by the story, the direction, and the characters, you allow yourself to forget that you're basically just looking at a big cartoon. All you're interested in is getting the audience to react. Sometimes they will react more if you allow them a glimpse behind the façade. The melon-head crushing in *Terror Firmer* gets a huge reaction, though it couldn't be more obvious if we'd painted the word MELON on the front of the head in big block letters.

And the easiest solution doesn't just apply to blood 'n' guts effects. On another episode of *Project Greenlight*, Porky decided he couldn't shoot a particular scene unless it was in a traveling car. So the crew wasted hours and hours and god knows how much money assembling a rig to mount the camera on and pull the car along. The easy solution, and the one we use, is to shoot the scene in a stationary car. Shoot the scene with the camera low and pointed up toward a blank patch of sky. Put production assistants around the car to jiggle it to make it look like it's in motion. Have additional PAs running past the windows in reverse with small trees to make it look like the car is passing by them and pull other cars up alongside to make it look like there's more traffic. Put some lights on a rig that you can move up and down and wave them past the windshield to complete the illusion. Voila: a traveling car that you can actually control and record the dialogue in. On our next movie, I'm planning on doing a whole car chase using this method, with the added joke of having joggers and little old ladies creep past the car once in a while.

If you do follow these recipes, remember to get all the food stuffs you need to create these recipes secretly. You don't want your crew to find out that you're using all the good food on fake heads and guts instead of in craft services.

1. **Fake Blood**—Not so much a special effect, really, as a staple of any good Tromatic kitchen. The key ingredients to any fake blood recipe are Karo syrup and red food coloring.* From there, you can add any number of ingredients depending on what you need to use the blood for. For

---

* For added realism, add a couple drops of blue food coloring for every mega-squeeze of red.

instance, if you're going to be spraying the blood through a tube or a fire extinguisher, Karo syrup will gum up the works pretty quickly. You'll need to thin the blood out with water so it's not too goopy and sprays well. If nobody's going to put the shit in his mouth, a finishing agent used in photo processing called Photoflow is also a good thinning agent. You can also put a few drops of soap in there to make the crap wash out of clothes and walls a little easier.

2. **Fake Vomit**—I consider myself something of an expert on vomit, seeing as how I often wake up in the gutter with a mouth full of the stuff around four o'clock in the morning. But recently I received this letter from Troma fan Andrew Mackay that made me rethink my position.

Dear Mr. Kaufman,

Greetings from London, U.K. I have been reading the past few pages of this book.* It's great, I can't put it down. However, I thought I should write to you and speak my mind. Having seen *Terror Firmer* many times, I have come to the conclusion that, although the excess gore in general is very good, the vomiting scene is not. Now, some have commented on this being down to certain actors not "bringing up the right consistency in their bile." But making your actors throw up and filming it is starting to look fake. The reason I am writing to you is to share with you a

---

* I was trapped in London during the September 11 attacks in New York and Andrew and his family saved my ass from sleeping on a bench in Piccadilly Circus by offering to put me up in their home until air travel resumed. Apparently the little bastard went through my briefcase when I was asleep.

secret recipe that I have invented. I refer to it as "Cell-u-Lloyd Vomit." Don't print this letter please, this is my own personal recipe and I intend to make millions from it.

Ingredients for "Cell-u-Lloyd Vomit":

10 × tins of Economy Value Carrot & Coriander soup
1 × Black currant jam flavouring.*

You simply open all the tins of the soup and pour it into a big bowl. The great thing about economy soup is that it actually tastes like vomit. So the expression on your "artistes" faces will be natural. The black currant jam is to darken the texture on screen—just use a smattering of it. Once everything's finished you'll find it's edible, reasonably low fat, very, very harmless, and looks great onscreen. Actually, you'll have noticed this for yourself when I invited to you to watch my short film *Poisoned*: that film about three blokes being sick everywhere.

I hope you find the contents of this letter of use. I also realise that a lot of readers are dying to read the rest of the book. Sorry for stealing the manuscript and delaying its publication.

Yours Tromatically,
Andrew Mackay
Founder and Editor of the U.K.'s Official Troma Fan
Web site: www.toxie.com

* For those of you who don't speak Limey, currants are berries. Good luck finding a jar of black currant jam in this country. Try asking for blackberry jam or something.

3. **Fake Excretory Fluids and Solids**—I think we all know what piss looks like and fortunately for cinema, there's a remarkable number of sodas and juices on the market that look just like it. If you can't afford soda or juice, there was probably a little bottle of yellow food coloring in the box when you got stuff to make blood. Add some to water and you're good to go. Shit is a little trickier to get the right consistency. For good solid turds, you can't do much better than a Baby Ruth candy bar. For more ambitious crap, mix chocolate pudding, corn, and brown gravy together. Because all these ingredients are edible, the shit is edible. But as Yaniv Sharon discovered while we were making *Terror Firmer*, edible does not mean the same as tasty.*

4. **Fake Semen**—You might think you can save money and have a little fun besides by simply using your own semen but that's extremely unsafe. Besides, if you've been jerking off while reading this book as much as I have while writing it, you're probably just shooting air out of your dick by this point. A white hand lotion is usually an adequate semen substitute. You can add water to it until you achieve the appropriate cum consistency for the character.

5. **The Meltdown**—Discussed in great detail in my last book but it is such an important effect, we'll recap the basics here. Mix one Dixie cup full of water with ½ tablespoon of green food coloring to achieve a dark green hue. Do not use red food coloring because you will never get an

---

* See the *Terror Firmer* DVD documentary for the explosive aftermath of Yaniv's shit-feast.

R rating with people exploding foaming blood out of their mouths. Place 1–3 tablespoons of Bromo Seltzer in your mouth without swallowing it. Place the green water mixture in your mouth, again without swallowing. Let it foam up inside your mouth. Wait until it's a huge, erupting volcano in your mouth and let the fun begin.

6. **Crushed Head**—Again, discussed in the last book but worth repeating. Hollow out a cantaloupe. Fill with hamburger, cranberry sauce, and fake blood. Top with a wig and crush till you can't crush no more. For fuck's sake, don't use watermelons. Watermelons are much too thick to crush properly, while cantaloupes will fall apart nicely and ooze gore in every direction. We recently shot some additional scenes for a project (tentatively) titled *Tales From the Crapper* and a production assistant mistakenly picked up watermelons instead of cantaloupes. The effect was more than disappointing.

7. **Torn Limb**—No doubt your project will call for several arms and legs to be ripped from bodies. This is easy enough. Just cut the sleeve off a long-sleeved shirt and attach the sleeve to a fake arm. You can make the fake arm for about $4.95 by using foam and a rubber hand or you can go down to the VA Hospital and steal a prosthetic limb from some senile old war hero. Have your actor tuck his real arm behind his back, then put on the sleeveless garment. Run tubes from a garden sprayer or fire extinguisher full of blood up under the garment to the stump on his shoulder. Attach the fake arm to the actor's shoulder, slopping on a bunch of

Ultraslime (a gooey mass easily available through any special effects supply house) and fake blood. If Ultraslime is not around, use string or spaghetti and chunks of toilet paper to achieve that realistic viscera that makes the effect so powerful. When the arm is ripped off, pump blood through the tubes like a motherfucker and have your actor scream until his voice breaks. It's exactly the same process if you want to rip off a leg. If you're really lazy, you can even use the fake arm for a leg and cover the hand up with a shoe.

8. **Severed Penis**—Once employed exclusively by gay snuff porn films, the severed penis effect has grown in popularity in recent years. All you need to do is paint a banana flesh colored, run a tube of blood through one end, and you've got yourself an instant dick to hack off. You just need to show a few seconds of the close-up of the banana. For the rest of the gag, just have your actor scream like a banshee while you pump gallons of blood out of his fly. Cinema magic.

9. **Chicken In the Ass**—Naturally, your movie will have at least one scene where someone is killed by being stabbed up the ass by a chicken. Most films do these days. To achieve the effect, simply cut a rubber chicken in half. Attach the rear to the actor's ass and stick the head out the actor's fly. Run tubes through both ends so that blood comes squirting out of the chicken's mouth and anus. Ted Raimi was killed in this manner in *Tales From the Crapper*, spawning legions of copycat effects. Accept no substitutes, however. Only Troma's Chicken-In-the-Ass is approved by both the ASPCA and the ACLU.

CHAPTER 10

Fix It in Post!

Wherein Once-Solid Relationships of Trust, Respect, and Mutual Admiration
Degenerate into Bickering and Pointless Name-Calling

I know what you're thinking. You're thinking, "Lloyd, all of this information has been invaluable and I will never, ever be able to begin to repay you for your wisdom. But dammit, when I plunk down hard-earned cash for a nonfiction book about filmmaking, I expect some obscure Russian film theory! This is the same goddamn problem I had with your first book, you fucking loser! Make with the Marxism or I'm putting this book down right now and walking out of this store I've been loitering in and reading the book without paying for it!"

Well, all right then.

Lev Kuleshov was a director, theorist, and mentor to better-known Russian filmmakers like Eisenstein and Pudovkin.* Today, he is best known for the Kuleshov Experiment, a study that proved once and for all the importance of film editing. Kuleshov's theory was that the same image conveyed different meanings to an audience depending on what

---

* Sergei Eisenstein is the film master you've seen ripped off in Brian De Palma's *The Untouchables* and satirized in Charles Kaufman's *When Nature Calls*. He (Eisenstein, that is, not my brother Charles) made such classics as *The Battleship Potemkin* and *Alexander Nevsky*. V. I. Pudovkin directed the dull *Mother* and the boring *The End of St. Petersburg*. Odds are you've probably never actually sat down to watch a movie made by either of these guys just for shits and giggles, but you can learn a lot about filmmaking if you do. This is why so many film professors show their movies to their classes instead of bothering to try to teach anything.

that image was juxtaposed against. He took a neutral shot of a Russian actress and cut that shot against a wide variety of different images: a bowl of soup, a crying baby, a coffin, etc. Viewers felt that the actress was conveying different emotions with each new juxtaposition, even though the shot of the actress remained the same. When it cut to the soup, viewers said she was hungry. When it cut to the baby, viewers said she was concerned. When it cut to the coffin, viewers said she was horny. The Kuleshov Experiment demonstrated to filmmakers everywhere that film editing was as important (if not more important) to the filmmaking process as cinematography, music, or craft services.

Basically, all this is a snooty way of saying that editing can either turn your film into a masterpiece or fuck it up so badly that it bears absolutely no resemblance to what you were trying to achieve in the first place. It can be the most creatively fulfilling part of the entire process . . . but it can also turn you into a light-fearing hermit locked away from society, forever tinkering with a project that really isn't going to get any better.

Because editing is so vital to the creative process, you simply must remain in control of the entire post-production process. The only excuse for losing control of the editing of a low-budget, independent film is your own laziness. On a studio film, though, the director can find control wrested from his hands at any time. In 1970, John Avildsen was removed from editing the movie *Joe*. Of course, this was one of his first movies and Hollywood is littered with tales of first-time directors finding themselves removed from the editing rooms of their pictures. But thirty years later, John, now an Academy Award–winning director whose films had grossed hundreds of millions of dollars worldwide, was directing a Jean-Claude Van Damme movie and the exact same thing happened. I saw John's rough cut of this movie and it was a very good John Avildsen film, containing all the Capravildsen* elements that marked his best movies like *Rocky* and *Cry Uncle*. But Van

---

* Frank Capra is the director of such films as *It's A Wonderful Life*. Both Capra and Avildsen's work is noted for its optimistic view of human nature and underdog heroes. Capra's terrific

Damme had Avildsen removed from the editing room so that Jean-Claude could recut the movie to his own specifications. What had been a good John Avildsen film became a very bad Jean-Claude Van Damme film.* So in the studio system, there are dozens of people looking for any excuse to kick the director out of the editing room and take control of the project. As an independent, you don't need to worry so much about people stealing control. What you should worry about is growing lazy and complacent and losing control through your own mishandling.

As worthy an experiment as it was, the Kuleshov Experiment was probably responsible for the common editing misconception of thinking of movies in terms of still pictures. Motion picture editing actually has very little to do with still photography. Rather, you should think of your movie more in terms of music. Imagine your movie as a piece of music and put it together with that in mind. A good movie should have the same elements as a good piece of music: rhythms, themes, crescendoes, decrescendoes, and a seventeen-minute-long drum solo.

Despite this, Kuleshov's theory still holds water today. However, Kuleshov himself was working with pointed sticks and stolen fire compared to the complex tools filmmakers now have at their disposal. Post-production nowadays involves a lot more than mere editing. To

---

autobiography, *The Name Above the Title*, is a great portrait of the filmmaker in despair, eventually becoming an extremely embittered soul who basically despises the industry he helped create. Of course, there is no way this could ever happen to the happy people at Troma.

* Troma got back at Van Damme on Avildsen's behalf at the Cannes Film Festival. Van Damme was scheduled to hold a dock-side press conference one afternoon and the Troma Team just happened to be in the vicinity at the same time. The Belgian Lunkhead cruised up in his boat, waved once at the collected media, and sped off without even touching land.† You can actually see this on the Troma DVD *All the Love You Cannes*. The press was so pissed off that they'd wasted their day that they turned their cameras on the Troma characters and the Tromettes, so at least they could get some useful footage out of the excursion. By day's end, the media at Cannes held the Troma Team in high regard as friendly, photogenic, and outgoing individuals, while Van Damme was cursed as an egocentric bastard who'd wasted everyone's time for no reason.

† We can neither confirm nor deny the rumor that Van Damme spied the Troma Team on shore and was frightened off like a wee little schoolgirl.

keep it simple for you,* we'll break post-production down into four general areas: editing, sound design, dialogue re-recording, and duplication.

EDITING

Once upon a time, editing was a horrible job that only miserable fat guys (and the occasional Dede Allen†) would be willing to do. Back then, you would develop your film negative and make a low-quality print called a workprint. Next, you would physically cut, mutilate, and re-arrange the workprint any way your twisted little heart desired—in other words, you would edit the movie. This system required a large number of fat assistants to keep track of all the trimmed shots and all the rolls of film.

Then came the digital nonlinear editing system, such as AVID‡ and various other systems. This reduced the number of miserable fat fucks in the editing room to one or maybe two. When you edit digitally, a computer organizes and keeps all of your footage on hard drives— readily accessible with just the click of a mouse. You don't physically cut any actual film until you've got the movie just the way you want it. This allows you the freedom to experiment with your movie and work much faster without fucking up the film any more than you did when you shot it in the first place. *Terror Firmer* was the first Troma movie to be cut on a nonlinear editing system. However, every Troma movie

---

* All right, to keep it simple for me. You're a young genius and can handle a lot more information than my acid-saturated, verging-on-senile brain.

†Dede Allen was Arthur Penn's favorite editor, working on such films as *Bonnie & Clyde*. She entered post-production at a time when gyno-Americans were rarely employed in such capacities, making her a real trailblazer for introducing women into another shitty workplace where they can become as stressed out and suicidally depressed as men.

‡The AVID is a high-end digital editing system currently used by just about every single movie and TV production, including Troma. Now that AVID has engulfed virtually every other editing system and become the standard, I suppose it would be too obvious to point out that the definition of "avid" is "eager" or "greedy." It's kind of like if Microsoft had named its operating system "Omnivore" instead of "Windows." But since it is so obvious, I won't even mention it.

made to date has been made with nonlinear writing, directing, acting, and distribution systems.

RAZOR BLADES, TAPE, AND SUICIDE ATTEMPTS: EDITING THE OLD-FASHIONED WAY
Frank Reynolds

Frank Reynolds came to Troma in 1995 and served as film editor on Tromeo & Juliet. *Despite this, Frank has gone on to great success as an editor, including the recent award-winning film* In the Bedroom *starring Sissy Spacek (star of Troma's non–award-winning film* Ginger In the Morning). *Here, Frank shares his experiences on editing in the days before we all had barcodes tattooed on our necks and computers took over the world.*

When I was a junior at NYU film school, I called Troma looking for a summer job.

"Do you have any openings in editing, maybe?" I asked. "Like for an apprentice or an intern?"

"No!" the girl on the other end of the phone said, and hung up on me.

Five years later, at 11:00 P.M. on a weeknight, I got a call from another girl at Troma. She was much more polite. They were looking for an editor for their new film, *Tromeo & Juliet*. Since they were calling so late, I assumed they were desperate.

I decided not to hold a grudge, and told them, yes.

I started editing *Tromeo* in June 1995. Digital editing systems were around by then, and I knew how to use them, but hey, this was Troma. Why were they going to rent me a hundred-thousand-dollar computer system when they already owned not one, but *three* film editing flatbeds? And did it really matter that none of the flatbeds had been properly serviced since the Reagan administration?

Actually, I didn't really care all that much. I was young (26) and hungry and I wanted to cut another feature. (The only other feature I had cut played for one week at a theater on Twelfth Street and never made it to video.) And I also knew how to edit on film really well. When I learned how to edit at NYU, just four or five years earlier, digital editing didn't exist yet. If you wanted to be an editor, you had to learn how to cut up your film with a razor blade and tape it back together. This might seem primitive and inefficient to those who are now used to editing on a computer, but back then there was no other way to do it. Did you complain about using a pay phone before cell phones came out? Exactly. Besides, if you want to be an editor, you'll quickly discover those razor blades come in very handy for other things, too.

A big difference between editing film and editing digitally is that when you edit film, you have to keep track of *all* the pieces of film that are not in your cut at that moment. When you cut digitally and shorten a shot, you can let those extra frames just disappear into cyberspace, but on film you have to take those extra film frames and file them away somewhere because you might need them later. Also, if you want to use a different shot or take in your movie, you have to know where to find it in all the rolls of film. So you need to be very well organized. Because if you can't find the shot you need, you either have to have the lab reprint the shot, which is expensive, or live without it. This has only happened to me once the entire time I edited on film, and it was while I was editing *Tromeo*. I was working on the scene where Murray and Benny were taunting the Capulet parents up on the balcony, and I wanted to change one of the cuts. But to do that I needed to get a certain two seconds of a shot of the Capulets. (Two seconds of film is about as long as your arm.) And we couldn't find it. I drove my poor assistant crazy for days, making her look in boxes and trim bins, even through the garbage, for that shot but no luck. I knew Troma wouldn't pay to reprint the shot, so I just gave up and left the cut alone. For the next two weeks or so though, it always bothered me that I couldn't cut the scene exactly as I wanted. (But, as I look at the scene now, over six years later, I completely forgot which cut I wanted to change.)

One of the things I love about digital editing is being able to save multiple versions of a scene. Whenever I edit digitally I always save all my old cuts in case I have to go back to them; and if I want to try something new, I save the movie the way it was so I don't have to worry about putting it back again if what I'm trying doesn't work. On film, you only have one copy of all the footage, so to try something new you have to rip apart your old cut to try it the new way; and if you don't like it, you have to remember exactly how you had it and take the time to put it back together that way. On *Tromeo*, when I made the first cut of the tattoo parlor scene, where Murray gets hit with the ax, Lloyd was very unhappy with it and we spent an entire afternoon ripping apart the scene and trying a whole mess of things, just trying to make the scene work. At the end of the day, though, Lloyd decided that he needed to shoot more footage of the scene to make it work, because none of what we tried was any good. So I had to take all the bits and pieces of film we had chopped up that day and put it back the way I had it originally, and just wait for the new shots. (We couldn't get the tattoo parlor back, so we dressed up the editing room to look like the tattoo parlor and shot there. When you see all those quick edits when Murray gets hit with the ax, half of those were shot in our editing room.)

There are a lot of other things I love about editing digitally. I love being able to play with titles and dissolves, and put in a lot of sound effects and music while I'm cutting, all of which are very tough to do on film. I love the fact that no matter how much I run the picture on a digital system, it doesn't get scratched or dirty. But there are a few things that are cool about editing on film. For instance, when you edit digitally, you have to make sure your system's hard drive is big enough to hold all your footage. Not a problem on film. If you have enough boxes and shelves to store all your film, you're fine. Gabe Friedman, the editor of *Terror Firmer*, which was the first Troma film edited digitally, told me that when Troma bought their first AVID digital editing system, they only got a hard drive big enough to hold half the footage. So he had to edit the first half of the movie, erase the drives, edit the second half of the movie, etc. That would have driven me crazy. I want to be able to look at the whole movie, beginning to end, any time I want. I'd rather cut on film than not have enough drive space. Also with digital systems, there's a question of resolution, which is how good the picture looks. If you want to use less drive space, you input your footage into the system at a lesser resolution, which usually means that your picture looks kinda fuzzy, and you have to look at that fuzzy picture the whole time you're editing. Again, not a problem on film. The film you're looking at while you're editing will be exactly what it will look like when it's finished. And any time you're editing, you can take the film, go to a theater, and project it on a big screen, so you can see all those little flaws that you couldn't see on the little screen. Like that boom mike that creeps into the frame, which you never would have noticed if you edited with a fuzzy digital picture on a seventeen-inch screen.

It's been almost four years now since I touched film, and I don't expect to do it anytime soon. Almost no one edits on film anymore, especially not independent films. I'm not really complaining, though every once in a while I miss the feeling of running the film through my fingers and seeing the multiple images go through the light and thinking that that's the stuff that movies are really made of . . . then I remember that afternoon with Lloyd, chopping apart that tattoo parlor scene; and I get down on my knees and thank all the gods above and below for digital.

Earlier in this book, Trent Haaga urged all of you to shoot your film on digital video. While this is certainly an option, I would strongly urge you to shoot on celluloid. Digital video is a young technology that, quite frankly, isn't at the point that allows you to make a professional-quality feature film (unless, of course, your name is Mike Figgis or Lars von Trier, in which case you can do pretty much whatever the fuck you want and it'll turn out great).

Now if you're making a documentary, then without a doubt you should use DV. If the Maysles brothers were making *Salesman* today, I'm quite sure they would use video. We've shot several documentaries (on Cannes, TromaDance, and behind the scenes on *Terror Firmer* and *Citizen Toxie*) and we would not have considered shooting them on film. Likewise, on *Citizen Toxie* we shot the newscaster segments and the final fantasy sequence with me on DV because the format gave us the look we wanted to achieve. But I simply cannot think of a single feature shot entirely on DV that's any good. They all look shitty, amateurish, and slapdash. So if you want to make a good-looking, professional-quality feature film, do yourself a favor and invest the extra time, money, and work in celluloid.

TRENT HAAGA REPLIES: Okay, Lloyd, I went to film school and understand that the latitudes of film are greater than video today, *but the technology is developing so quickly that DV (particularly the 24P DV* that's being used right now) will some day become the standard. Regardless of its story quality,* Star Wars II *film was shot on digital video[†] and I suspect that people will line up to see it despite the fact that it wasn't shot on film. We're trying to inspire people to go out and make their own damn movie no matter what and, let's face it, the best way to get that done is to use what you have access to. DV cameras are affordable and are more widely available to most people out there.*

As I said before, I shot a movie less than a year ago on digital video for about \$35,000. It's already made \$750,000 in domestic *sales alone. With that \$750,000, the company (I won't mention their names because they're considered to be direct competitors of Troma and manage to sell their \$35,000 DV films to Blockbuster whereas Troma can't sell a single copy of their \$450,000 35mm films there)[‡] can now go out and make two or three 35mm films. It's a matter of pure math that DV will be preferable to the young filmmaker.*

Also, Lloyd, I don't think that telling the people reading this book that they aren't—and never will be—as talented as Mike Figgis or Lars von Trier is very inspiring.

LLOYD KAUFMAN RESPONDS: All right, skinny, I don't know what the fuck this so-called *Star Wars* thing is you're talking about but listen up. I know you think you know it all and that you're Mr. Wave of the

---

* EDITOR SEAN MCGRATH RESPONDS: 24P is *not* Digital Video. It's video capture. Sure, George Lucas can afford 24P but right now, it's way more expensive to shoot on 24P than it is to shoot on film, you fucking asshole. This sounds like advice given by somebody who just read a b.s. fluff piece about digital technology in *Entertainment Weekly.*

[†] SEAN MCGRATH RESPONDS: No, it was shot on \$35 million video capture.

[‡] Lloyd here. Why can't we mention the company? It's Full Moon and they've gone bankrupt any number of times since they started filling the world with their evil puppet flicks. And the movie you keep bragging about is *Killjoy 2.* Why don't you read the IMDB review of your DV *Killjoy 2* and then read the reviews of the shot-on-film *Terror Firmer.* Then come back and you tell me which is better.

Future, but video's been around for a long, long time and, quite frankly, it hasn't improved one iota. Hell, when I was a kid, everybody would gather round on a Saturday morning and eat a great big bowl of frosted videos (though I think back then, it was spelled Viddy-Os). So I think I know a little bit about what I'm talking about here.

As for these DV movies you produced, I believe that *you* believe they've made a huge profit and are in Blockbuster stores coast to coast. But I have yet to see a single copy in the stores, and I go to a lot of Blockbusters in order to have plenty of material to rant and complain about. The pure math you keep talking about seems to be *2 + 2 = Trent's an ass.*

But, of course, I didn't mean to imply that the readers of this book aren't as talented as Figgis and von Trier. No doubt they will all surpass them in every way. But even those guys didn't start out making digital video features. Their first films were shot on celluloid. You've gotta learn the rules before you can break 'em, son.

TRENT HAAGA RESPONDS: First off, I prefer to think of myself as svelte. Secondly, if you want to know all about this Star Wars *thing, tell your beloved editors to take off their Stormtrooper helmets and Greedo masks for a second and explain it to you. Thirdly, Lloyd, I thought you were supposed to be Mr. Wave of the Future . . . isn't "Movies of the Future" the Troma slogan?* Well, guess what you geriatric son of a bitch? Movies in the future will not be shot on celluloid. I don't know what Blockbusters you're going to, but there are more movies in Blockbuster with the name "Trent Haaga" on them than "Lloyd Kaufman" and I'm less than half your age. Maybe you should check the New Release section. If you're suggesting that people learn the rules, then what better way than a cheaper format?*

By the way, Lloyd, your pictures aren't known and loved for their stunning cinematography. If the kids want to make a "good-looking, professional-quality feature film," then I would suggest that they put this book down right now. Any of

---

* Editor's Note: Lloyd should reply that Troma's *Redneck Zombies*, directed by Perry Leunes, is probably the first movie shot on video to be widely distributed—but he probably forgot.

your films could've been made on digital video and done just as well—if you think that melons full of cranberry sauce look more like heads when you shoot them on 35mm, you're even more delusional than I thought.

LLOYD KAUFMAN RESPONDS: Listen, shit-wit, I have checked the New Release section and I don't see *Killjoy 2* anywhere. Don't think for one fucking second that you're impressing anybody with your Blockbuster bullshit. You'll find the name Penny Marshall all over the goddamn place in Blockbuster and her movies suck huge fucking donkey dicks, so you can shut your little piehole about the whole "my name's in the store more than your name" crap. And it seems like your math is getting fucked up again. If you were less than half my age, I'd be ninety-two. And who are you to say what format movies are gonna be shot on in the future? You think you're Kreskin or something? Don't forget, buddy-boy, my name's first on this goddamn book. You're only here 'cause I asked you!

ADAM JAHNKE RESPONDS: Guys . . . can we maybe just agree to disagree on this issue? After all, the chapter's supposed to be about editing and post-production. This should have been resolved months ago.

LLOYD KAUFMAN RESPONDS: Butt the fuck out, Jahnke, unless you want a piece of this, too!

TRENT HAAGA RESPONDS: Okay, Lloyd, why don't you and Penny Marshall continue to make your beautiful and professional 35mm films? Why don't we go ahead and tell the readers that if they want to make a "professional quality" film then they should hire Tom Hanks and Rosie O'Donnell and that it should cost several million dollars and be backed by the Weinstein fucks? Hell, if you're gonna tell em they'd be better off shooting film, then you might as well tell 'em to get on their knees and suck the corporate dick. I'm disappointed in you, Lloyd.

And Adam—I can fight my own fucking wars, thank you very much, you bookish freak.

LLOYD KAUFMAN RESPONDS: That's *not* what I was fucking saying and you goddamn know it, you word-twisting douchebag! I always knew you sucked ass but I didn't know just how hard until right now, you ungrateful dickweed.

ADAM JAHNKE RESPONDS: Fuck both you assholes. I'm getting the hell outta here. Let's see you two hyperactive dimwits try to finish this thing without me around to make it vaguely comprehensible.

TRENT HAAGA RESPONDS: Good, Adam, you do that. I don't know why you're even involved, anyway. Not like you've ever made a movie.

And as for you, Lloyd, you talk a pretty mean game but now I see the truth: You wish you were sitting next to Penny Marshall at some fancy bistro while polishing your Blockbuster Video Lifetime Achievement Award and since you aren't, you've decided to bankrupt every filmmaker who is reading this book by telling him/her/it that they've got to spend all of their hard-earned cash shooting a film on 35mm film when you know goddamn well it won't get theatrical release since every theater in the nation is owned by your Devil Worshipping Conglomerate buddies. Get out of film school, Lloyd, and quit listening to those NYU film school brainwashed ... er, educated ... editors of yours. Elitist scumbag.

LLOYD KAUFMAN RESPONDS: Elitist?!?!?! Hey, only one of the editors went to NYU and he's got a job, smart guy. Sean McGrath went to Jersey City State College. And Brian McNulty went to College of Staten Island, home of the largest fresh-kill garbage dump in the world, and he got in by drawing a turtle off a matchbook cover.

Y'know, maybe if you'd pull your head out of your sphincter, you'd get to see some truly independent art. Inexpensive movies by Warhol,

Cassavetes, and Robert Bresson . . . all of which are masterpieces and all of which were shot on *film*!

TRENT HAAGA RESPONDS: But would have been shot on digital video *if the fucking technology had existed at the time, you stale fart!*

LLOYD KAUFMAN RESPONDS: *They fucking would not have shot on video!*

TRENT HAAGA RESPONDS: Would so!

LLOYD KAUFMAN RESPONDS: Would not!

TRENT HAAGA RESPONDS: Would so!

LLOYD KAUFMAN RESPONDS: Would not!

TRENT HAAGA RESPONDS: Would so!

ADAM JAHNKE RESPONDS: This is exactly the kind of incomprehensible bullshit I was talking about. Good luck, dipshits.

EDITOR'S NOTE: *At this point, the collaboration between Kaufman, Haaga, and Jahnke broke down completely. When the manuscript for this book arrived at St. Martin's, the following fifty pages were nothing but Kaufman and Haaga continuing the "would not/would so" argument, with the only variation being the occasional addition of the word "asshole." We at St. Martin's felt the book was not publishable in this stage and our legal department swung into action, reminding the authors that they would not receive the rest of their advance until a publishable manuscript was delivered. Kaufman, Jahnke, and Haaga immediately put aside their differences and returned to work, eventually delivering the text that follows, which admittedly meets only the barest minimum definition of the term "publishable."*

According to Trent Haaga, whose opinion I respect and admire more than anyone's on this earth,* at no point in the filmmaking process will you be happier you shot on video than when you start editing. If you're working with video, you can watch your dailies[†] the same day you shoot the footage. Hell, you can even start editing while you're still in production if you really want.[‡] If you're shooting on celluloid, there are all these other expensive chemical processes that you have to go through before you can even see what you've done. You need to get the film processed. If you're editing on an AVID or any other computer-based editing system, you need to get the negatives transferred to Beta videotape.[§] You need to worry about syncing your sound up to the image. If you shot on DV, you just dump the tapes into your computer and you're ready to roll.

Probably the best thing to come out of the digital revolution, aside from free downloadable porn, is the ability to edit a feature film at home. While you can certainly go out and rent time on an AVID, this will cost an assload of cash and result in a film that's not discernibly better than a film that was edited on a home editing suite. If you've enjoyed the process so far and hope to go on to make other damn movies, investing in a high-quality editing program is a very good idea. In the long run, it will save you money and time. Since this isn't an issue of *Consumer Reports*, I won't go into the pros and cons of the various systems on the market. The information changes so quickly anyway that by the time this book sees print, you'll probably be able to edit a movie on your wristwatch.

---

* TRENT HAAGA RESPONDS: Thank you, Lloyd. The feeling is mutual, I assure you.

† Dailies are simply all the footage you shot on a production day. You should watch them every day and use them as a guide to fix what you fucked up. Do not let your actors watch dailies, because they will never be satisfied with their performances and will always want another chance to do the scene. You will always say fuck no and this will lead to bitter resentment between you.

‡ You'll probably drive yourself completely insane if you do, but it is possible.

§ This process is known as telecine.

TRENT HAAGA RESPONDS: It's also known as a complete fucking waste of time because if you'd known you were going to end up transferring your film stock to video eventually anyway, you wouldn't have bothered with it and would have shot on DV in the first place.

EDITOR'S NOTE: Don't start, Haaga.

TRENT HAAGA RESPONDS: Sorry, sir.

Before you start editing on any digital system, whether it's an AVID or a home editing system, it's very important to make sure that you have adequate hard drive space for all your footage. Otherwise, you'll have to work on the movie in pieces. We ran into this problem on *Terror Firmer*. We didn't have enough hard drive space to keep all the footage on at the same time, so we had to work on the movie in halves. The Troma editors and I never saw the movie as a whole piece until the first test screening, at which time we saw it as a whole piece of shit.*

One of the great advantages of editing digitally is the ability to preview and experiment with optical effects. Opticals are things like split-screens, dissolves, credits, and star wipes. The split-screen sequence at the end of *Terror Firmer* was designed and completed during the final week of editing.† In the old days, we would have had to plan that sequence methodically from day one and we wouldn't have known for sure what it was going to look like until it was too late to do anything about it.

When you're editing on an AVID (or any other digital nonlinear system), you're editing on video but theoretically you'd like for your finished product to be on film. For this to happen, you need to create a database. Every frame of film is identified by a number called a keycode. Every frame of video is identified by a number called a timecode. A database brings these numbers together and tells you which video frame's timecode corresponds to which film frame's keycode. The negative cutter needs this information to match everything back up to the

---

* Of course, this was the first rough cut of the movie with all the pointless garbage that I'd insisted stay in the movie left in, despite the fact that the editors were constantly telling me that we needed to eliminate the pointless garbage. Editors are excellent at disciplining the director. I find that in the rough cut, I don't want to lose anything because I think it's all great at that point. The editors can look at it and tell me I'm completely and utterly wrong, that the scene I love so much is really a poorly filmed, humorless diversion with no point that must go if we have any hope of saving the movie. On *Citizen Toxie*, we shot a scene with Warhol superstar Taylor Mead presenting the Oscars. I adored this scene but the editors convinced me that it had nothing to do with anything and we deleted it. The scene will be included on the DVD, so you can see for yourselves how right or wrong the editors were.

† I had rerun *Carrie* one night and, urged on by a pint of Popov, I thought it would be a stroke of genius to replace Sissy Spacek in the dominant spot of the *Carrie* split-screen with a large close-up of the dripping hermaphrodite genitalia attached to actor Will Keenan.

original camera negative. This database can either be created by the negative cutter or the lab that made your video dailies. It's extremely important that this be done correctly. Otherwise, your film will be chopped up into an unrecognizable mosaic. This very nearly happened on *Citizen Toxie*.

Our database for *Citizen Toxie* was being done by one of the most prestigious labs in the business. If that's the case, you might ask yourself, what the fuck was Troma doing there in the first place? Well, because your sound mix is so vitally important to the impact of your film, I try to use the very best labs and sound labs possible. But you can do this without spending a gazillion dollars. Oftentimes, major productions will book the best laboratories and you can piggyback on these guys. All you have to do is be willing to go in at odd times and get your shit out of the way whenever Martin Scorsese wants to come in and work on his movie. So if Scorsese's working during the day, Troma's probably using the same place at night.

On *Citizen Toxie* we were using one of the top-of-the-line sound houses but Sean McGrath, the movie's associate editor, noticed early on that there was a problem matching the codes in the database. We had a big meeting at the sound lab and were assured that this was just a minor glitch, there was no problem with the database and everything was going to be hunky-dory. Well, as it happened, there was a problem. A big one. As we started to wind up and do the optical effects, Sean realized that the database was totally fucked. We had to create a new database, at a cost of about $50,000. Still, this top-of-the-line lab insisted this was not their fault. It wasn't until we sued them that they graciously agreed to reimburse us the cost of the new database. So when you're dealing with major entities like those that deal with big Hollywood productions on a daily basis, be prepared to be treated like shit. And if you see Sean McGrath at a bar sometime, be nice to him. He'll be the one in the corner drinking bottle after bottle of milk, taking care of the bleeding ulcer he got as a souvenir of *Citizen Toxie*'s post-production (see Sean's vivid recollection of his medical problems in the sidebar).

THE DARK, MYSTERIOUS REALM OF THE ASSOCIATE EDITOR

Sean McGrath

Sean McGrath was associate editor on both Citizen Toxie *and* Terror Firmer. *Here, Sean explains that associate editing is a skill that requires patience, discipline, and good health insurance. Contrary to popular belief, the job extends far beyond simply being the editor's coffee bitch.*

A lot of people may wonder what an associate editor does exactly. I know I sure did before I became one. Well, once the editor has made all of the creative decisions, the associate editor has to make sure they are executed by the negative cutter, optical house, sound designer, and the lab and that they don't get fucked up. To put it another way, an associate editor worries a lot. I worried a lot on *Terror Firmer* mainly because we had a tight deadline for Cannes and because I had to learn how to do all this stuff while I was doing it. As stressful as *Terror Firmer* was, *Citizen Toxie* was worse.

The overwhelming fear that the negative might be chopped up into random pieces by our lab was enough to give me a duodenal ulcer. If that wasn't bad enough, the doctor told me I also had a colon polyp. Now I really had something to worry about. When they removed it, the laxative they gave me didn't start working until after the procedure. As I lay in my hospital bed filling bedpan after bedpan with explosive diarrhea, my IV decided to come out causing blood to shoot of my vein and all over me. As I lay wallowing in my own feces and blood I realized this was life imitating art since I was re-enacting both the scene in *Citizen Toxie* where a diaper mafia punk shits himself to death and the scene where Tito squirts blood out of veins. The bitter irony almost made it all worthwhile.

Apart from doctors and male nurses across the greater New York metropolitan area, nobody really knows who the associate editor of a film is. In fact, I would venture to say that most people who worked on *Citizen Toxie* didn't even realize there was such a position. While Gabe Friedman, the editor of *Terror Firmer* and *Citizen Toxie*, got to live it up on set and be treated with near rock star reverence, most people didn't know who I was and still don't (which sometimes is a good thing, especially at screenings where an irate actor wants to know why a fart noise was surreptitiously dubbed in during their stirring monologue. They'll usually walk right past me and start yelling at Gabe).

One person who did know who I was (unfortunately) was Patrick Cassidy, the associate producer of *Citizen Toxie*. He knew full well who I was and that my job required me to stay at the Troma Building in New York until the wee small hours. So it was on the Friday before Labor Day around 11:00 P.M. The phone rang and there on the other end was Patrick. Since I was pretty sure this wasn't a booty call, I was dreading what he was going to ask me to do. He told me they were running out of film and probably wouldn't have enough to last until after the holiday. This wasn't a big problem since more film was being delivered the next day. What was a big problem was that the brainiacs on the production had it sent to the Troma Building in New York City instead of the production office in Poughkeepsie. Patrick asked if I would be so kind as to wait for the delivery and then drive it two hours up to the set. He promised me a free lunch at McDonald's if I did. I agreed, and drove the film to the set the next day.

Not only did Patrick welch on the promise of lunch, I got an unexpected bonus when the still photographer smashed into my car. I found out later that she quit the production the very next day, and probably knew full well that she was quitting when she put the big dent in my car. So, Patrick, if you're reading this, I'm still waiting for my Big Mac.

For some reason, while the physical task of film editing has gotten easier, the editing itself has gotten much, much worse. Now that you can cut and recut a scene without damaging any of the original materials, people tend to overedit and create TV commercials or music videos instead of feature films.* These days, holding a take for twenty seconds is considered daring and avant-garde. If you're working on celluloid, all these extra cuts are going to cost you money. *Terror Firmer* has 2,437 cuts in it. A "normal" film will have approximately 1,400 cuts. Since I shoot so much coverage of every scene, I tend to use a lot more angles than most directors. So while somebody like Otto Preminger will shoot a dialogue scene in one continuous take, I would have done the same scene with about 62,000 different shots. This style comes at a cost, though. *Terror Firmer* had so many cuts that the negative cutters, who get paid by the cut, were able to take a six-week vacation in Hawaii.† It's best not to overthink the editing process. Follow your gut. More often than not, you'll find that your first instinct regarding how to cut a scene is the correct one.

Conventional wisdom will tell you to edit quickly, get your movie finished and out there as soon as possible. I say bullshit on this. Take as long as you want. Nobody's really beating down your door and demanding to see your work, so you'd might just as well take your time

---

* GABE FRIEDMAN RESPONDS: And this is bad because . . . why, exactly?

† And I'm sure they sorely needed that vacation because the movie was in all likelihood a logistical nightmare to assemble.

and make the movie as good as you can. It's not as if you're got to rush out the movie for a Christmas release to capitalize on fast-food tie-ins and toy deals. Marcel Duchamp said the artist of the future must go underground and in post-production, "underground" is going to be your new permanent address.* We often take a year or more to edit our movies† and I believe the care and extra time pays off in the finished product . . . not to mention the personal satisfaction that you have done your absolute best.

Troma employs three brilliant, silken-lipped editors: Gabe Friedman, Sean McGrath, and Brian McNulty. Because these three guys are much, much smarter than I am and have been with Troma for a long time,‡ I trust them with much of the initial editing, after I give them a good idea what I think the best takes are. Because I have exotic film festivals to visit and people to infuriate, I don't sit in the editing room day in day out until after we've settled on a rough cut.§ Unless you've cloned yourself in an unholy attempt to create the perfect editor, I would not recommend just handing over your footage and going on a six-week vacation. During post, you should be your editor's Siamese twin. This can be accomplished with a needle and thread or, if you don't want that kind of commitment, duct tape should bind you together for as long as necessary to complete the project.

In theory, you and your editor should be able to sit down with your footage and your meticulously prepared script notes and use them to quickly and easily create a beautiful cut of the film. In theory, piss should taste like lemonade 'cause they're both yellow, but it doesn't. More often than not, your script notes will just look like *Baby's First Book of Scribbles.*

---

* EDITOR'S NOTE: A number of critics have compared Kaufman to Duchamp, presumably because Duchamp hung a urinal on a gallery wall, signed his name to it and called it art.
† If you saw any of the first teaser trailers for *Citizen Toxie* (released in fall of 2001) that optimistically promised that it was "Coming Summer 2000," you know I'm not exaggerating.
‡ Troma math tells us that six months of regular human time = eight years of Troma time.
§ Also, because they don't drink 800 cups of coffee before they lock themselves into the editing bay like I do, they have a much longer attention span and are better suited to watching the same footage over and over and over again without kicking a hole in the wall.

The script notes for *Citizen Toxie* were so fucked up that, as of this writing, one year after post, they're collecting dust in the same corner as the editors' first box of condoms—never opened, never used.

A couple paragraphs up I mentioned something called a rough cut. This is not a jagged throat wound made with a broken bottle.* The rough cut is the very first assemblage of footage in linear order. The rough cut is also where you discover that whoever came up with the formula of one page of script equaling one minute of screen time was out of his mind on methamphetamines. The screenplay for *Citizen Toxie* was eighty-five pages long. The first rough cut ran about two hours and forty-five minutes.† Once you sit down and watch your first cinematic diarrhea, you'll have a pretty good idea where to start fine-tuning.

The hardest thing to do in the entire editing process may be letting somebody watch your movie in its raw, unfinished state. Unfortunately for your ego, it's one of the most important things you can do. It simply isn't possible for you or anybody who's been working closely with you on your project to keep watching the movie with fresh eyes. You're going to need to discover what works and what doesn't (or if anybody can even understand the damn thing at all) and that means sucking it up and bringing in an outsider. For your first movie, your test screening audience will probably be your mom, your cousin Doreen, and the fat, creepy guy who lives across the hall and collects *Mork & Mindy* memorabilia.‡ You should try to make it a little more formal than that. If you can, try to show it to twenty to thirty people who really don't

---

* Though it's not unheard of for the editing process to result in a number of these kinds of rough cuts.

† Being a weak-willed, cheap son of a bitch, I seriously considered for a time turning *Citizen Toxie* into a three-hour, two-part movie, where you would come see Part One on Monday and return on Tuesday for Part Two. The editors humored me on this score and allowed me to watch the long version of the movie with a focus group. I quickly realized what the editors had known all along. Instead of making one pretty good movie, I would have made two really shitty movies. About halfway through the screening, I sheepishly turned to Gabe and said, "Nevermind."

‡ That guy's name is Ian, by the way. If you introduce yourself and make friends with him, he probably won't post those pictures he's been taking of you in the shower on the Internet.

give a shit if they hurt your feelings by telling you the whole thing sucks. To make absolutely, positively sure that they feel free to be as brutally honest as possible, give them questionnaires asking them about their favorite/least favorite scene, favorite/least favorite character, and if certain scenes should be cut out. Find out what they liked, what they hated, and what they didn't even realize was in the movie because they'd fallen asleep ten minutes earlier. Also, give them a choice of two or three titles and ask them to pick their favorite one. Focus groups overwhelmingly chose the title *Citizen Toxie*, though I wanted to use the title *A Tale of Two Toxies*. For the first time in Troma history, I wanted to go with the logical choice and use the title that actually had a little something to do with the story.

Whatever you do, do not give out copies of your rough cut to your actors. All this will accomplish is giving you and your editor a series of migraine headaches that can only be cured by a bullet to the cerebellum.* Some well-meaning Troma employees took it upon themselves to bring the actors up to speed on *Citizen Toxie* and provide them with rough cuts of the unfinished film. For weeks, the editors' phone rang off the hook with actors complaining about takes that had been chosen, angles that were unflattering and assorted other minute bullshit that had nothing to do with the quality of the movie and everything to do with the actors' egos. The only people you should show your rough cut to are audiences at a test screening, fuckable young men or women that you want to impress, or potential investors from whom you hope to squeeze money.

When Troma holds a test screening, we rent a screening space and start recruiting random audience members, just like the Hollywood studios. Screening spaces are one area where film schools actually come in handy. They all have 'em and most are willing to rent them out for fairly cheap, especially if school isn't in session. For that mat-

---

* I leave it to your discretion whose cerebellum to apply the bullet to, whether it's your own or your actors'.

ter, we've done focus group screenings as a part of a class (and consequently, for no money at all) at NYU and at the New York Film Academy. Two NYU professors in particular have been extremely nice to us: David Irving, the head of the film department,* and Jeremiah Newton, who heads up the Directors' Series. The Directors' Series has brought students into close, personal contact with such filmmakers as the Coen brothers, Frank Darabont, and yours truly (though I imagine I tried to get a bit closer to the students than the Coens did).

To get a good mix of people to bolster the students (who are usually rich, spoiled brats who don't particularly enjoy Troma films), we post someone out on the street to pull people in with the promise of a free movie starting right this very second. Of course, most of the people who have nothing better to do than go see a movie on the spur of the moment are homeless crack addicts just looking for a warm place to rest for a couple hours. For one test screening of *Terror Firmer*, we booked a two-hour block of time at MagnoSound in New York. Our naïve assumption was that since we paid for two hours of time, we would be able to stay in the theater for the full 120 minutes. The manager of the MagnoSound screening room had other ideas. It seems that the golden gods at Miramax had booked the space for the time immediately after us and the manager wanted us out of the theater the second the movie ended even though we still had seventeen minutes left on the time we'd paid for. We wanted to stay for the full two hours and talk to our audience. This was, after all, why we'd rented the damn theater in the first place. The manager, who was a real snot-bastard while he was trying to give us the bum's rush, told us we should have rented two and a half hours if we'd wanted to do that. We told him we didn't have the budget for that and the fucking shitbag sniffed and said, "If you don't have the budget, don't make the film." We were

---

* Incidentally, David Irving is actress Amy Irving's brother. Amy Irving is Steven Spielberg's ex-wife. So it may be that David brought Troma in to spite his ex-brother-in-law.

appalled by the sentiment but amazed that he had unknowingly quoted a line of dialogue from the movie we'd just screened, delivered by Will Keenan's Spielberg-loving character, Casey, to us.

We did have some revenge on the piece of shit manager. We had some filthy, smelly homeless guys in the audience for the screening and they didn't really want to leave the warm theater and go back out on the freezing-cold streets. After the manager ejected us, Gabe and I told the stinky bums it was perfectly okay for them to go back into the theater (now filled with Miramaxers) and stay as long as they'd like.

If you've ever been to a major studio's test screening, you know that they make you swear on your grandmother's tit that you will never, ever say anything about what you're about to see on the Internet. To which you probably reply, "Internet? What's this you're speaking of?" Then once you're in the theater, you whip out your laptop so you can send your review to Harry Knowles' Ain't It Cool News in real time as the movie's unspooling. Studios hate it when Internet spies infiltrate test screenings because they know that bad word of mouth will kill their multi-zillion dollar investment. It's perfectly okay by us if they come to our test screenings and spread the word about what they've seen. For one thing, we know we've made a good movie that the mainstream press will ignore, so sites like Ain't It Cool are one of the few places to spread the word about truly independent cinema. It isn't like we're making *The Avengers* and people are going to warn the public not to waste their time.

With these questionnaires in hand, you can go back to the editing room and fix where you went wrong. Sometimes you'll just need to recut or eliminate something. Other times, you might need to go back and do some reshoots. Something might be unclear and need clarifying. There may be something that you intended to shoot in production but just plumb forgot. Or there may be something that you shot but it really, really sucks. A good example of this are the newscaster segments in *Citizen Toxie*. After we put the movie together, the editors realized I'd royally screwed up filming these segments and since they open the picture, this was a major fuck-up. While I was obsessing over how I could have been so stupid, I went to Minneapolis for a book signing. One night, I was invited by Rock 'n' Roll Ray, the Minneapolis-based director of *Go to Hell*, to a comedy club to see the Sklar Brothers perform. They were major Troma fans and let me in for free. I thought they were hilarious and realized they could fix the awful newscaster segments. So they came out to New York where, in return for letting me in the club for free, we let them work for free and completely reshot the scenes. We created a T.V. station in the dilapidated judo studio we'd been using as a production office. Now, the newscaster scenes are a highlight of the movie. Stephen Holden singled them out in his *New York Times* review, saying their "gleefully snide asides make Chevy Chase at his airiest seem funereal."* Moral: it's never too late to reshoot. Lesson: keep some money in your budget for post-production reshoots. Ralph Rosenblum, the editor of such films as *Annie Hall*, was an editor I admired very much. When we were in post-production on *Stuck On You*, I discovered his name was listed in the New York telephone directory. I took a chance and called him to ask if he'd help with our movie. Much to my surprise, he agreed and became supervising editor. While we were working on the movie, Ralph told me that Woody Allen also keeps money reserved in his budgets for reshoots in post-production. This confirmed to me that I wasn't totally insane and/or miserly for doing this all these years.

Once you've recut, reshot, recut, retested, and recut some more and you're satisfied that the movie won't get any better, you can lock the picture. Unless your name is George Lucas, in which case you'll just keep fucking around with the same shitty, pointless movie, trying to make it more and more juvenile until the day you realize you've wasted your entire adulthood working on the same boring thing and take your own life.

---

* High praise indeed, as I have always considered Chevy Chase to be one of the most bitterly sarcastic towns in all of Maryland.

ADR, AKA LOOPING, AKA FIXING THE SHITTY SOUND YOU RECORDED IN PRODUCTION

ADR stands for Automatic Dialogue Replacement, which is odd because our editors, at least, have to do it all manually. The most common use of ADR is to replace dialogue that was poorly recorded in production, because of background noise, a drunk boom mike operator, or an actor who had a stroke the night before filming. But you should also use ADR as a way to continue improving the script and raising the level of the movie. If a character's face is turned away from camera, you can give that person a line that didn't exist before. If there's a scene with a large number of people, you can add a line and the audience will understand it's being delivered by an off-screen character. These lines can be throwaway jokes,* they can clarify confusing plot points,† they can be used in any way you can imagine.

You're almost guaranteed to have to do some ADR work on your movie, either to replace poor location sound or to improve the script. If you shot your picture in a working coal refinery, you may have to loop every single line of dialogue. The tricky part (if you're replacing dialogue in a specific necessary shot that shows the actor's face) is getting the new dialogue to sync up with the actor's lip movements. The even trickier part is convincing the actors to come in and record the dialogue weeks or months after they dropped down on their knees and thanked god they'd never have to see your fucking face again as long as they lived. To prepare for that eventuality, you should have written into the actors' contracts a clause that commits them to returning for at

---

* In *Terror Firmer*, the totally illogical line "Oh, my God, he's got an Afro!" after the bald black guy is killed by a falling 2K light was created in ADR and always gets a huge laugh. The incandescent 2000 watt (2K) tungsten light, by the way, was a workhorse twenty years ago. Today, HMI lights render these beasts virtually obsolete, which means the 2K lights are cheap and plentiful and still basically in working order. Troma uses them a lot . . . not out of nostalgia or because we think things were built to last in the good ole days, but because we can't afford HMI lights.

† Also in *Terror Firmer*, we added the line "Moose, that's a goofy knife" to clarify that Moose was using a fake knife to stab Casey.

least one day of free ADR work. So if your hypnotic power of persuasion fails to bring them in, the threat of legal action should do the trick.

Troma has a multitude of creative uses for ADR. On *Citizen Toxie*, Dave Mattey, despite his powerful physical performance as both the Toxic Avenger and his evil doppelganger the Noxious Offender, lacked the distinctive vocal quality that had come to be associated with the character in the first film. On the original *Toxic Avenger*, we replaced Mitchell Cohen's voice with a deep, bass voice for Toxie. People loved it so much that I stupidly decided they all must be wrong and left Ron Fazio's voice alone on *Toxie II* and *III*. Troma fans hated the new voice, so for the fourth movie, we decided to go back to what worked in the first place. This necessitated a nationwide talent hunt to find Toxie's voice. We found the perfect match in Salt Lake City radio personality Clyde Lewis. We flew Clyde out to New York and looped all of Toxie's and Noxie's dialogue, improving the movie a thousand percent.*

The Plastique Palace scene in *Citizen Toxie* was intended to poke fun at plastic surgery mishaps but, in its original form, was actually an example of bland dialogue over bland visuals. It was made more interesting by dubbing the sexy gyno's† voice over with an extremely masculine one, suggesting that this gorgeous woman was once a guy.‡

As I mentioned, Troma also uses ADR as a rewriting tool, constantly tweaking and perfecting scenes right up until the very last minute. Sometimes this means just tossing in an offhand line delivered by somebody off-screen but other times, it's a lot more work. In *Terror Firmer*, Popo's

---

* Also, I believe Dave pissed off the editors during production, so they even dubbed Dave's voice during Dave's momentary cameo out of makeup. The big guy who cums in Joe Fleishaker's mouth in Amortville? That's Dave. The extremely gay sounding voice? That's Gabe Roth, the brother of Troma alumni and director of *Cabin Fever* Eli Roth.

† If you're anything like me, you probably don't remember anything from Chapter One at all, so if you don't remember what the term "gyno" means, check out the footnote on page 8 in Chapter One.

‡ We've just realized that the term "gyno" contains the homonym "guy," making it a totally unacceptable substitute for females in today's politically correct society. Henceforth, we will no longer use this potentially offensive term. Instead, we shall call Gyno-Americans "XX-Chromosome-Americans."

death scene was completely re-written and re-recorded no less than three times in post-production. We had this scene where the serial killer (wearing bloody panties) kills the perverted ventriloquist by stretching his dick out to a truly grotesque length.* But the scene simply wasn't working as originally written. A brilliant cartoonist named Mike Shapiro (creator of a terrific comic called *The Book of Sick*) was working for Troma at the time and he saw the scene and instantly observed that we had filmed the ultimate scene of female empowerment. We totally rewrote the dialogue to where it is today, basically creating a brand new scene that was never there before. My brother Charles did this on a much grander scale with *Ferocious Female Freedom Fighters*, on which we completely redubbed an Indonesian female wrestling movie. The new movie was much funnier and also made Charles the target of Indonesian assassins for the better part of a decade.†

You don't need to rent expensive studio space to record great ADR. All of Troma's ADR is recorded in the editing room where, if we remember to do it, we hang filthy, cum-stained sound blankets around to improve the acoustics. Then, armed with a mike and a Beta deck (speaking of Beta deck, I need a better dick),‡ we get people from the office to do the voices (if we don't need or can't get the original actors back for some reason). In *Citizen Toxie*, Toxie's growl was simply Gabe growling into a pitch shifter (or was it a shit pitcher? Maybe it was a

* Although men with small penises have told me they find nothing grotesque whatsoever about the scene.
† It's no coincidence that shortly after *Ferocious Female Freedom Fighters*, Charles left filmmaking entirely and opened the Bread & Cie, San Diego's premiere French bakery. When asked why he left movies for the bakery, Charles will respond that both horror movies and bread have sharp, lethal knives in them, so there really isn't that much difference. And speaking of French bread, did you know that *Terror Firmer* star and co-writer of this book Trent Haaga is hung like a baguette? I should know, because I had to grab a handful of his manly area in episode five of *Troma's Edge TV*.
‡ Once upon a time, we owned a beautiful Nagra tape recorder that we used exclusively for recording post-production sound. Until the digital age, Nagras were the standard for recording on-location sound. They were magnificent Swiss-made models of engineering. Our Nagra was used as a prop in *Terror Firmer* and disappeared from Times Square while we were filming Yaniv Sharon's naked run. There was absolutely no reason for the Nagra to be in Times Square

snitch picker). Most of the fart sounds were generated by Gabe's ass. And speaking of fart sounds . . .

SOUND DESIGN

Sound design incorporates everything on the soundtrack of your movie that isn't dialogue, which basically leaves music and sound effects. In Troma, the entire spectrum of sound effects can be summed up with three essential cues: the cat,* the fart, and the cowbell. These three indispensable sound effects will satisfy every comedic need you will ever have. In olden times, I would personally create these sounds live in the studio. This procedure was extremely taxing. I would often end the day having crapped my pants at least twice and having strangled or mutilated the tails of dozens of innocent cats. Fortunately, those days have been replaced (at least for the low-budget filmmaker) by voluminous CD libraries that contain virtually every sound effect known to the human ear.

Troma puts a lot of care and effort into creating a truly magnificent sound mix. This is one area where we do not skimp. On *Citizen Toxie*, we hired Bernie Hayden from Sound Dimension, one of the best sound people in New York. In the end, all of the expense and hard work really paid off.†

For some reason, a lot of first-time filmmakers decide if they need to cut corners somewhere in post-production, it may as well be the sound design on the chopping block. This is a bad idea. Sound accounts for up

---

in the first place, since we didn't use it to record location sound and the prop didn't figure into the scene we were shooting, but that's the last place it was seen. If you have any information on Troma's Nagra, please contact me at lloyd@troma.com. There is no reward other than the satisfaction that you've helped restore a piece of Troma history.

* Whenever something falls or is thrown on screen, we add the sound of a screeching cat to suggest that whatever it is has just struck the innocent feline. Speaking of cats, did you know we had to cut the word "pussy" out of *Terror Firmer* in order to get an R rating? Meanwhile, Disney's R-rated *Scary Movie* got away with showing a penis penetrating someone's head.

† EDITOR'S NOTE: Yeah, it really paid off. In an otherwise favorable review of the movie, the newspaper *LA Weekly* singled out *Citizen Toxie*'s "porno-incompetent sound" as one of the hallmarks of Troma's "defiantly cheap" style.

to 52.358983% of your movie's impact, maybe even more if somebody's half-watching it on video while they go to the kitchen to fix themselves a grilled cheese sandwich. A good sound mix can draw the audience back into the picture. A bad sound mix will surely alienate them and make them decide to go give their pet rabbit a bath instead of finish watching the movie you've put all your blood, sweat, and semen/quiffing fluid into.

Giving your movie a professional-quality sound mix is time-consuming and detail-oriented but it is the best and most inexpensive way for a low-budget filmmaker to enhance the production value of his film. Just be conscious of the fact that you're going to need many, many more effects than you think you will at first. Every door that opens or shuts, every car that screeches to a halt, every punch that is thrown, every testicle that is kicked, and every birdie that's singin' from a tree needs a sound.

Each scene should be densely layered with sound.* A good example of sound layering is a fistfight. Too often, low-budget filmmakers will throw in the sound of the impact of a punch or kick and call it a day. This will sound fake and empty to the audience's ear. Each punch needs at least three sounds. First, you need to hear a grunt of effort from the guy throwing the punch. Then, you hear the impact of the punch hitting the chump. Third, you hear a grunt of pain from the chump himself. One action, three sounds. Remember that sound is dynamic and complex, especially if you're dealing with action, machinery, or the good ol' fashioned bump 'n' grind.

And remember, if a scene seems too quiet and you need some background noise but you just aren't sure what's appropriate, you can always throw in a cat screeching, a nice juicy fart, or a hilarious cowbell to liven things up. During the sex scene between Jennifer and Jerry in *Terror*

---

*Unless, of course, you're intentionally using silence as an effect, in which case you should be extremely aware of the impact even the tiniest sound will have under these conditions. The brilliant visual artist Stan Brakhage and I once had a conversation about John Cage's use of silence in music. I thought it would be interesting to find a visual equivalent, so on *The Girl Who Returned*, I occasionally cut to an entirely silent black screen. This backfired totally, as audiences always turned in their seats and started yelling to the management that the projector had broken.

Firmer, we added a cowbell every time we saw Jennifer's tits bouncing around. This infuriated Alyce LaTourelle, who played Jennifer. She was humiliated, mortified, and out for blood. Until, that is, she saw the movie at the San Sebastian Film Festival with an audience of 2,000 people who thought the cowbell was hysterical. Once she saw how the scene played and that people really did think it was funny, all was forgiven.

The other element of sound design is music and here is where the novice filmmaker can run into some monetary problems. Before you spend five days brilliantly editing a bank heist scene to the tune of "Can't Buy Me Love," consider the fact that Michael Jackson (who owns the rights to all the Beatles tunes) might want a couple hundred thousand dollars before he lets you use the song in your movie.* Believe it or not, music executives are about twenty thousand times sleazier than movie executives. If you're lucky enough to be in contact with a band that likes what you're trying to do, you may be able to get around the dickheads who control the purse strings and secure a song or two from the artists themselves. And while it's not unheard of for big-name rock stars to do the right thing and allow their music to be used for nothing on a project they believe in,† these are exceptions, not the rule.

Be extremely careful when you're securing the rights to music. Having the bass player drunkenly tell you that it would kick ass to have his band's song in your movie is not a legally binding contract. On *Citizen Toxie*, we attempted to contact a musician who had been begging us to use one of his songs in the movie. We called him, his management, and his lawyers repeatedly but never heard back from any of them.

---

* I know, in a fair and just world, Michael Jackson would tell you he already has more money than the entire country of Kazakhstan and would give you the song for free to support independent art and cinema. But that's not gonna happen. Plastic surgery is expensive.
† Bryan Sipe was able to use Bruce Springsteen's song "Sad Eyes" for his first, ultra–low-budget feature *A Million Miles* simply because he asked politely and persistently and Springsteen liked the story. And Troma's been very lucky to have musicians donate music to our movies simply because they're fans. Motorhead, Sublime, Lunachicks, Flipp, and Ass Ponys (or as Kenneth Branagh calls them, Arse Ponys) are just a few of the bands who have contributed tracks to Troma movies.

Time went on and we forgot about it until the movie was finished, at which point we received an angry phone call from the musician's lawyer, saying that he was going to sue us for using his client's song without permission. In my opinion, this was done deliberately. The lawyers had attempted to convince us that we could use the song but didn't sign anything so that they could shake us down for a big payoff later. The joke was on him, though. Since we never received a signed contract, we never put the song in the movie.

Be aware that if you *do* secure a band's permission to use a song in your movie, you need to have them sign two different contracts. One contract is for publishing rights. That is to say, the maestro who wrote the song is giving you permission to use it. The other is for performance rights. This means the band (or orchestra or street performer) who performs the song is giving you permission to use their rendition of it. If the songwriter's dead, don't assume you can skip the publishing rights. Songs written by people who are dead and famous are often protected more carefully than Colonel Sanders's eleven herbs and spices, so be careful.

You might think that a piece of music you want is in the public domain (that is, no longer protected by copyright). Be sure to look into this carefully. It's highly possible that the music itself is public domain, but the performance of the music is not. When we used Puccini's "Un Bel Di" from *Madame Butterfly* in *Sgt. Kabukiman NYPD*, we did not pay Puccini a dime. We did, however, have to pay the opera company that performed the tune. Later, when we wanted to use a selection from Puccini's *Turandot*, we were startled to discover we'd have to pay both the orchestra and Puccini's estate. Apparently, *Turandot* was recent enough that it had not fallen into the public domain. Needless to say, cheap bastards that we are, we immediately lost all desire to use *Turandot* in the movie.

Copyright law is a tricky thing, made even trickier by the U.S. Copyright Law of 1998. Copyright was intended to protect the artist during his, her or its lifetime and give the artist the freedom to explore and advance the arts and make a living doing it. Today, it seems that laws exist to allow big monied interests like Disney to control intellectual property for eternity. This is not what the founding fathers intended when they enacted copyright law in the first place. But little by little, the intent has been subverted and changed, particularly now thanks to the law passed by Disney's pimp, Bill Clinton. By rights, Mickey Mouse should now be in the public domain. But the Clinton/Disney Copyright Law of 1998 changed that so Disney can protect its rodent for years to come. I am not saying that copyright law should be abolished. Far from it. But you and I both know that Disney is still going to make a pantload of cash with or without Mickey Mouse being protected by copyright. In fact, it doesn't seem like Disney has a whole fuck of a lot of interest in Mickey Mouse anymore, since he's been relegated to being a hydrocephalic concierge at their theme parks. Since they're not really doing much with him anyway, wouldn't it be interesting to see what people like Trey Parker or Mike Judge would do with the public domain Mickey Mouse? Even Shakespeare cribbed most of his work from existing poems, plays, and histories. If Shakespeare was working under the U.S. Copyright Law of 1998, he would not have been able to write *Romeo & Juliet*, arguably the greatest piece of dramatic literature ever written. He would have been sued by the writer of the original Italian play that had appeared less than eighty years previous. And it isn't just artistic work that's affected by this. Academics and science are being constrained by copyright laws. These medical patents they have today are unconscionable, allowing big corporations to get rich off of research and pharmaceuticals that should benefit the entire world! None of this has much of anything to do with sound design, but by god, it pisses me off! GIVE ART BACK TO THE PEOPLE!

Hey . . . Adam Jahnke here. Sorry about all that. Lloyd's taking a time out right now. He got so worked up there that he had actually stopped typing about five minutes ago and when I came in he was just standing there, shouting at the computer about conglomerates getting rich off his wife's breast cancer and something about organ harvesting. Anyway, I gave him a couple of pills and told him to go watch a few minutes of Princess Yang Kwei Fei. *It's one of his favorite movies and usually calms him down. Okay, here he is. Remember Lloyd . . . we're talking about sound design and music. All right?*

Sure, sure. I got it. Now if you want original music in your movie, that's another matter entirely. If half the population of the free world wants to be an actor, at least as many fancy themselves to be musicians. It's not too difficult to just hang around a coffee shop on open mike night and find somebody whose work you like. Just like with screenwriters, most musicians will be so flattered to be asked to work on a movie that money won't even be an issue. Besides, if there's anybody who will be able to relate to trying to create something out of nothing, it's a struggling musician.

Not too damn long ago, Napster permitted unknown bands from around the world to be discovered by music-hungry fans everywhere. File sharing could have been a great boon to both low-budget filmmakers and struggling musicians, putting artists together who otherwise never would have found each other. Unfortunately, sleazebag record executives and a handful of greedy musicians who already had more money than they could ever spend decided this wasn't sharing, it was stealing and succeeded in shutting Napster down. Troma's support of Napster has been well-documented so I won't go into it much here.* Suffice it to say that independent art, artists, and a public starving for music other than the Backside Boys lost one of their most beneficial tools the day Napster died.

The only other thing to keep in mind with music is start thinking about it early on. Music will either enhance the mood you're trying to create or totally subvert it and make the scene something it was never meant to be. Get started early in the process and work closely with

---

* Get me started on it and I'll add another forty pages to this chapter. Adam Jahnke and I wrote a number of essays in defense of Napster and the curious reader can find them all lovingly archived in the "Lloyd's 'Roids" section at www.troma.com.

both the composer and the editor to make sure that the music is doing what you want it to do. Because we at Troma believe music and film are so closely related, we will often edit a scene to a particular piece of music with the intention of removing the music later on. The music guides the editing and tells us where the beats and crescendoes should be. We edited the famous Clown-Chasing-the-Taxi scene in *Stuck On You* to the William Tell Overture, fully intending to remove it and use original music later on. However, we liked the scene so much that we ended up using the temporary music in the final film.

After the sound is designed, recorded and up to par, the final step is mixing. All this means is creating a layered soundscape with the dialogue, sound effects and music at appropriate levels so they don't drown each other out. It's a very good idea to have a sound booth or an extra mike available during the mix, in case inspiration strikes for any last minute lines* or fart noises. Just make sure you pay attention to how your film is being mixed. Mixing engineers are notorious for mixing music too loud so that it obscures the dialogue. And remember, dialogue always sounds clearer in the studio than it will on your release print or video master.

CREDITS, DUPLICATION, AND FINISHING UP

Once picture and sound are locked, mixed, synched, and ready to go, your very last step is adding the credits. One reason this is last is because you're going to be pulling in investors, favors, and dates right down to the wire and you always want to make sure you can offer someone a credit on the movie for their assistance. Don't be afraid to approach celebrities you happen to meet and ask them for help. I never expected Ralph Rosenblum to help out with *Stuck On You*, but I certainly never would have known one way or another if I hadn't taken the chance and called the number in the phone book.

---

* This, of course, would be lines of dialogue. If inspiration strikes for any other kinds of lines, you should probably quit the film industry and start a band. While cocaine and other drugs have inspired hundreds, if not thousands, of great songs, they don't do too much for movies except provide free publicity after you're all arrested.

Another, equally important reason is that your credit sequence may be all that stands between your calling your movie a feature or a short. By definition, a feature film must be at least sixty minutes long. If it isn't, the major, prestigious film festivals, video stores, and distributors will consider it a short subject and, for the most part, won't touch it. If you run into this dilemma, you can prolong your credit sequences as long as it takes to pad the movie out to feature length. Chad Ferrin's *Unspeakable* may very well be a milestone in cinema history. Besides being the darkest film in the Troma library since *Combat Shock* (1986), it boasts the longest end-credits crawl imaginable, clocking in at a whopping seven minutes.*

For the last several years, we have also hidden jokes in our end credits. God knows this ain't because we need to make our movies any longer. Rather, these are like little rewards for the Troma faithful. We figure if somebody likes our movies enough to sit through the end credits, they deserve to at least get a laugh or two while they're staring at a bunch of names they've never heard of before.

Once you've cut your negative, you need to make a print of the finished product (with sound) known as an answer print.† You will then spend the next several days of your life locked in a dark room with a surly fat lab guy‡ looking at the answer print and telling him where you think the colors are wrong (including some shots that are either completely blue or green) and what it's supposed to look like. You should ask your DP to join you in the tiny room for advice and support. After all, it's his career on the line if all the flesh tones in your movie look light green instead of pink. Jocko, the angry lab guy, writes down your changes in some cryptic runelike scrawl that only he can understand and makes the

---

* The opening credits don't exactly whiz by, either.
EDITOR'S NOTE: Neither does the movie.
† The question it is answering is, "What the fuck did I think I was doing when I sat down and started writing the screenplay to this damn movie?" Hopefully, you will be satisfied with your answer.
‡ You'll quickly discover that there are a lot of fatsos in the wide world of post-production. Come to think of it, though, pre-production and production have a pretty good selection of chubbos, too.

corrections. This process is called timing the print. You can do this as often as you want, but each answer print costs a pantload, so you'll be lucky if you can do it more than once. Whether you shot on film or video, you still need to color correct the print, so be sure to buy some air freshener to disguise the aroma of Jocko's "editorial comments."

With the movie in the can, now it's time to start duplicating your masterpiece so that people can watch it without you lurking in the background, waiting to grab your one and only copy back. If you've shot on DV, this is a piece of cake. All you need to do is start cranking out VHS copies. If you're really ambitious, you can even get your movie burned onto DVD and impress all your prospective distributors and festival committees with how forward thinking you are.

If you've shot on film, things once again get a little tricky. After the answer print, you can either strike as many release prints as you can afford* or start cranking out the old VHS tapes again. To do this you'll need to create a video master from what's known as a low-contrast print. These run anywhere from $2,000 to $4,000. The good news with the low-contrast print is that you can use it to strike a new negative in case, god forbid, anything catastrophic should happen to the original.

TRENT HAAGA: Once again, just shooting on digital video in the first place will simplify your life. Most people are going to be watching your movie on video. A growing number of film festivals use video projection. And of the thousands of movies that are made each year, only a fraction of them get any kind of theatrical release. If you're one of the very, very lucky ones, you can always make a celluloid print from a video master.†

---

* And at around $2,000 a pop, I'm guessing you'll be able to afford one, if you're lucky. If you do it more than a few times, you also get to experience the joy of spending $10–20,000 on creating what's called an interpositive or internegative. This is because you don't want to make too many release prints directly from your negative. If something happens to it in the machine while the print is being made, like an ash from the lab guy's smoke falls in, you're fucked. An interpositive is struck so that you can continue to make prints without putting your negative in jeopardy.
† Actually, if you're that lucky then whoever is picking up your movie for distribution should be able to pony up the dough and make prints from your video master.

Editor Sean McGrath proves that at Troma the editor is
king . . . or at least queen.

Once you're finished, you may be tempted to purge your life of the
detritus of your movie by throwing out all the outtakes, audition
tapes, location scouts, and various other footage you shot that didn't
end up in the movie itself. Fight that urge. With DVD overtaking
VHS as the format of choice, every piece of footage you have is a
potential bonus feature. Years ago, Michael Herz decided we needed
to conserve our storage space since space is so expensive in New
York. To this end, he threw out years and years of footage that was
useless then but would have been a gold mine today. If we'd saved it,
you could see *The First Turn-On* on DVD with the Super-8 film audition that got Madonna rejected. You could see *Sizzle Beach USA* on
DVD with additional footage of a young Kevin Costner that was cut
from the movie. You could see *Squeeze Play* on DVD with bonus hot
lesbian action. Alas, these are all gone now and of all the movies
Troma has released on DVD, Michael never asks why *The First Turn-
On, Sizzle Beach USA,* and *Squeeze Play* aren't bigger sellers when he
reads the monthly sales figures.

So there you have it. You've been face down in the trenches, led the
troops through an ordeal second only to a Japanese prison camp, and
emerged on the other side with your own damn movie! Take a second
and enjoy the feeling that you have done what you set out to do. Show

the movie to your nearest and dearest and bask in their admiration (or confusion if they just don't get your movie at all). Savor the moment because this will be the easiest audience you get. If you think you're done, guess again. You've scaled the mountain, but now you've got an even bigger one looming in front of you. Getting your movie seen.

CHAPTER 11

Marketing, Publicity and Distribution—Whoring Yourself Out for Your Art Yet Again

Hey, remember back in the pre-production chapter where we said that the last few days of prep before production would be the hardest time you will ever experience as a filmmaker? Well, we lied. It was for your own good, though! If you'd known way back when that the really, truly hard part was going to come at the very end, you wouldn't have come this far, now would you? So quit your goddamn blubbering and act like the independent filmmaker you now are! I expect to see that kind of behavior from the pussy directors at major studios, not hard-core, sharp-as-a-razor, genitalia-of-steel independent film mavericks like you.

This stage of the game, which you could refer to as post–post-production, basically boils down to separate but equally daunting tasks. The first is promotion. You have to get the word out and get people to watch your movie; otherwise you've wasted a lot of time and money for nothing. The second is distribution. You want to get your investors' money back to them, if for no other reason than so you can hit them up for more money and make another movie. But first you need to promote this movie, so your potential distributors can hear all about how great it is and feel like if they don't see your movie, they're missing out on the opportunity of a lifetime.

How well you are able to promote your movie after it's done really doesn't have anything to do with your ability as a filmmaker. So if you've just made a colossal piece of shit but you sold the most candy bars back in fifth grade band class and have a gift for getting people to buy crap they don't really want or need, you will probably be able to get your movie seen. Likewise, if you just made a movie so brilliant it makes a legitimate claim to being the heir to *Citizen Kane* as the most auspicious debut film of all time but you're so quiet and reserved you don't even complain when a clerk shortchanges you by ten bucks at the gas station, you're gonna have a hard time getting people to sit down and watch.

The sad truth is that we cannot teach you how to sell your movie. Troma has staggered on for three decades now and much of our success has had to do with the fact that we owned the negatives to our films. This allowed us to derive immediate and continued revenue as new technologies came along.* For instance, in the early days of cable television, there were around thirty different pay-TV systems all competing for subscribers. They were desperate for product and simply couldn't get it from the major studios. The majors, you see, were still contractually obligated to sell their movies to network TV. So for a period of about two years while these outdated contracts played out, independents like Troma were able to sell anything and everything to the nascent cable channels. We were able to sell *Squeeze Play* (which had a budget of less than $200,000) to Showtime for an exclusive run for half a million dollars. KA-CHING!

Those days are long gone. Not only have the major studios entered the fray, but most of the cable channels from those early days have

---

* A main element of Troma's business strategy since 1974 (and yes, smart ass, Troma DOES have a business strategy) has been to build a collection of company-owned films. The autobiography of Charlie Chaplin details how he was able to do very much the same thing and, with this financial security, was able to continue directing films well into his 70's. Compare Chaplin's fate to that of Buster Keaton, who did not own his own negatives, and ended up virtually broke and did not have complete artistic control over any film after 1927's *The General*.

either gone out of business or been absorbed by AO-Hell/Slime-Warner (which owns the inbred HBO family of channels) or Viacom (which owns Showtime and its subsidiaries). These days, we're lucky if we can get Showtime to return our calls. An outfit like Showtime will spend millions on the rights to big-budget schlock and then will turn around and say there's no budget left over for Troma or other independents.

Perhaps the most egregious example of this in recent years is the fact that Trey Parker's *Cannibal! The Musical* has never aired on Comedy Central (co-owned by Viacom and HBO). *South Park* is one of the only successful shows in the history of Comedy Central. Even a chimp would realize that programming the first film by the Academy Award–nominated creator of *South Park* would be a good move. Well, apparently Comedy Central is programmed by mammals with less intelligence than chimps, because we've been told time and again that they have absolutely no interest in airing *Cannibal! Cannibal!* has sold a huge number of units on DVD alone. To an independent like Troma that has to fight tooth and nail to get product into video stores, a movie like *Cannibal!* is a major success. *Cannibal! The Musical* is Troma's *Lord of the Rings.**

The other major technology to come along in the early 1980s was home video. As soon as it started to become popular, Jack Valenti and the major studios freaked out and refused to release very many titles, fearing that home video would be the downfall of copyright law. They envisioned a world where everybody and their decrepit grandma would be pirating copies of *Orca, The Killer Whale* and bankrupting the studios. Companies like Vestron and Media Home Entertainment rushed in to fill the gap, discovering a huge new market for independent films. While the Hollywood studios did their best to ignore this new development, Troma was able to make an assload of cash selling

---

* Of course, *Cannibal!* has much better music than *Lord of the Rings* and has fewer elves, ogres, and magic pixies.

Alison Deck modeling the latest in Troma fashion. The video tape bra . . . which is a lot more comfortable than the Troma DVD toilet paper. (Doug Sakmann)

video rights to movies like *The Toxic Avenger* and *Bloodsucking Freaks* to distributors around the world. Michael Herz is fond of saying that we could have sold his bar mitzvah films at that point.* In fact, *The Toxic Avenger* was one of the films that proved that the video rental business was here to stay. Up until Toxie, video had been considered the domain of musical acts, how-to instructional tapes, and aerobics for fat chicks.

The Toxic Avenger helped prove that a feature-length genre movie could attract a wide audience at the rental counter. At something like $125 per tape, we made a fuck of a lot of dough.

Troma thrived in the early days of video, just as older independents had capitalized on the drive-in market twenty years earlier. Of course, eventually Valenti and the majors realized how much money there was to be made in video and swooped in, effectively ending the feast. But once we had our big, swollen, pustulant foot in the door, it was pretty damn hard for the majors to kick us out.

Not that they haven't tried. More and more movie theaters are being merged and consolidated into humongous chains that are con-

---

* I've seen Michael's bar mitzvah films and I think we could probably sell them today. They're pretty standard home movies until the naked inbred hooker crashes the party wielding a 14" machete.

trolled, and in some cases owned outright, by the studios. They dictate what movies will be shown where and how often. This has made it virtually impossible for independents like Troma to get a formidable theatrical release for their movies. Back in 1980, *Waitress!*, one of the pre-Toxie sex comedies that Michael Herz and I directed, played in ninety-two theaters in New York City alone. In 2000, the universally acclaimed, and clearly superior, *Terror Firmer* had to swallow a lot of semen to get just one screen in New York.

As video became accepted, the studios realized that not only would they not lose money by releasing the collected works of Chevy Chase on video, they would in fact gain a significant new source of revenue. To aid the lining of the megaconglomerates' pockets, the video chain store was born. Huge chain stores muscled their way into towns and drove the independent mom and pop video stores that created the business into bankruptcy.* These chain stores kneel down to suck corporate dick at the drop of a zipper, stocking their shelves with hundreds of copies of *What Women Want*† and virtually shutting out the independents entirely. This isn't really too much of a surprise. Blockbuster is owned by Viacom. Viacom also owns Paramount Pictures. Paramount released *What Women Want*. So it's in the parent companies best interest to push the unwatchable Mel Gibson shit-fiesta and either bury something like *Terror Firmer* on the bottom shelf or just not stock it at all. The jazz musician Charles Lloyd once told me that he was informed that record stores wouldn't put his albums in the front window because jazz doesn't sell. His response to this was, "But if the records aren't in the window, nobody's going to know they exist, so of

---

* Megan Powers, Troma's brilliant and alluring diretor of marketing, suggests that if I ever want to sell movies to these giant chains again, I probably shouldn't name any names. But the worst one rhymes with Cockbuster.
† I don't mean they actually stock what women want, which would be intelligent films made with passion and care by people who truly love the art of filmmaking. I'm referring to the cinematic emetic starring Mel Gibson and Helen Hunt.

course they won't sell." This is the situation that exists with chain stores today. They don't believe independent films sell, so they bury them. But if the films are buried, how are customers going to know they're there?

There are actually two types of video/DVD rental chain stores out there. There are the corporate stores, owned and operated by the parent company, and these rarely if ever take any independent titles, Troma or otherwise. Then there's the privately owned franchise stores. These stores will actually order independent titles if they find out about them and the reason is simple. They actually have a profit motive and they can see firsthand that these titles rent. They won't order very many copies, but at least they get the movies in the stores. In my opinion, Viacom (which owns Blockbuster and thus controls the corporate stores) is not interested strictly in profit. Their main goal seems to be to increase market share and kill off competition. Life is easier in a top twenty world. If the only titles you have to worry about are *Harry Potter* and *Shrek*, things are much simpler than if you have to deal with a hundred independent titles and actually need to think a bit. The franchise stores are concerned with profit, so they're willing to think and try to market movies that are outside the norm. They will stock movies like *Ichi the Killer* and *Terror Firmer* because they know there is an audience for them.

Not only do the chain stores perpetuate this economic blacklist, they have the balls to dictate the content of the films they bring in. Most will not accept a movie with an X rating or an NC-17 rating or an I-8-PP rating or whatever the fuck the MPAA calls their "adult" rating these days. And they sure as fuck won't accept a movie without any rating at all. This makes it basically impossible for Troma to get into these chains without disemboweling our movies to get the sacred, fun-for-the-whole-family R that the big chains look upon as a *Good Housekeeping* Seal of Approval.

Contrary to popular belief, DVD has not been the godsend that independents were hoping for. It's done pretty well for itself but it's nothing like the video rental business of the early '80s. DVD is more like the music business with product aimed at selling directly to consumers rather than to rental stores. Because of this difference, it's difficult to get independent DVD product into stores. It goes back to Charles Lloyd's argument. If the independent DVDs aren't positioned up front alongside studio crap like *Pearl Harbor*, how are they going to sell? Also, there is the apparent incompetence factor at play with the stores' own employees. How many times have we at Troma had to call HMV music stores to inform them they have no Troma DVDs in stock. It isn't because they never ordered them in the first place. It's because they've sold out and their own idiots at the store don't give a shit and haven't bothered to reorder them.

It's also interesting to note that the exact same arguments that were once made against home video* are now being made against the Internet. At Troma, we hope and believe that one day soon the technology will exist to make Internet distribution a reality and when that happens, we jolly well may see a return of the free market that existed in the early days of cable television and home video. The great devil-worshipping conglomerates are doing their best to keep this from happening. They killed Napster. Bertelsmann (which is one of the only privately owned devil-worshipping conglomerates) bought out and reinvented Napster as its docile servant when it seemed that upstart company was getting too big for its britches. But technology evolves so quickly today that countless other file-sharing services have sprung up to take Napster's place. Nevertheless, the fact that Napster was castrated in the first place is totally insane. *The Wall Street Journal* reported that 60 percent of Napster's users went on to buy albums by the artists whose music they allegedly "stole" via Napster. The very premise that Napster was encouraging music theft is flawed! Every single one of

* By the MPAA, the president of the United States, and the communications cartel.

these conglomerates uses this kind of fuzzy logic to further their agendas and people buy into it! It's all intertwined, Napster, video-on-demand via the Internet, all these great new technologies that could save the independent artist are being smothered by conglomerates that simply want to engulf the world and turn it into one giant soulless strip mall! If these things continue to happen, if independent technologies get swallowed up and neutered by the industrial, corporate, and bureaucratic elite, I swear to fucking Moses on the mount I'm gonna blow my fucking brains out!

EDITOR: Okay, Lloyd, so you've had a hard time of it over the last few years. We're very, very sorry. But need I remind you that this book isn't about you. This is an inspirational book for young filmmakers and right now you're depressing the shit out of everybody. So if you want to see the rest of your advance, either get back to passing along your "wisdom" or wrap this thing up. You're already about 5,000 words over your limit and paper is extremely expensive.

Okay, okay, fine. All I was trying to say is we've been doing this for a long time now. Troma has a lot of fans and a thirty-year reputation and even we have trouble getting our movies into theaters and video stores. Selling your movie takes luck, skill, faith, and more luck. There are no guarantees. It's a crowded field and if you go about pushing your movie in a half-assed way, it's going to get lost in the shuffle. So your first step is getting your movie noticed.

Probably the first thing you should think about doing is creating a Web site. The Internet is becoming the primary place to get buzz about your movie going. The thing to remember is make the Web site entertaining. Your Web site should be better than your movie. The Web site for *The Blair Witch Project* is the biggest and best example of this recently. Their site was amazing, terrifically entertaining, and a lot better than the movie. And then the suits got involved. When it came time to make the inevitable shitty sequel, a new Web site turned up. But the new site sucked. It lacked originality and interactivity, the key elements that made the original site so compelling. I'm not suggesting that the piss-poor Web site is solely to blame for the disaster of *Blair Witch 2*. The fact that the movie itself was less interesting than a bucket of sand had a little something to do with it. But a good Web site will entice audiences into checking out a garbage movie. Thanks to the Troma brand name, we get a lot of hits to our site despite the fact that it isn't nearly as good as it should be. But Troma links to a lot of other sites that really are great, like newgrounds.com.

After launching a Web site, the first thing most filmmakers try to do is to submit their movie to film festivals around the world, hoping that festival attention will attract buyers and distributors. You will not lack for festivals to submit to, since nearly every city in the world these days hangs up a stretched-out bedsheet and hosts at least one film festival at some point. However, from a business perspective, the only festivals really worth a dam* are Cannes, Berlin, and Venice. It's our opinion that most of the movies in the big festivals (like Sundance) are controlled by monied interests and already have distribution. Sundance 2002 seemed more like HBO-Dance, with movie after movie boasting the HBO Films logo on their poster. But having said that, miracles do happen and if your movie's really good, it might just have a shot at breaking in.

When shopping your movie to markets and distributors,† obviously the best drawing power you can have is a big star. Barring Russell Crowe's participation (or even Wings Hauser, for that matter), if you've made a movie that's heavy on violence and/or sex, you've got a much better shot than if you made a dialogue-heavy character piece about a left-handed (fully clothed) gay mattress worker's search for

---

* "Dam," of course, is a macro-economic term coined by John Maynard Keyes in his position as exchequer of Churchill's cabinet. "Dam" refers to a film distribution deal with a cash advance of at least $250,000. This offer will induce the filmmaker to exclaim, "Damn!" And while there are very few festivals that are worth a dam, there are no festivals that are worth a hot dam.

† The first markets you should try are AFM or MIFED. If those do not bear fruit, try Ralph's or A&P, both of which have a constant need for baggers.

spirituality in modern-day Topeka. Even with snooty, highbrow festivals like Sundance, sex and violence will put asses in seats.* A lot of festivals have begun to schedule midnight screenings and I don't believe they've done that out of love and affection for genre movies. They've done it because these movies sell tickets and help make it possible for the festivals to stay afloat. Kicking, screaming, and moaning translates into any language. Angst-ridden dialogue is barely understandable in English. Of course, if you don't believe in these elements, you shouldn't force them into your movie just to make a buck. Personally, I believe in sex and violence more than I believe in God and Santa Claus, so *Terror Firmer* and *Citizen Toxie* have more than their share of t, a, and g (tits, ass, and gore). Not that it's helped us get the movies accepted into competition at Sundance.†

As with post-production, do not rush the festival circuit. Take your time and try to get accepted to the best possible festival. If your movie's good, the big festivals will ask to have the world premiere. If you can give it to them, super. But some of this "world premiere" crap is absolute bullshit. We heard that the Toronto Film Festival wanted to play *Citizen Toxie*, but only under the condition that they had the North American premiere.‡ For this to happen, we would have had to pull out of the Fantasia Festival in Montreal a few months earlier. Toronto argued that attendance at their festival would be down substantially if

---

* Please note that I have just used every amount of restraint I can muster and did not say puts "assholes" in seats, even though if you consider the unbelievably large number of cell-phone-toting, balding-with-a-ponytail, dressed-in-black Hollywood fuckheads in Park City during Sundance, it would be perfectly appropriate.

† EDITOR'S NOTE: It should be noted that Kaufman and his films are constantly invited to important film festivals around the world. In fact, the recent Cinematheque Francaise premiere of *Terror Firmer* led to Kaufman's radio appearance with French director Claude Chabrol. The publicity gained by their on-air discussion of the political meanings of vomit and menstrual blood led to a distribution deal for Troma and possibly a reappraisal of Monsieur Chabrol's work by the French press.

‡ I should point out that I personally never spoke directly to anyone involved with this excellent festival.

we premiered the movie in Montreal. For this argument to make any sense, you have to ignore the fact that an entire season would have changed by the time the Toronto fest rolled around, not to mention the minor point that half the population speaks an entirely different fucking language in Montreal than they do in Toronto. Besides all this, Troma believes in a little thing called loyalty. Fantasia discovered Troma years ago and we weren't about to screw them out of *Citizen Toxie* just to make the Toronto festival organizers feel like they had the biggest Canucks in the Yukon.* So we said thanks but no thanks to Toronto, stayed loyal to Fantasia and had a packed screening in Montreal, just as we'd hoped.

You may also find yourself going broke (again) submitting to festival after festival, since nearly every film festival charges a processing fee just to submit your movie, ranging from $30 to $250. Because we think that it's a crime for filmmakers to be charged again after they've sold their kidney just to afford to finish their movie, in 1999 we founded the TromaDance Film Festival. TromaDance is held every January in Park City, Utah, concurrent with about 800 other festivals with the word "dance" in their names.† The inspiration for this came from Trey Parker, Matt Stone, and Jason McHugh. One year, they submitted *Cannibal! The Musical* to Sundance. After going through the time and not inconsiderable expense of submitting the film, they got bupkiss in return. Not even a letter saying, "Fuck you. Your movie's unwatchable and we wouldn't screen it at our festival on a dare." So they decided to go to Park City and set up their own festival with just one movie: *Cannibal! The Musical.* I went myself and stayed in a condo with a bunch of other young, idealistic filmmakers who had similar

---

* Mitch Davis and Karim Hassain, the organizers and creators of Fantasia, recently produced their first damn movie, by the way, a mini-masterpiece entitled *Subconscious Cruelty*.

† Some of the other notable "dance" fests include Nodance, Lapdance, which was founded by *Cannibal! The Musical* producer Jason McHugh, and, of course, the festival named after one of Robert "Leatherface" Redford's most popular movies, Bagger Vancedance.

stories of being treated like shit by Sundance. Inspired by these people (and the fact that the screening of *Cannibal!* was a huge success), we decided to establish TromaDance as a viable alternative. TromaDance has grown each year, becoming one of the most popular and antici- pated festivals in Park City thanks to the many enthusiastic orgy- makers . . . I mean, volunteers who gather at the Troma condo, our grassroots publicity campaigns and a wide variety of outstanding films.*

Once your movie is accepted to a film festival, the biggest mistake a first-time filmmaker can make is to assume that now the work is done and all you have to do is find a comfortable spot next to the phone to wait for appreciative festival-goers to call and congratulate you on your cinematic vision. Believe it or not, most film festivals screen more than one movie and unless you get your ass out there to convince people to invest a couple hours in your particular screening, nobody's going to show up.

The first rule of festival attendance is to actually attend the festival. If your movie is an official selection of the festival, negotiate with the organizers to get them to pay for your transportation and lodging. But if that doesn't work for whatever reason (they don't have the budget, they screen 100 movies and don't pay for any of the filmmakers to visit the festival, your movie frightens them and they suspect you might be dangerously unstable), get out there on your own dime. Film festivals are magnets for distributors and media and if you can get your movie in front of one, it will make it easier for you to get it in front of the other.

You may at first think you can't afford the time and expense of trav- eling around the country and/or world to promote your movie. But if you're serious about getting your movie seen, you can't afford not to. If you can convince other people who worked on the movie to come

* For more information on the festival, including how to submit your movie, visit www.tro- madance.com.

with you, the cost of a motel room can be whittled down to just a few bucks per person. Sure, you might have to teach someone how to sleep vertically against a wall, but it can be done. Troma squeezes dozens and dozens of bodies into condos and hotel suites all the time, from Park City to Cannes. Not only does this save us thousands of dollars, it brings the Troma Team closer together and allows us to explore our own sexuality in a way few filmmakers ever dare. Even if you're unable to find a patch of floor to crash on, you should still attend the festivals. You can always sleep in your car, if necessary.*

Before you hit the festival circuit, invest some money in printing up slicks, flyers, postcards, and publicity material for your movie. A well-designed, eye-catching poster can be the most potent weapon in your publicity arsenal. Be aware, however, that many of the towns that host festivals are cracking down on handing out flyers and putting up posters. Park City is definitely the worst in this regard. If you're going to Park City with any festival other than Sundance, before you even arrive you receive a three-page list of rules and regulations. One of the more prominent rules relates to handing out flyers. It reads: "Handouts for films and parties are not exempted by the First Amendment regulations and it is a violation of code when handed outside of a building." So basically, Sundance and the city of Park City get to decide what the First Amendment means for ten days every January. Even if somebody on the street asks you specifically for a flyer, you are not allowed to give them one. You have to ask them to go into the nearest place of business with you so you can hand it to them on private property. During TromaDance 2001, filmmaker and volunteer James Lynch spent a night in jail for the heinous offense of handing out leaflets on the street.

As for hanging posters and flyers, all of the non-Sundance festivals

---

* Sleeping in your car is not a particularly good idea during the Park City festivals, however, where the average nighttime temperature hovers around two degrees. Try it there and you'll be sleeping in your car for a very long time.

and filmmakers are permitted to post bills only on two or three minute designated poster kiosks. Post on a Sundance kiosk and you face arrest. Hand out flyers and you face arrest. Shout "Robert Redford can suck my cock," as TromaDance director of events Doug Sakmann did in January 2000, and you will also be arrested.* This situation results in nearly every independent filmmaker in Park City circling the same "legal" kiosk, continually stapling their flyers on top of someone else's. On average, you get about three minutes of kiosk time before somebody comes and covers your flyer up.

The threat of incarceration by Park City's finest should not deter you from having flyers and posters made. You will always be able to use these, even after the festival is over. Send them out with copies of your movie to prospective distributors, future investors, and video buyers. The accumulation of these little promotional details will help these people take you seriously.

SEMI-LEGAL WAYS TO GET NOTICED AT FESTIVALS
Adam Jahnke

Filmmaking is an art, a skill, and a business. While you can develop the skill and hone the art independently, there's really no way to learn the business without jumping into the deep end. You can find no better guide to the business than Lloyd Kaufman and Troma. For one thing, you quickly realize that if those morons can make a movie, anybody can. Once I became one of those morons, I discovered that making a movie is at most only half the

*As an experiment for *Troma's Edge TV*, Doug went out in the middle of Times Square and shouted, "Robert Redford can suck my cock" repeatedly through a bullhorn. No arrests were made, leading us to believe that Park City is the only town in America where this sentence is verboten.

battle. There are thousands of independent features lying unseen next to their makers' VCRs. Once the movie's made, you have to get it noticed. On the first full day of the Cannes Film Festival, Lloyd hectored . . . I mean, inspired me with the following tips on making your movie stand out from the crowd. Fortunately for the readers of this book, upon the advice of Troma alumni like James Gunn and Trent Haaga, I began taping all my conversations with Lloyd about two days after I started working for him. What follows is a transcript of our conversation in Cannes.

LLOYD KAUFMAN: Adam! Adam Junkie!* Wake up! It's time to get going!

ADAM JAHNKE: Lloyd, it's four in the morning. And what the fuck are you doing in my sleeping bag?

LK: Just, uh . . . making sure you're comfortable.

AJ: Yeah, right. That's a first. I still don't see why I couldn't have had a bed until the other volunteers get here.

LK: Oh, no no, you don't want to get used to that kind of thing. You'll go soft. Anyway, get up. We've got a lot of ground to cover today.

AJ: OK, OK. What's up?

LK: We've got to start getting the leaflets out. Slide one leaflet under the door of every room in every hotel along the Croisette. And hurry, before these nasty fat ponytailed fuckers start to come out of their drunken stupor. By 9 A.M., I want everyone in Cannes to have seen the title *Citizen Toxie: The Toxic Avenger Part IV* at least once.

---

*Ever since I met him, Lloyd has had an annoying habit of mispronouncing my last name in this way (the correct pronunciation is "jang-key"). He also had an annoying habit of biting his fingernails, spitting them into my coffee cup, then insisting that I not waste money and finish my coffee. I've asked him to stop doing that, so I guess I'll live with the mispronounced name.

AJ: Won't I get arrested doing that? Or at least stopped by security?

LK: No, no. You're small and stealthy . . . you'll be able to sneak right past the guards. Besides, this is France, not Utah. Sure, you hand out leaflets during the Park City festivals like TromaDance or Nodance or Lapdance or that other one that got started by that leathery bastard who used to be a movie star . . . Flashdance or something like that . . . sure, you hand out leaflets at any of those and you'll get your ass tossed in the clink. Like (Troma employee) Doug (Sakmann) was at last year's TromaDance. And that's not such a bad thing either. "Troma Employee Busted For Promoting Independent Cinema!" You can't buy that kind of publicity! But you shouldn't have to worry about that here. Just stay off of the guards' radar. You don't want to get tossed in the Bastille and have nothing to live on but wine dregs and stale croissants.

AJ: Gotcha. Speaking of which, what's for breakfast?

LK: Wine dregs and stale croissants. Anything you find on the room service trays in the hall is fair game. You should be happy you're up so early. You get first pick.

AJ: Swell. So after I leaflet the Croisette and eat other people's table leavings, then what?

LK: First parade of the day at 10 A.M. We should have about forty Troma volunteers here by then, so get 'em organized and dressed up like Toxie and Sgt. Kabukiman NYPD and Killer Condom Man and go marching up and down la rue with the big Troma picket signs. Use the megaphone and for god's sake, keep saying Troma and the name of the movie. They've got to keep hearing the title. *"Citizen Toxie!! Citizen Toxie!!"*

(At this point, Trent Haaga, apparently roused by Lloyd's chanting of the words "Citizen Toxie," woke up as if suffering from a horrible nightmare and joined the conversation.)

TRENT HAAGA: *Citizen Toxie!! Citizen Toxie!!*

LK: Good morning, Trent. Sleep well?

TH: Yeah, I always sleep well on a cold marble floor. What the fuck's going on?

LK: I'm just giving Adam here the drill on today's events.

AJ: You got any pearls of wisdom to drop in here? After all, you're the big writer/co-star of the movie.

TH: Yeah, right. So I make a couple of Troma films and now, years later, I get to bask in the glory of being a bona fide writer and movie star. Lloyd here invites me to come to the beautiful French Riviera for sixteen days and nights at the Cannes Film Festival. Where the stars gather, where the beaches are topless, and every hotel room is a deluxe suite with a hot tub and a sauna, right?

AJ: I'm pretty sure you're gonna tell me that it's wrong.

TH: Wrong with a capital what the fuck are you thinking! If making a movie is like going to war, then Cannes is guerrilla terrorism. Your odds of getting arrested while promoting your film, be it at Cannes, Sundance, or any other festival, are ten times greater than getting arrested for shooting a film.

LK: True, but the cops usually tend to zero in on the costumed characters, so you should be in no danger. That's why we try to put European volunteers who speak French in the costumes and we always have a lot of volunteers. The trick in Cannes is numbers. Numbers get noticed. The big studios are content to just slap a hundred-foot billboard across the front of the hotel and call it good. And sure, everybody and their Seeing Eye dog stumbles across the billboard but the billboard doesn't move around and it doesn't make noise. We can. It's a festival, right? So be festive! Call so much attention to yourself out there that nobody even notices the billboards anymore. Of course, at smaller festivals you don't need as many people. If you're an independent filmmaker and you've got a movie screening at the Ainsworth Film Festival in Nebraska, you can probably recruit four or five friends or film students to come and help you get the word out. We get most of our volunteers through our Web site, www.troma.com. That's what's great about the Internet. Anybody can build a site to promote their movie, get the word out, stream trailers, recruit like-minded volunteers or whatever. Have you seen some of these things on the web, Adam? They're amazing.

AJ: Yeah, Lloyd, I know how the Internet works. So we're out on the Croisette doing the parade. Any suggestions for what we should do other than shout the name of the movie through the megaphone?

TH: That megaphone's broken, by the way. You're just gonna have to scream at the top of your lungs. And all that parade activity will attract street urchins from miles away, so you're gonna have to beat them off of the Tromettes, so they don't become traumatized from being groped by dirty French kids. And that beautiful, romantic sun that's just rising out there? By noon, it'll be like a flamethrower, burning us all to a crisp.

LK: Yeah, good point, Trent. Be sure to wear sunblock out there. But as for your question, Adam, you can't just do the same thing every day or people will get used to you. So you've got to keep topping yourself out there, doing different stunts and coming up with different ways to attract the media. Every single entertainment media outlet in the world is here right now and everybody's vying for their attention. But if you do something outrageous or visually interesting enough, you can always pull crews from E! or Canal Plus or MTV away from the boring Miramax red carpet to support some truly independent cinema. Naked women and dousing yourself in a bucket of fake blood is always good. It's also a good idea to recreate the more exciting scenes from the movies out on the Croisette. We had Yaniv Sharon recreate his thrilling naked run from *Terror Firmer* here once. I told him he had to be running around naked for five minutes and then every five minutes he could run over to the trash can and pull out a *Terror Firmer* mini-poster to cover his privates.

AJ: Now what do you want me to do with all these global warming and recycling press releases you made me write?

LK: Well, another way Troma calls attention to itself is by making fun of current events. We hold mock press conferences and demonstrations and things to sort of warp the world so that everything has to do with whatever movie we're promoting. So for instance, when EuroDisney opened over here, we came to Cannes as EuroTroma. So that global warming press release is a perfect excuse to get some Tromettes to take their clothes off out there. It usually isn't too difficult for us to reflect current events and hot topics, since our movies always touch on major issues. *Citizen Toxie* deals with abortion, school shootings, racism . . .

AJ: Not to mention the growing threat of alternate universes.

LK: Indeed. In the fullness of time, Troma will most likely be seen as a trailblazer for alerting the world to this danger.

AJ: Okay, so we've got leaflets under every door, windshield wiper, and Perrier bottle in Cannes. People have heard the name *Citizen Toxie* so often it haunts their dreams. And we've got the

Toxic Avenger, Kabukiman, and the rest of the guys and Tromettes running around either naked or covered in gore commenting on issues of the day.

LK: So far, so good.

AJ: So are we ever gonna show the movie or what?

LK: Oh, yeah. Very important to do something like that. Now with Troma, we've got a twenty-eight year track record, a rabidly loyal fan base, and a recognizable brand name, so we'll probably get a few asses in seats tonight. But if you're just starting out, it can be a lot more difficult to make people actually sit down and watch your movie. You can promote the hell out of it, trumpet your genius to the heavens, and ensure that everybody knows the name of your movie, but if nobody comes to see it, you're basically screwed. And while I'm against the whole preening Hollywood star system, even I have to admit that having a recognizable name in your movie does add some legitimacy to it. You can get people who are recognizable without selling out to the star system. There are a lot of genuinely good, talented people with some measure of celebrity that will lend their name in support of a project they believe in. I was in a movie called *The Tunnel* made by a guy named Ramzi Abed. Ramzi got both myself and Mark Borchardt from *American Movie* to appear in his movie. And Ramzi is now in touch with David Lynch and Penelope Spheeris, in part because my support of his project suggested to them that maybe this guy has some talent. So if Ramzi can get his film seen by using a universally despised nonactor like me, think what somebody can do if they're able to use a genuinely talented performer like Ron Jeremy or Julie Strain . . . both of whom are in *Citizen Toxie*, by the way.

AJ: I know. I've seen it. What exactly does that have to do with Troma promoting *Citizen Toxie* at Cannes?

LK: Well . . . nothing, really. But it's interesting, don't you think?

AJ: Yeah, why not. So the movie wraps up around eight or so. Is that it? We're done for the day?

LK: Just getting started. After the movie, it's time to hit the parties!

AJ: We're not invited to any parties.

LK: I've got your invitation right here. Press passes!

AJ: Lloyd, this is a press pass for the *Troma Times*.

LK: Which is a legitimate newsletter! I wouldn't encourage anyone to blatantly lie . . . just stretch the truth a little bit. And, you'll see here, we've each got two (*see illustration*). This one has my real name and picture on it and this is the one to try first. But if this doesn't get me in, I'll try this one.

AJ: Gerard Depardieu?

LK: Yeah, the French just wave you in with one of these babies. Here's one for you.

AJ: This says I'm supposed to be Lance Bass from *NSync. Nobody's going to believe that.

LK: Sure they will. Later on, when we have some privacy, I'll coach you on how to act just like Lance.

AJ (WHISPERED TO TRENT): Do not leave me alone with him on this trip.

LK: Besides, the press pass is laminated! Lamination is the key. Dress nice and act like a bigshot and you'll have no problems. If it doesn't work, find a TV crew, pick up a cable and follow them inside. Once you're in, head straight for the buffet because by then you'll probably have worked off whatever energy you got from this morning's hallway scavenger hunt. After you've eaten, drink all the free booze you can. I like to replace the pockets of my suit jacket with sandwich baggies so I can fill them up with canapes and liquor, too. And keep handing out flyers and talking up the movie. *Citizen Toxie*!! *Citizen Toxie*!! Get it?

AJ: Got it.

LK: Good. Now what the hell are you still doing here? Get out there and get those leaflets under the doors! Time's wasting!

AJ: All right already, I'm going! Would you *please* get out of my sleeping bag?

LK: Fine. Trent, give Adam a pep talk while I go try to scrounge up some coffee dregs for us from the hall.

(Lloyd leaves the room.)

AJ: Jesus fucking Christ. Is this gonna be as hellacious as I think?

TH: Worse. I know what you were thinking. You'll get to meet all kinds of famous people and check out topless beaches, right? Fuck that. Last time, I didn't meet or see one "famous" person while at Cannes. And topless French girls are hard to pick up when Dolphin Man and The Killer Condom dog your every step. And those press passes are a joke, and not a very funny one. We didn't get into any "good" parties (i.e., parties with free food). We just ended up pissing off the doormen instead. I don't even drink and yet felt hung over every morning.

AJ: So what's the point? I mean, does all of this yelling, provocation, and quasi-legal promotion work in the long run?

TH: A couple of years ago I went to a friend's wedding. I ended up being seated at a table with a bunch of people I didn't know. The conversation got around to what we did for a living. I said I worked on low-budget horror movies.

"Oh yeah? What kind?"

"Ever heard of *The Toxic Avenger*?"

I got the usual clueless smile.

"Well, he's a mutant superhero. I work for the company who created Toxie. It's called Troma."

"Troma?"

"Yeah."

"Hey! I know you guys! You're the ones with that stupid guy who looks like Mel Brooks with the ugly socks and the bow ties! You guys are on the E! channel all the time!" So there you have it. After all the hell of making the movies and the hell of promoting the movies, all you need is a paisley bow tie to get your work noticed.

You will also probably want to get your movie reviewed at the festival. While there are outlets like *Film Threat* who will review truly independent movies, if you've got your eyes on a personality like Roger Ebert,* you're in for an uphill fight. It's been our experience that unless a kabillion dollars is spent on advertising (which only the major studios and their vassals can afford), Ebert doesn't review or bother to see independent movies. One of our fans wrote Ebert a letter once asking why he hadn't reviewed such Troma movies as Dario Argento's *The Stendhal Syndrome.* His response was that *Stendhal* hadn't played in Chicago and it was Troma's own fault for being such piss-poor distributors.

---

*Roger Ebert, of course, is the dipshit critic whose partner, Gene Siskel, died of a brain tumor, possibly brought on by Ebert's inane yammering. Ebert's only legitimate claim to fame is the screenplay to the Russ Meyer classic, *Beyond the Valley of the Dolls.*

PLANET CANNES
Sonya Schultz

For years, Troma has attracted a brigade of volunteers from around the world at film festivals, conventions, and bail hearings. One of the most coveted positions on the Troma Team is that of Tromette—women with very large minds and very small clothing. At Cannes 2001, Sonya Schultz traveled from her home in Berlin to become an official Tromette.

One afternoon in Berlin. A girl is sitting on a balcony. She is surrounded by empty coffee mugs and chocolate bar wrappers. Her feet rest on two piles of books from the library, most of them long overdue. The girl is balancing a small computer on her knees. She is supposed to write something for her university. Instead, she has been staring at the Windows screensaver for forty-five minutes now. Then she reaches for another chocolate bar and stuffs it into her mouth. The telephone rings. The girl gets up and picks up the phone:

"Mmmmph?"—"Hey, Sonja, you okay?"—"Mmmh!"—"I see . . . Are you still working on that paper about gender roles in Julia Roberts movies?"—"Yethh . . ."—"Listen, switch on the TV! This will cheer you up! On that cultural channel there's a feature about this really independent New York film company. You got it? I think you can learn a lot by studying their business strategies, besides there's lots of tits . . ."

I got that channel. This was my first contact with Troma Entertainment. And while the sweet chocolate melted inside of me, I knew I discovered something special.

After that I developed crazy dirty fantasies containing the Tromettes. I still have these. But there was something else. The people at that New York company actually seemed to have fun doing what they did. And they had a philosophy. Surprisingly that philosophy was not: "Make money, make more money, make a Julia Roberts movie!" but: "Don't make compromises—make true independent art!" I wanted to get to know these people. I wanted to support them in exchange for some of their energy. Because what I had seen on TV that afternoon was more energetic than my whole two years of film studies had been.

When I read on the Troma Web site that volunteers for the Cannes film festival were needed I applied immediately. It was a chance to meet the Troma team and experience the *other* side of Cannes. They told me I could come. They told me I would get some floor space to sleep on. So I bought an airline ticket. All volunteers had to pay for the trip and their food themselves. But it was worth it. And—you know—eating isn't that important. I want you to close your eyes, so I can tell you more about Troma's mission at Cannes. And about the side effects. Maybe you might want to go there sometime. Relax.

Imagine the Côte d'Azur in May . . . beautiful warm weather . . . and Cannes, a lovely French town by the sea with a population of 70,000—most of them friendly old people with baguettes for walking sticks who always say "merci" and "s'il vous plait." Now imagine the Croisette, the main strip at Cannes, with the small beaches next to the promenade, the palm trees . . . and then the Carlton. It's located in the center of La Croisette and that's what they say in their catalogue:

A unique hotel where hospitality, coupled with courtesy and the treasured art of discretion, reign supreme. Boasting panoramic views of the Bay of Cannes, the Carlton International provides the perfect setting together with the perfect luxury experience.

You get the picture? Now imagine the Carlton, the Croisette, the whole town plastered with advertisements for the stupidest movies ever. There are overdimensional posters for such masterpieces as *Josie and the Pussycats* next to every palm tree. The time-honored Carlton Hotel, opened in 1912, is covered in propaganda for Jean Claude Van Damme's new piece of art: *The Monk*. He is wearing a hare-krishna sheet, mediating, and fighting.

Welcome to the Cannes Film Festival—Europe's most important film event. For 2001 the logo is a man with the globe for his head. And in the small garden of the Carlton there is another big billboard with an appropriate interpretation of this. In stiff typewritten letters it says:

RULE THE PLANET.
The Planet of the Apes. Our Planet.

Those that rule Cannes are the advertising agencies, the big film studios, the mega-moviemakers, the ones with the most money and the crappiest films. Everybody is trying to sell the glamour. Worship the surface! You have to, because there's nothing underneath it. Shut up, smile and sell.

This is what the mainstream film business does. They rule the planet.

This is what the Troma Team does: they happily sing, scream, and puke. Their dresses are stupid looking stinky costumes or bare flesh, their makeup is made of the fake blood and real sweat they give for Troma's sake. They make fools out of themselves in public and they do it proudly. Because deep down they know that this is what Hollywood is trying to do to them anyway. The

Troma spirit leads you under the surface of things. Troma knows the cleansing powers of puke and blood, slime and shit. These—plus sex, violence, and stupid jokes—are the weapons against Hollywood and their planet of apes.

Each year Lloyd Kaufman and his company pay an enormous sum to rent a suite on the Carlton's first floor so the Troma Sales Office is located next to Paramount, Universal Pictures, and all the others. Someone told me that Troma gets that suite every time only because Lloyd has been friends with the hotel manager for quite a while. And because he speaks French *fluently*. I guess you and I both know what that means . . .

But at the end it's a small sacrifice when you are fighting for the independent way of life, isn't it?

Another important part of Troma's activities at Cannes are the volunteers. Troma has what other film companies don't have: fans. People who are willing to work for Troma and show their breasts on the streets (or what they have instead) without getting paid, without getting credits, without getting fed. The volunteers come from all over the world. They are film students, unemployed would-be writers, waiters, and waitresses whose leisure-time activity is shooting black-and-white horror films; there are some lunatics and some sincere young people that want to support Troma, experience the festival, meet other independent filmmakers or live out their exhibitionism.

And that's exactly what made me join the group: The spirit of independent art taking hold of my heart! . . . and maybe a tiny bit of exhibitionism.

Each day the stinky Troma movie characters led by Sgt. Kabukiman and the Toxic Avenger arm themselves with flyers, signs, whistles, megaphones, stickers, and special invitations for nice looking people and on a good day a bucket or two full of shit or chicken innards—depending on the occasion. Trimmed like this, the Troma Team parades up and down the Croisette. On their way they only stop to rip off an arm now and then, give interviews and help blind grannies cross the street. The aim is to gain as much publicity as possible for the Troma screenings at Cannes—and it works. The parades are equivalent to a multimillion-dollar ad campaign. They are supposed to attract interested buyers that might want to bring Troma movies to other territories throughout the world. After that they can proceed to the serious part and enter into business negotiations at the office down the Carlton. Or they can just try to get as many free DVDs and Troma baseball caps as possible because they love this stuff. But that's part of the business, too, I guess.

If you come to Troma's Carlton office at the wrong time you might at first think you are visiting a company just like any other on that floor. Then you might notice the group of Japanese businessmen gathering in the hallway staring into the room in a state of rapture. Their eyes widen as they watch the Troma promotion video on the TV inside and when the screaming begins a tender smile appears on their faces. You might wonder why there are always so many hotel security guys passing by the office mumbling into their headsets. And maybe you even witness the end of a parade. There's a racket downstairs. The very important people in the lobby try to ignore the head-high flesh-colored condom stuck in the revolving door at the entrance. Other members of the promotion team are already in and head upstairs. Still outside are the ones that are covered in blood or shit and are stopped by the security staff. It's really a pity: if the glamour inside and the shit outside would be allowed to mix, it could be an inspiration for both. But who cares for inspiration if you can have that "luxury experience" instead. And remember: "hospitality" is always for those who pay.

In short these are the two frontlines at Cannes and in general. The best strategy to be a real nuisance to your enemies is to have more fun than they can ever have. If they rule the planet—at least you can rule the party. Make it an orgy. Make sure that they see. After all, Troma is what pulsates under Hollywood's perfect skin. And most people can't stand to see their own blood and guts. But you and I know that blood means life.

If the notion of parading around Cannes in either a bizarre costume or no costume at all turns you on and now you want to be an independent artist yourself, there are several things you should bear in mind:

- Do not expect to make any money.
- Make art!
- Always be open and devoted toward the things that happen to you. They might expand your mind.
- Life is too short to pretend you are cool.
- Do not be afraid of real emotions!
- Exploit yourself and exploit the others. But make sure they get some love and respect in return.
- Never fake an orgasm.
- Take good care of your friends. You will need them.
- Someday you will have to tell your mother. Be kind.
- But for now: start working. Out of the closet and onto the screens!

Now go out there and make the world a little more independent.

DOIN' TIME FOR INDEPENDENT CINEMA
Doug Sakmann

Besides production and pleasuring Lloyd with my sweet lips, a big part of my job here is marketing and promotion, which is why I've been asked to contribute something to this part of the book. I wanted to write something about pleasuring Lloyd but Adam and Trent explained to me that since it's so damn easy, there's no real point in writing anything about that.

Every year, there are two major film markets where Troma goes to promote our independent art. The Cannes Film Festival (in Cannes, France) and the TromaDance Film Festival (in Park City, Utah, during Sundance). Being European, the folks at Cannes are slightly more amenable to the Aroma du Troma than the Park City crew. Cannes has its problems, though. In 2001, I ran around yelling a lot and dousing myself in fake blood, including the place where our offices were, the Carlton Intercontinental Hotel. At the Carlton, I spit a little bit of blood on the wall and floor, which washed right out. Because of that, I was not allowed into the Carlton twice in 2001, was strangled by the Carlton security, got charged over $1000 in blood damages, and this year we are not allowed back into the Carlton at all. We get a lot of publicity doing things like this but if you don't have a grand to drop on damages or don't want to risk having your neck wrung by security's girlish hands, I'd try to avoid spilling blood, fake or otherwise, in the lobby of any luxury hotels.

On the other hand, it is my belief from my experiences in Park City that Robert Redford and his Sundance goons are running Park City like a Nazi war camp. Even though Robert Redford has not been too involved directly with the Park City events in recent years and sightings of him during Sundance are about as common as Bigfoot, Redford is the figurehead who represents Sundance and its ethos. Sundance is trying to kill real independence and is succeeding to some extent because the truly independent festivals are dropping like flies. The Park City authorities give a list of rules to all independent filmmakers and festivals not affiliated with Sundance. Below are some excerpts from the Park City Rules.

- During the film festival, the exclusive Master Festival License holder is the Sundance Institute.
- Handbills, which are defined as papers, stickers, flyers, posters, pamphlets, or other type of medium distributed by hand for identification, advertisement, or promotion of the interest of any person, entity, product, event, or service, are prohibited by the Park City Municipal Code. Handouts for films and parties are not exempted by the First Amendment regulations and it is a violation of Code when handed outside of a building. (In other words, your First Amendment right is *illegal* in Park City during Sundance.) Please use the City designated kiosks to advertise events and films.

There are three city-designated kiosks. The rest of 'em are owned by Sundance. The result of this is that filmmakers outside the Sundance system all end up fighting for the same three spaces to promote hundreds of different things that are created independently. A lot of festivals and filmmakers are deciding it's just not worth it and dropping out of the Park City scene.

It wasn't always this way. The first year we went to Park City with TromaDance (2000), we had just come up with the concept of TromaDance after seeing what was happening with Sundance. We'd organized the whole thing about three months before going to Park City, so Sundance wasn't prepared to deal with a truly independent film festival like TromaDance. In 2000, we came and promoted TromaDance in grassroots style (with massive amounts of flyers and Troma heroes in the streets) without any problem. Besides TromaDance, there were many different independent films and film festivals, which were being promoted by all types of people, with flyers in hand.

However, after all the truly independent film festivals had converged on Park City in 2000, Sundance realized that true independence was leaking into Park City. Now they had a full year to prepare for it. So when all the film festivals not affiliated with Sundance came back in 2001, they were handed this list of rules specifically for the two weeks that Sundance is in town. All of the indie fests and filmmakers, TromaDance included, didn't really think twice about it, and we went about our business as we did the year previous. However, in my opinion, the Park City Police, whose paychecks are paid for by Sundance's money, were instructed to crack down on independent filmmakers. Myself and a TromaDance volunteer, James Lynch, were arrested for disturbing the peace and handing out leaflets. (See my essays at www.tromadance.com for the full scoop.) Because I work for Troma and not Miramax (or McDonald's for that matter), I couldn't afford bail and got stuck in jail for a couple days. On the upside, while in jail, I got to hang out with a chain gang of illegal aliens on their way to being deported to Mexico, and they taught me the proper way to "wrap a burrito." (We did a dramatic reenactment of this horrible, *Midnight Express* scenario for "Troma's

Edge TV". It can be seen on *The Best of TromaDance* DVD.) As if this wasn't bad enough, we heard from Troma-friendly witnesses that our condo was under surveillance by the "Sundance" authorities, who were apparently itching for any excuse to shut us down.

So after being arrested and fucked with in 2001, we had a full year to study the rules and regulations and retaliate. We came back in 2002 and were able to promote our festival, not be fucked with, and prove that Troma has seen the rise, rape, and deterioration of true independence in Park City. We went back to the place where we were arrested the year before and I recited, at the top of my lungs, the First Amendment. I then went on to explain how Sundance says this is illegal. We made a flyer printed with the First Amendment and handed it out to everyone and put it on all the kiosks. A lot of people agreed with us. Not just filmmakers and festival-goers but also Park City residents who didn't give a shit about movies one way or the other but felt that Sundance was giving them a bad name.

I'm sure you would never find an executive in my position working for Miramax or Disney running through the street shouting the First Amendment, or "Robert Redford can suck my cock." It's a pretty sure bet you would not see people who are employed by Universal crawling around on the sidewalk or foaming at the mouth like a rabid dog (well, not as part of their job, anyway). In my opinion, these corporate studio executives would probably love to do that kind of stuff. However, I doubt their employers would stand for it, as it goes against the status quo. That's part of the charm of working for Troma. (Another big part is hooking up with all the fine foxy ladies.) We are allowed to be artistically and creatively free with whatever we do.

Sure sometimes it may get me in trouble, but I love it, and wouldn't have it other way. Only in Tromaville can one be arrested and strangled while on the job, and still be employed the next day.

In the case of *The Stendhal Syndrome*, we're the first to admit that we're morons who have a hard time distributing a cold. But *Terror Firmer* and *Tromeo & Juliet* played in all national markets, including Chicago. Ebert didn't bother to review any of these movies. Regarding *Stendhal*, Ebert apparently does not find it newsworthy to report that the only way a world-class director like Dario Argento could get his film released uncut in the United States was to give it to Troma. And while *The Stendhal Syndrome* may not have played in Chicago, it definitely opened in Los Angeles and New York. So even if Ebert didn't review *Stendhal* in the *Chicago Sun-Times* (which, frankly, we don't care about 'cause nobody reads his shitty newspaper anymore anyway), there's no reason he shouldn't have reviewed it and every other worthy independent movie to receive a theatrical release on his nationally-syndicated (and, perhaps not coincidentally, Disney-owned) TV show.

Now I don't expect Ebert to go on TV with a big cum-stain on his pants because he thought *Citizen Toxie* was so great it sent him into multiple orgasms. In fact, judging from his taste in films, I'd be surprised if he had a single kind word to say about a Troma movie. What I *do* expect is for him and critics like him to report on the movies that are released. All of them, regardless of corporate parentage or marketing budget. But that seems about as likely to happen as a zombified Gene Siskel returning from the grave to eat Richard Roeper's brains on national television.

Promoting your movie and getting it seen is a lengthy, potentially arduous process, but it's a goal that can be achieved. Grassroots publicity has worked for Troma for years and it continues to, in large part because the major studios are so obsessed with fast food tie-ins and multizillion dollar marketing campaigns they've forgotten how to promote a movie cheaply and efficiently. Independents can get a lot of attention out of no-frills publicity because we're the only ones who are still doing it. And this type of publicity transfers to every situation, whether you're promoting a screening at a film festival, a regular engagement at a cinema, or at a film market. In other words, as I told John Stossel, who was reporting on Troma from Cannes for Disney/ABC's *20/20*, it's a little thing called *showmanship*.

Film festivals and markets are two separate but related beasts. Festivals are exhibition places for films that are selected by the festival's organizing committee. So even festivals that do not give out awards or prizes have an element of competition to them, even if it's only the competition to get accepted. Film markets are exhibition places sort of like conventions for anybody who has the cash to rent a screening venue. Buyers and distributors attend both festivals and markets, but more actual business goes on at the markets than at festivals. Festivals are open to the public as well as to industry people (and, as I've already said, a lot of the movies that screen at major festivals tend to have distribution deals sewn up by the time they get there). Markets tend to be industry-only affairs, with business (usually) taking precedence over skiing, nude sunbathing, and drinking yourself into an unholy stupor.*

Cannes has both a festival and a market going on at the same time, which makes it an ideal place to seek distribution, but there are others that are less well known and equally important. Two of the biggies are

---

* Actually, I take that back. Drinking oneself into an unholy stupor usually takes precedence over everything else in the entertainment industry.

the American Film Market (AFM)* in Santa Monica every February and MIFED,† which is held in the fall in Milan. Independent studios from around the world rent booths and screening venues at these markets to showcase their product and, if you've got the bucks, there's no reason you can't do the same. A filmmaker named Barak Epstein volunteered to work for Troma at Cannes in 2001, learning the ropes and figuring out how the market worked. He then returned to Dallas and made a movie called *Cornman*.‡ In 2002, Barak went back to Cannes on his own. He has rented his own Cannes market (Marché du Film)§ booth and a screening venue and sought global distribution for *Cornman* at the festival. Having learned the Troma way of doing business, Barak will now attempt to do it correctly. Even if you don't go whole-hog and rent office space or screening time, markets are still great places to meet with key distributors and buyers. Get yourself a day pass and you have access to hundreds of potential outlets for your movie.

All the ballyhoo and grassroots publicity in the world will not guarantee that your movie will be distributed. You can get everybody from Disney and Blockbuster to Troma and Bob's Discount Video to watch your movie and if it sucks, they're all going to tell you so. Troma is quite literally the last stop on the distribution train for most people and

* EDITOR'S NOTE: AFM is run by AFMA, the American Film Marketing Association, a trade association of independent entertainment companies. AFMA seeks to do for its members what they cannot do individually. For most companies, this includes things like lobbying local, state, and federal government agencies regarding tax incentives for filming. For Kaufman, this includes things like tying his shoes. Lloyd Kaufman is currently vice chairman of AFMA's board of directors, a further indication of the dire straits independent film is currently in.

†MIFED is presumably an acronym for something unspellable in Italian but their Web site gives absolutely no indication what that might be, so fuck it.

‡Barak asked me to act in this movie, so *Cornman* is another movie to showcase my pathetic abilities as a lesbian . . . I mean, thespian. Incidentally, *Cornman* should not be confused with *Roger Corman*, my proposed biopic tribute to my independent film mentor.

§ Marché du Film—an ancient French phrase from the fourteenth century epic poem *Chanson du Roland*. Roughly translated, it means "I wish to fill your chocolate starfish with marshmallows."

even we pass on a lot more movies than we actually acquire. And sometimes a distributor's reasons for passing on a movie will have nothing to do with the quality of the movie itself. They'll tell you it isn't marketable to their key demographic. They'll tell you they're not currently looking at whatever genre your movie happens to be. They'll tell you their acquisition budget for the year is spent. And a lot of them will tell you they're not interested unless your movie has a name star in it. Right about now you'll be wishing you'd ponied up the extra hundred grand to get Rutger Hauer to make a cameo.

The distribution food chain basically breaks down to four separate options. Now, before we look at these one by one, it's important to understand that a book twice as long as this one could be written just on the subject of distribution and it still wouldn't cover the whole territory. So before we rush into an admittedly rudimentary look at distribution, let's dumb the subject down just a little bit more and look at the pros and cons of each option in handy-dandy chart form (see following page).

THE DISTRIBUTION FOOD CHAIN

Option	What this Means	Pros	Cons
Acquired by Major Distributor (Miramax, Sony Classics, etc.)	A major "independent" distributor gives you a huge advance for the rights to your movie.	You get a shitload of $$$. You get in the door at a major studio and possibly get a deal to make another movie.	You're working with a vassal of a devil-worshipping conglomerate. About as likely to happen as sixteen donkeys farting the national anthem at the Super Bowl.
Acquired by Mid-Level Distributor (Artisan, Lion's Gate, etc.)	An up-and-coming independent distributor offers you a deal for the rights to your movie.	You're working with a legitimately independent company. You are likely to receive some kind of theatrical release.	Mid-level distributors go out of business with more regularity than Joe Fleishaker's bowel movements. Company might become a vassal of a devil-worshipping conglomerate. In either case, your movie is likely to get swallowed by the cracks.
Acquired by Small Distributor (Troma, Roger Corman)	One of the few remaining, small distributors offers you a deal for the rights to your movie.	Companies are well established and are not going to vanish overnight.* Might actually meet Roger Corman.	You would make more money by working for a week at Burger Barn. Might actually meet Lloyd Kaufman.
You Distribute the Damn Thing Yourownself	You book theatrical screenings and/or sell videotapes directly to consumers.	You are in complete control and maintain total independence. Any money you make goes directly to you.	The cost of making prints and duplicating videos is entirely yours. A fuck of a lot of work falls on your shoulders and yours alone.

*Troma might be exempted from this particular "pro." Speaking of pros, if you're in Cannes and are looking for pros, Monique and her transsexual friends come highly recommended and can be found on any given evening out in front of the Hotel Grey D'Albion.

The first, most desirable option is to have your movie picked up by one of the five or six giant, so-called "independent" distributors that are owned by big conglomerates like Disney, AOL/Time-Warner, or Viacom. You might think it's hypocritical of me to call this the most desirable option but from a purely economic viewpoint, it makes perfect sense. I mean, who doesn't want to win the lottery? An interviewer once asked Jerry Garcia why the Grateful Dead never sold out. His reply was, "We've been willing to sell out for a number of years but nobody's been buying." That's kind of Troma's philosophy, too. We're certainly not against making money . . . we're just not used to it.

The primary drawback to selling your movie to one of these companies is that you're going to be entering the homogenized, corporate world of the mainstream. This is not in and of itself an awful thing. Trey Parker, James Gunn, Jon Voight, and John Avildsen all work squarely within the confines of the mainstream and they're some of the greatest people I've ever met. You're not going to burn in movie hell if you happen to make a lot of money and win Academy Awards.* The mainstream is going to exist with or without you, so the best you can hope for is to get in there and be a good influence on it, like Trey Parker or James Gunn. If Disney offers you a fistful of dollars and you think you can take the money with all the strings attached and not let the huge corporate bureaucracy get to you, then take it by all means.

One thing to watch out for when signing with the big boys is the backend deal, so named because the filmmaker usually ends up taking it in the backend. A major distributor will probably offer you either a big advance or a small advance plus a percentage of whatever the movie makes. This percentage will either be gross points or net points. Gross points are not how critics like Joe Bob Briggs estimate the worth of Troma movies. They are what are given to people like Tom Hanks on a

---

* The only way to burn in movie hell is to make a truly hideous piece of shit like *A.I.* or decapitate Vic Morrow and a couple Asian kids with a helicopter while making a big-budget movie version of an old TV show.

regular basis. Your percentage kicks in the second the first dollar comes in. Net points, or "monkey points" as they are also called, are virtually worthless. Your percentage kicks in once your movie starts making a profit and, according to the creative accounting Hollywood studios use, no movie has ever made a profit in the history of the medium. So don't think you just got a great deal if the studio offered you an armload of net points, 'cause odds are good you're never going to see a penny of it.

Option two is to sell your movie to one of the mid-level distributors. On the surface, this may seem like the best of both worlds. You get to maintain the street cred of independence while enjoying the free-flowing cash that young up-and-coming companies invariably throw around like so much used Kleenex. But you should be very, very careful before agreeing to option two. Mid-level distributors declare bankruptcy and go out of business with shocking regularity. It's no coincidence that this chapter on distribution is Chapter 11. Orion, Canon, Carolco, Live, Vestron, Cinema Shares, and Shooting Gallery were all major players in this arena at one time and now they're all history.

The death throes of each of these companies are long, complex, and of interest mainly to chartered accountants and students of poorly run businesses. But essentially, each of these companies becomes smothered in bank debt over the years. They borrow millions to get their companies up and running, so much that even the interest on the loan is more than they can bear. They will promise filmmakers a lot of money and never pay it, assuming that the filmmaker will be too intimidated by the goliath bank that controls the studio to ever call them on it. Eventually, however, the bank comes calling and nine times out of ten, the studio can't afford to pay back the loan and the studio disappears.* Hundreds, if not

---

* One exception to this might be the remarkable run Menahem Golan and Yoram Globus enjoyed with Canon Films. By leveraging debt and fucking around with numbers, they were able to create a relatively long-lived studio and acquire a library of movies that rivaled the major studios. They also managed to produce the greatest number of shit movies in the history of cinema. Inevitably, Canon fell apart but it lasted for a surprisingly long time, even landing Golan and Globus on the cover of *Newsweek*, a position that has never been occupied by Herz and Kaufman.

thousands, of movies have basically vanished from the face of the earth because they had the misfortune to be scheduled for release at the same time their distributors folded their tents and called it a day. Now if one of the few remaining companies in this category like Artisan or Lion's Gate offers you an advance, you're probably okay. But I would not advise anyone to sign a deal based on back-end profits with a mid-level distributor. There's just too great a risk that the company will disappear before your movie comes out.

The next stop is one of the very small distributors and these days, that basically boils down to Troma or Roger Corman's company New Concorde. Here, you don't have to worry about the company disappearing in a miasma of bank debt. Troma's been around for thirty years. We have no bank debt. We own the Troma Building in New York free and clear. We're not going anywhere,* no matter how badly our critics might want us to.

The bad news is that in this present cartel-controlled environment, you'll make little or no money. At least, that's the case with Troma. You'll receive a tough but fair deal, perhaps, with a very, very small amount of good faith money up front. But your movie will be released on VHS and DVD and, if nothing else, you'll have a calling card with your movie on it to show people in the future.

But the biggest misconception first-time filmmakers have about distribution is that you have to go big to make any money. If your movie isn't in Blockbuster, you've failed. In fact, there's no reason that you can't distribute your movie yourself if you're willing to absorb the costs of creating prints and duplicating videos. Frank Zappa distributed his own music and, for years, Russ Meyer has distributed his films himself out of his house with the aid of a giant-breasted assistant.

For theatrical distribution, you can do exactly what Troma does and

---

* Well . . . at least, Corman isn't going anywhere.

approach independent theater owners yourself. There is a dwindling but extremely vital number of independents out there who are willing to deal with big studios, tiny studios, and filmmakers themselves and whose only criterion for showing a movie is the quality of the film itself. Laemmle and Landmark Theater chains are both willing to book movies from any source as long as they're good. And besides these, there are plenty of individual movie theaters you can deal with. The Music Box in Chicago, the Royal Oak in Detroit, the Alamo Drafthouse in Austin, the Heights in Minneapolis, Coolidge Corner Theater in Boston, the Times Cinema in Milwaukee, the Bloor Cinema in Toronto, the Two Boots Pioneer Theater in New York, and Jumbo's Clown Room in Los Angeles are all great theaters that are more than happy to book any good movie that comes their way, no matter how it gets to them.*

With video distribution, it gets a little trickier but it is still not insurmountable. Some of the larger video chains like Tower and Virgin are reticent to deal with individuals who have just a single movie to sell them, so you might need someone with an existing relationship at these chains to get in. And it's still fairly expensive to produce DVDs with all the packaging. On the other hand, Scott Beiben of the Lost Film Fest Collective says that collectives of filmmakers are being formed that pool their resources in order to mass-produce and sell DVDs. If you can get in on something like this, it might be a viable option. Otherwise, you're looking at least at an additional couple grand to get your movie on DVD.

If you've managed to keep your budget low enough, you can bypass the entire traditional distribution system altogether and sell your movie direct to consumers. Set up a Web site and sell directly to consumers through that. The back pages of *Fangoria* are full of tiny ads taken out by guys who've made a movie and are selling it copy by copy to anyone

---

* Sorry . . . Jumbo's Clown Room isn't actually a movie theater. It's a legitimate performing arts space, exploring the frontiers of erotic dance. They won't book your movie but on any given weekday afternoon, you'll probably find most of the Troma West staff hanging out there.

curious enough to shell out $14.95. Are you going to get rich doing this? Probably not. But if your budget is low, you can make enough to defray the cost of making the movie and earn enough to make another one. And if you're passionate about filmmaking, that should be all you really want to do anyway.

The simple fact is if you have a good movie, someday, somewhere, you will sell it. Whether you sell it to a studio, a foreign distributor, or to individual movie fans from a table at a comic book convention, you will sell it. You might sell it immediately or you might sell it several years down the road. That's one of the real pluses in filmmaking. Movies don't have expiration dates. The movie that you make today might not be appreciated until much later. *Combat Shock*, directed by Buddy Giovinazzo, was reviled when it was first released back in 1986. In the fullness of time, it has come to be appreciated as a mini-masterpiece and one of the truly great films in the Troma library.

The odds are against your getting rich off your first movie, but if you entered into this process hoping to make a lot of money, you've completely missed the point. Independent filmmakers should first and foremost be artists and storytellers who firmly believe there is no greater way to express oneself than through the combination of moving pictures and sound. If you don't truly love movies, you shouldn't bother putting yourself through the hell of trying to make one. You will make a bad, indifferent movie and the world is already stuffed full of those as it is. But if you have an idea for a movie and it eats at you day and night, setting you on fire with the urge to see it on screen, don't let anything stop you from making your movie.

If you're really lucky, everything will come together and a strange magic will occur. For Troma, the magic came together on *The Toxic Avenger*. This is a movie that not one theater was willing to show at first. But we didn't give up on it. I knew when we were filming that something great was going to happen with this movie. Kids would come up to Toxie on the street while we were filming. They didn't know who or what this thing with the mop was supposed to be. All

Doug Sakmann displays the length of the nightstick that we believe was shoved up his ass by the Park City cops after he was arrested for passing out flyers at the TromaDance Film Festival. (Zafer Ulkucu)

they knew was that they loved him. Eventually, we broke through and managed to get one small theater to play *The Toxic Avenger.** On opening day, there were lines around the block. Word had spread somehow and people felt they had to come see this strange, unprecedented horror/comedy/erotic/superhuman hero† movie.

This magic has spread around the world. Once, I was in Venice for a festival. At the time, we were shooting a DVD "interactive adven-

---

* This theater was the historic Bleecker Street Cinema in Greenwich Village, now unfortunately defunct. Jackie Raynal, the legendary filmmaker and owner of Bleecker Street Cinema, was an oddity amongst theater owners in that she genuinely loved movies and actually bothered to watch the movies she programmed for her theater. Jackie watched *The Toxic Avenger* and got it. She realized that it was a comedy, a minor point that had eluded most of the other theater bookers up to that point.

† By the way, we are required to use the term "superhuman hero" because the word "superhero" is jointly owned by Marvel and DC Comics. When Marvel was publishing *The Toxic Avenger* and *Toxic Crusaders* comic books, Toxie was a superhero. The second that licensing agreement expired, he was kicked out of the *Super Friends* or whatever the fuck superhero club is allowed to use the term "superhero."

ture" showing Toxie in all these exotic locations around the globe called "Where In the World is Toxie?" In Venice, I didn't really have a big guy to be Toxie so I made my eleven-year-old daughter Charlotte throw on the mask for a few pictures while we were floating along in a gondola. As we went under the bridges, people gathered and recognized Toxie and started calling his name. Sure, Charlotte was confused and possibly traumatized, but I was overjoyed. The same thing happened in Paris, with locals shouting, "Toxique!" whenever we passed by. This is the kind of magic that studios can't buy, no matter how much money they toss into the publicity machine.

For all the frustration and difficulty it presents, I believe that making movies is the greatest feeling on earth. It's like taking a really satisfying dump and having the best sex of your life all rolled into one. That's why when I'm on the set I often say, "Shitfuck!" The Troma Team knows when they hear me say "shitfuck," I'm the happiest man in the world.

Epilogue

The Big Emotional Spielberg Ending

Back in New York, sitting at my desk alone in the Troma Building. It's late on a Friday night and all the Troma employees have either gone home or passed out at their desks. Once again, it's been a piss-poor day. *Citizen Toxie* has become a major success, with theaters calling from across the country to book the movie. Of course, in the world of independent cinema, a "major success" is relative. Most "major successes" in the film world are movies that gross over $100 million and play for months theatrically. In Troma, a major success is a movie that plays at more than one theater, usually for about two or three days. And even this paltry release seems to be beyond our capabilities. Because we can't afford to make more than seventeen prints, we're double-booking *Citizen Toxie* left and right, pissing off theaters, media, and promotional partners from sea to shining sea. Only Troma could instantly turn a hit movie into a major scheduling disaster. We're getting some good reviews when we can get it reviewed at all. But for every bit of unexpected praise we get from papers like *The New York Times*, there are half a dozen major players like the *Los Angeles Times* that ignore the movie completely.

At the same time, we've been working on getting money for our next movie. We have two projects in development: *Saving Private Toxie:*

The Toxic Avenger V and a Troma zombie movie about fast food tenta- tively titled *Poultry Geist.* My preference would be to do the zombie movie, so of course the potential investors have shown considerably more interest in the Toxie sequel. But interest isn't the same as investors, so right now, we have absolutely nothing in the pipeline and even if we did, we don't have anything even remotely close to a filmable script for either project.

In fact, the only thing we're working on is the DV Dogpile 95* fea- ture *Tales From the Crapper.* We've been working on this fucking thing for what seems like an eternity now. So much for Trent's big theory that shooting on video is faster and more efficient. On one of my last visits to Los Angeles, we shot a significant amount of additional footage. The new scenes were funny, controversial, and, according to the editors, completely superfluous. Sean McGrath and Brian McNulty, who are editing the films, were extremely pissed off at me for shooting a bunch of shit with rabbit-fucking and people dancing in Osama bin Laden masks instead of the simple inserts and establishing shots they actually need to finish the goddamn stories.

We also received news from Canada that Rod Gudino, the editor- in-chief of *Rue Morgue* magazine, took it upon himself to phone up the Bravo television network in Canada to encourage them to program some Troma films. He didn't get far, though. The acquisitions person at Bravo told Rod that Bravo won't deal with Troma "on principle." So somehow the Troma name has stigmatized over 950 movies, including films starring Sissy Spacek, Robert De Niro, and Dustin Hoffman, and

---

* Dogpile 95 is the Troma equivalent of the Dogme 95 film movement launched by Lars von Trier. Dogme is supposed to be kind of a vow of cinematic purity, using only available, natural lighting, employing nonprofessional actors, shooting handheld, and producing only dull, incomprehensible movies that nobody wants to see. Troma, of course, has been following most of these rules (except for the last one) for years. We just didn't realize we could build a whole movement around it. The main difference between Dogpile and Dogme is a filmmaker must pay a fee to submit his film for Dogme certification. Anybody who's willing to get lumped in with Troma can slap a Dogpile tag on his or her movie.

also films directed by Trey Parker, Brian De Palma, and John G. Avild-sen. Just by being associated with me, I have prevented these people's films from being shown on Canadian television. I can't imagine what principle we've violated to prevent Bravo from showing these movies but it must have been something truly horrendous.

It seems that a lot of people refuse to be associated with Troma "on principle." The Tromadu sequence in *Citizen Toxie* was shot at the Playboy Mansion at a cost of $25,000 for the day. While we were there, we shot a tiny cameo appearance by Hugh Hefner himself. A few months later, we received a letter from Hef's lawyers threatening us with litigation unless we cut Hefner out of the picture. Apparently he was concerned that his squeaky clean image would be compromised by appearing in a Troma film. I guess our money was good, but our movies were not. Not only that, but we offered a role to porn star Jenna Jameson, who, I was informed, flat-out refused to have anything to do with the movie once she read the script. Apparently having a stranger's cum dribble out of your engorged asshole is more respect-able than appearing for five minutes in a Troma film.*

8/11/02
RE: "Epilogues"
Dear Mr. Kaufman,
It's Andrew, the British bloke, here again from page 213. I write in urgency to denounce the allegation that I went through your bag while you were staying with me in September of 2001! Nat-urally, I refute your every implication. It was my brother.

So far the book has been an invaluable source of information

* EDITOR'S NOTE: Could it perchance have also been the fact that El Cheapo Kaufman was offering Ms. Jameson less money for a month of Tromindetured servitude than she earns in an hour of cock slapping and pussy lapping?

on how to make one's own damn movie. I am now reading this last chapter: the "epilogue" of the book.* And suddenly, a thought occured in my brain.

May I suggest that you write a "how to write your own damn epligoue" *for your* epilogue? It might be an idea to outline why exactly one writes an epilogue. For example, *Tromeo and Juliet* has a fantastic epilogue to juxtapose the prologue and round out the story satisfactorily. I live in the UK everyday and have been brought up on all of Shakespeare's novels and Dickens's plays and stuff, so I know what I'm talking about. Please try to include a brief guide on how to write one's own damn epilogue and also, perhaps, outline why prologues are necessary after that. I feel this would be an invaluable resource for your readers.

Another final thought. Right now the book end on page 322 with the line "However, I believe they flipped me off good-naturedly." In my experience in book writing, which is lots, I find it better to end on a witty and amusing sentence such as "The End" or "Fin". A quick, concise and witty conclusion to any text, at least for us Britons, is of paramount impotence.[†]

Yours Severely,
Andrew Mackay
editor and founder of toxie.com
The Official UK Troma Fan Site

---

[*] Lloyd replies:- "Dear Andrew, it baffles me entirely how you are able to have read up till this point while I am still writing this paragraph. Are you spying on me or some-thing?"
[†] Lloyd continues:- ". . . what the fuck is going on? Please stop reading material I haven't yet written!"

But the best news of the day came from overseas. The Carlton Hotel in Cannes, Troma's base of operations for as long as we've been attending the festival and the nerve center of the entire Cannes market, informed us today that Troma will not be allowed back this year. The excuse is that the hotel is already booked to capacity. This strikes me as curious, considering it's about half a year until the festival and the entire world is currently in the grips of a recession. It seems far more likely that the hotel is still pissed off about the events at last year's festival, when Doug Sakmann traipsed through the lobby drenched in fake blood and the big wheels across the hall at Warner Bros. bitched constantly about the noise and activity coming from the Troma office. But according to the Carlton, it has nothing to do with any of that. It's simply that every studio, distributor, and independent filmmaker, including those teetering on the brink of bankruptcy, have already planned ahead and booked costly rooms in an expensive French hotel. For the first time in decades, Troma is homeless in Cannes.

I look across the mountains of shit on my desk. Videotapes, DVDs, bills, faxes, memos, invoices, purchase orders, and more bills. To the left of me, the fax from the Carlton that, in its polite-concierge way, suggests we eat *merde* and die. To my right, the manuscript for this book. Hundreds of triple-spaced pages, encouraging young people to get out there and do as we've done. Make independent cinema the way you want to and fuck the consequences.

Inside my desk drawer is a pearl-handled Derringer revolver. About half the people in the office think it's a cigarette lighter, despite the fact that I don't smoke. Everybody else knows it's a real gun, but they figure I have it because I'm paranoid about staying in the office late at night. They assume it's either not loaded, or doesn't work, or that I'm too stupid to figure out how to make it work. Nobody has ever made the connection between the gun in my desk and my frequent threats to "blow my fucking brains out."

Well . . . they're about to.

After thirty years of work, Troma is no closer to respectability than we were in the 1970s. If anything, we've retreated farther onto the fringes of the film industry. Video buyers won't stock our tapes and DVDs unless they receive a satisfactory, full-swallow blow job from me personally. Theaters won't book our movies and in the rare instance we make a movie they actually want, we can barely pull our heads out of our asses long enough to figure out how to get it to them and promote it properly.

Besides which, I'm pushing sixty. Not long ago, I had a cancerous melanoma removed from my face. Years of filming outside in the hot sun have left me with dozens of movies nobody wants to see and skin cancer to boot. Now I've either got to smear rank-smelling sunscreen all over my face every day for the rest of my miserable life or become a recluse and never leave the house, an option that Pat and our children adamantly refuse to let me pursue. Sooner or later, my body will start to fail completely. With my luck, I will get sick in the most painful and disgusting way possible and die only after I spend years in stench-filled agony.

Better to leave spectacularly and keep people talking than to slowly decay, I think. I pull the revolver out of the drawer and check to make sure that nobody's stolen the bullets. Luck is on my side for a change. A full chamber. While it may be true that I wouldn't be able to figure out how to use the gun against an intruder, I'm pretty sure even I can find my open mouth long enough to shove the barrel inside it.

With the gun in my mouth, I pause. My death will probably increase interest in *Citizen Toxie* by 1000%. Shit. Then we'll really be fucked. There's no way we'll be able to get prints to all those theaters. On the other hand . . . good! Fuck 'em! I'll be gone, so it won't be my headache. Let the rest of these fuckers figure out how to deal with the mess. So long, assholes!

Wait a minute . . . turning around, I notice several vintage Troma posters on the wall behind me. Hmmm . . . will their eBay value be increased or decreased when my blood, brains, and skull get splattered all over 'em? Better not take any chances. I put the gun down and take a few seconds to carefully roll up the posters from *Troma's War, The Toxic Avenger*, and *Class of Nuke 'Em High*.

Okey-dokey, then. I think we're good to go. Put the gun back in my mouth, set my finger on the trigger. So long, assholes! I've had a miserable fucking time!

BLAM!

I wake up screaming. "Fuck! I'm alive!" My crotch is dampened by something I suspect isn't blood.

I look around, more confused than usual. The other passengers on the plane look at me with a range of emotions in their eyes. Annoyance. Irritation. Vexation. Yep, pretty much the whole rainbow of feeling is being directed at me right now.

In fact, the only two people on the plane who are determinedly *not* looking in my direction are Adam Jahnke and Trent Haaga. They've been pretty mad at me for awhile now, since I insisted that they fly from Salt Lake City (where we've just finished TromaDance 2002) out to New York with me so we can finish the book. Of course, their anger is fractional compared to the wrath I assume is brewing in my wife, Pat, and her deputy director at the governor's office, Jerry Stoeffhaas. Since Troma couldn't afford to buy tickets for Trent and Adam, I stole Pat and Jerry's tickets from our hotel room and gave them to the guys. Surely the great state of New York will understand why this was necessary when they read the book. My brilliant plan is kind of backfiring, however, since Adam and Trent are so pissed off about being dragged across country that they haven't spoken to me once or done a lick of work since they got on the plane. Right now, they're seated directly behind me, trying desperately to look as if they have no idea who this insane, possibly incontinent man in front of them is.

Looking down at my lap, I'm more than a little relieved to see that the wetness is nothing more than a spilled drink. Not my own. The fat guy crammed into the seat next to mine sleeps soundly, unaware that he's treated my balls to a Jim Beam and Coke. He seems to be the only person on the plane who wasn't awakened by my girlish screams.

So I didn't shoot myself. Fuck. It was just another in a series of fucked-up dreams I've been having since returning from Africa. For the Christmas holidays, the Kaufman family journeyed to the Cameroons, where I had spent some time back in the '60s. When you come back from Africa, you have to take a wonderful anti-malaria drug called Lariam. Besides preventing malaria, Lariam provides headaches the size of Jupiter and vivid dreams that never fail to disorient and cloud the mind. Well, I can always try to make my dreams come true tomorrow. For now, back to work. "Work," in this case, is a blank legal pad and one phrase that keeps repeating over and over in my brain . . . *I must wrap up the book, I must wrap up the book, I must wrap up the book . . .*

How? It's gotta be inspirational or nobody's going to go out and make their own damn movie. It has to be a great, triumphant, all-encompassing metaphor for the journey of filmmaking, proving once and for all that independent film is a battle worth fighting for. It's got to prove that I haven't been talking out my ass for the last 300 pages.

Shit on toast. This is never gonna work. Well, maybe we can do something about TromaDance. That's still fresh in the memory.

This year's festival was an enormous success with no arrests and only minor harassment by the Signage Police at Park City Municipal. Park City's laws regarding signage are more detailed than most cities' laws regarding kiddie rape. No more than 30 percent of a building's façade is allowed to display signage. So when a film festival takes an existing space for a screening venue, as TromaDance did with the incredible Phat Tire Saloon in Park City, you are required to take down the business owner's sign in order to put yours up, so that you both meet the 30 percent. Casey Calm, owner of the Phat Tire, basically said, "Fuck that shit" and allowed us to hang four signs on his building in addition to his own. Park City Municipal tsk-tsk'ed this and said we'd have to take two signs down. Casey and TromaDance said, "Make us." Nobody did, so our signs stayed up throughout.

For me, TromaDance is an annual reminder why independent art and cinema is worth creating. Each January, independent filmmakers and performance artists from around the world travel to Utah on their own nickel to volunteer for TromaDance. When they get to Park City, the only thing they're guaranteed is a roof over their heads. We can't even promise a comfortable patch of floor to stretch out on. Volunteers end up sleeping on countertops, on tables, and curled up in hardwood chairs.

The reason these young people put up with this shit is for the opportunity to meet and exchange ideas (and possibly bodily fluids) with like-minded artists. These people make films because they love it, not because they're hoping to land a three-picture deal with MGM (although they wouldn't turn one down if it fell in their lap). When I talk with these filmmakers, I get the feeling that they would keep on doing what they're doing even if no one ever saw their work. And every one of them is extremely grateful to TromaDance for making it possible for them to reach an audience.

The gratitude I receive from the TromaDance attendees and volunteers is in stark contrast to the reception I get at the industry parties. Every night during the Sundance Film Festival, Park City boasts at least two or three industry-only galas where the Hollywood contingent assembles to eat shitty free food, drink the watered-down Utah equivalent of alcohol, and complain about how cold it is. Ordinarily, the Troma Team doesn't even learn about these parties until the next day, much less get invited to them. But every so often, one will slip through the veil of secrecy and Troma will attempt to get on the invite list.

One such party this year was hosted by the industry trade magazine *Variety* at the ultra-posh Stein-Ericsson Lodge. I actually managed to get into this shindig. Not because we had an invitation. Not because I am a filmmaker with a thirty-year track record. Not because I am the president of one of the oldest independent film studios in the world. Not even because Troma and TromaDance are paying advertisers in *Variety* and they were giving away free copies of the issue with our advertisement. No, the only way I was able to weasel my way into this party was by riding the coattails of the New York State Film Commissioner.* The party was huge, with 2,500 of Park City's finest freeloaders stocking up on food and drink. Apparently, the people at *Variety* did not consider me to be in the top 2,500 most important people in town.

Once inside, I scanned the dimly lit ballroom. For a second, I was back in the Troma basement, watching hundreds of rats gnawing at boxes of Tromabilia. The stench of rat piss and shit filled my nostrils as I looked around in a panic for a shovel so I could kill these fuckers and start cleaning. I shook my head to get rid of the Lariam-inspired delusion and saw what was really happening. Hundreds of black-clad Hollywood types were gnawing on plates of buffet food. The smell of rat excrement didn't fade, though. Turned out I was smelling the dangerously undercooked prime rib sandwiches and icy cold egg rolls that the elite were chowing down. My stomach turned and my headache pounded.

Over the next hour, I schmoozed with the best of 'em, talking to anybody who'd listen (and quite a few people who wouldn't) about TromaDance and independent film. While just about everybody knew about TromaDance, it quickly became apparent that most of them didn't give a shit. Some people thought it was a joke. Some took it seriously but weren't about to break their plans to go see some "real" independent cinema, sponsored by Miramax or HBO. And if they were indifferent toward TromaDance, they were downright hostile toward my career as a filmmaker. Sure, I hadn't made *Citizen Toxie* to please these fucks, but the very least they could have shown me was polite

---

* Adam Jahnke led a contingent of TromaDance volunteers to this party separately. When he was asked what name the invitation might be under, he wisely just said, "Kaufman." The List-master at the door asked if he meant Pat Kaufman and Adam immediately replied, "Yep. That's the one."

ambivalence. These bastards acted as though my foisting another adventure of the Toxic Avenger on an unsuspecting public was a personal affront to them and the entire film industry.

So, in the end, all your hard work and sacrifice will earn you the respect and admiration of your artistic peers, but will apparently count for less than nothing in the world at large. Real independence is treated as a social stigma, an aberration that should be ignored and eventually wiped out. Media conglomerate–sponsored independence is the only kind of innovative thought that is encouraged and admired in today's society.

I hand the legal pad back to Trent and Adam, pleased with myself and pretty sure that I've finished the book. Within moments, the pad comes sailing back over the seats and hits me on the head.

"What the fuck are you thinking?" Trent asks.

"You can't end the book with that," Adam adds. "People will be discouraged at best."

I re-read what I've done and decide they might just have a point. I rip the pages off the legal pad and toss them onto the lap of the sleeping fat boy next to me. I figure if he used me as a sink, the least I can do is use him as a trash can.

All right, think inspirational. What about the trip to Africa? Maybe I can use that as a metaphor for the filmmaker's journey. I reflect on the trip for a moment, then realize that it's pretty unlikely that I'll be able to avoid making any *Heart of Darkness* comparisons. That being the case, I should probably avoid the subject altogether.

Maybe I'm just too old and broken-down to actually inspire anybody. Well, fuck, isn't that why I asked these two young people to co-write this book with me? Shit, I shouldn't have to write this epilogue at all. This should be entirely written by somebody who I've actually inspired. That's it . . . I'll make Adam do it. He was at TromaDance. Maybe he can explain why we independents must fight the good fight.

I hand the legal pad back to Adam and explain what I want him to do. He doesn't say anything . . . just gives me a sad, slow shake of the head like the old man has finally succumbed to the last ravages of Alzheimer's and takes the legal pad.

Adam Jahnke here. Yeah, I was at TromaDance all right. A film festival that managed to come together and be a success in spite of itself. Ten days of nonstop drinking, drug use, and fucking. And none of it, I'll have you know, was enjoyed by me. I was the sober one. The responsible one. The one who had to try to keep the train from careening off the tracks and killing everybody onboard and maiming innocents in Park City.

The very first evening the volunteers arrived, an impromptu party swung into action. Within hours, most of the condo's inhabitants were spectacularly drunk. One guy got particularly violent and smashed the glass stovetop with his fist, slashing a deep, gaping wound into his wrist. Despite all our efforts, he refused to go the emergency room and stormed through the place, coating walls, windows, and doors with blood. He simply could not be stopped, so a few of the other volunteers decided the only way to subdue him was to beat the shit out of him.

Meanwhile, one young, allegedly straight male volunteer allowed his virgin asshole to be deflowered by another female volunteer with a strap-on dildo. Most of the sexual activity took place in the hot tub, so within a short time the water had turned into a brownish-black cloud. Within about forty-eight hours of the TromaDance Team's arrival, the brand new condo we were staying in had been forever altered.

Somehow, the team pulled together long enough to promote the festival and get things underway in Salt Lake and Park Cities, but thanks to Sundance's iron grip on the Master Festival License, our promotional efforts had the undesired side effect of turning filmmakers from other non-Sundance festivals against us. They despised TromaDance's relentless flyering, since we had to cover up other flyers to post ours. At least half my time every day was spent talking to individual filmmakers and calming them down, assuring them that TromaDance was not the enemy.

Besides working on the festival, Lloyd and I sequestered ourselves from time to time to work on this book. The thing is, you can't be too damn sequestered when you're sitting at a table in a crowded restaurant. Lloyd's attention would focus on the book for maybe three minutes, tops. Then, inevitably, someone would catch Lloyd's eye and he'd be off on another tangent. I know, I know . . . from reading this book, you'd never believe that Lloyd suffers from attention deficit disorder. But while we were working on the book, we were interrupted by (or, more accurately, Lloyd would interrupt us to go talk with) Mark Borchardt and Mike Schank from American Movie; *Andrew Weiner, associate producer of* Tromeo & Juliet *who was now working with Universal; and just interesting looking people that Lloyd thought should be invited to TromaDance. If you spend ten minutes with Lloyd in public, you realize pretty quickly that Lloyd knows everybody. Which, depending on your mood, is either pretty impressive or pretty irritating.*

At any rate, I did spend ten days in close quarters with an impressive array of truly independent filmmakers and artists. For a little while anyway, we succeeded in giving art back to the people. Was it worth it? I dunno . . . ask me again in a year or so. Right now, my feet are hobbled with pain from walking miles in sub-zero temperatures in my leaky $9.95 boots (the only ones I could afford on a Troma salary). I get physically sick if anyone even mentions the word Jacuzzi, since all I can picture is the brackish, biological soup the volunteers created in Utah. I still haven't found out what the final cost of the damage to the condo will be. When the bill comes in, I assume I will either be fired or killed and honestly, I'm not sure which one I would prefer. The filmmakers whose work was on display at TromaDance all seemed to think their hard work had paid off in the end. As for me, I don't even want to see a movie again until all memory of my time in Park City has faded into a gentle blur.

Adam hands me the legal pad and settles back into his seat. I read over it and turn back to him.

"Thanks a whole fucking lot for that, Jahnke," I bark at him. Adam just shrugs and shuts his eyes. Well, there's always Trent. Good old reliable Trent Haaga. He's told me time and again that he's been watching Troma movies since he was dick high. If he can't inspire us all, no one can.

I hand the legal pad over to Trent. He won't even take it from me. He shakes his head firmly and spits out, "Fuck you, Kaufman."

"What did I do?"

"I'm still pissed about the whole digital video thing. I can't believe you'd tell people to shoot on film instead of video. That is, without a doubt, the single most idiotic, stuck-in-the-past piece of advice I have ever heard.

"And inspiration? Jesus, man . . . my wife's about to pork out our first kid and I am seriously unemployed. I just turned $35,000 into three-quarters of a million with *Killjoy 2*. They *should* sign me to a six-picture deal so I can make *Killjoy Part 6*. They *should* give me a little back-end taste of the money they've made. Instead, I can't even get a job interview at a goddamn courier service. Not a job . . . an *interview*! Sure, the economy's in the toilet right now but fuck, man! On top of that, my car's been fucked up for about a month now. I just had to shell out three grand because the repair shop wouldn't let us take the car until they got paid and I can't wait ten days for the insurance company to cut a check. And the car's *still* not fixed! The repair-monkey fucked up the electrical system while they were working on it, so now it's back in the shop. And back at the airport, I got into a shouting match over a parking space with some bitch and I swear to fucking god, if I'd had a knife I would have stabbed that cunt right in the eye.

"So write your own goddamn epilogue, Kaufman. I feel about as inspired as the crack addict that sleeps outside the unemployment office I visit every goddamn day."

I take the legal pad back and slump down in my seat. Fuck . . . maybe I can talk the editor into forgetting about the epilogue. I think I've said all that needs to be said, anyway.

Just as I'm slipping into my daily 10:00 P.M. pit of despair, I hear the captain announce we're making our final approach into New York. Since my head has smacked against the window anyway, I decide to open my eyes and look out the window, just in case any more landmarks have been obliterated by insane terrorists.

Manhattan glistens below me like a miniature jewel. I'm stunned . . .

I've been flying in and out of this city for decades and it's never looked so beautiful. The air is crisp and clear and makes the cityscape stand out in intensely sharp focus. The city looks vibrant and new . . . so much so, it almost looks fake.

"Y'know," I say to nobody in particular, "it's pretty fucking amazing when you think about it. For a film studio to survive thirty years, totally free of corporate interference, in a city thousands of miles removed from the cancerous heart of the movie industry. We've done exactly what we wanted to do, and we've reached a pretty goddamn big group of people. Not just entertained them, which would be enough, but inspired them to do some amazing things. Troma can't go anywhere without an army of volunteers appearing to help in whatever way they can. These fans don't want money . . . they just want to be a part of something that has spoken to them in a way nothing else can. Let's see Harvey Weinstein and his Miramax buddies make that claim."

The fat sleeping guy in the seat next to me has woken up enough to hear my speech and he looks over. "You're absolutely right. I can't."

I look the fat man up and down. "You aren't Harvey Weinstein."

"Sure I am."

"I don't believe for one second that the head of Miramax would fly coach."

"Miramax? What the hell are you talking about? I own a dry cleaning shop in Queens."

"Oh . . . sorry. Wrong Harvey Weinstein. No offense."

"None taken. Beautiful city, isn't it?"

"Yeah, actually. It really is. And y'know, I think we're making real progress. Truly independent cinema is finally making a mark and finding an audience. International filmmakers like Takashi Miike and Gaspar Noe aren't exactly household names, but they definitely have a following. I mean—"

"Yep. It sure is a beautiful city."

With that, Harvey stuck his headphones in and pretended to listen to the in-flight music which, by this time, had been turned off. But I had a point and by god, I was going to make it. Even if I had to write it on a legal pad to do it.

Truly independent films are as difficult to track down as a virginal cornhole in a public bath. But, like the virginal cornhole, they are well worth the effort it takes to find. And people do find them. Why else would a one-night-only showing of Alex de la Iglesia's brilliant movie *Common Wealth* be totally sold out at the American Cinematheque in Los Angeles? Why else would a Troma retrospective play to capacity crowds throughout Europe? Audiences find good movies. They don't believe the corporate hype spewed out by critics like Roger Ebert and Peter Travers of *Rolling Stone*. The critics have begun to marginalize themselves by praising every major studio movie to the sky. When ads for dozens of different movies are running and Travers calls every one of them the best movie of the year, even the dimmest bulb on the Christmas tree starts to figure out that something's not right.

So is it worth it? The hard work? The frustration? The humiliation of having to grovel for every dime? Oddly enough, yeah. It is. If you surround yourself with the right people, you will forge partnerships that will last the rest of your life. You will bring a vision that existed only in your head to life. That vision might be funny, it might be horrifying, it might be erotic.* Whatever it is, if it's deep within you, it's worth fighting for and making a reality. Make it happen and do not let anything stand in your way. In the plagiarized, Capraesque words of Jerry in *Terror Firmer*, sometimes lost causes are the only ones worth fighting for.

As I finished writing these words, the plane finished taxiing down the runway. Harvey Weinstein, the Queens dry cleaner, wedged his bulk into the aisle and tried to free his carry-on from the overhead compartment. Filled with new resolve, I decided to take my own advice.

---

* Personally, I'm hoping it's erotic, but don't let me influence you.

"Outta my way, Weinstein! I've got art to make!"

I shoved Harvey Weinstein's fat ass out of my way and strode confidently to the terminal, Adam and Trent trudging along behind, discussing what horrible thing they could possibly have done to get stuck with somebody like me.

Down at the baggage claim area, I receive a call from Michael Herz that confirms that this new feeling of enthusiasm isn't just the Lariam talking. I look around to find the guys. Trent is talking to someone on his own cell phone, while Adam is scanning the departures board, trying to figure out how soon he and Trent can get back to L.A.

"Trent! Adam! Great news!" I shout while I hurry over to them. They both attempt to look like they haven't got the first clue who Trent or Adam might be but soon realize that I'm not going to give up that easily.

"Big news from Michael Herz! We have an investor for our next movie! The long-awaited sequel to *Sgt. Kabukiman NYPD*: *Sgt. Kabukiman LAPD*! We'd better get our asses over to the Troma Building and get to work."

Trent and Adam look at each other, then the floor, then back to me.

"Lloyd," Trent says, "that's great, but I was just on the phone with the hospital in Los Angeles. My wife's water just broke. She's going into labor. I have to get back immediately."

"That's no big deal! You've got plenty of time to work on the script between contractions. Believe me, I've gone through this three times. Y'know, I wrote the entire first draft of *Troma's War* while Pat was delivering Charlotte. If you wrote the script for *Citizen Toxie* on your honeymoon, there's no reason you guys can't do this one in the delivery room."

Adam and Trent give each other another look, then Adam cautiously asks, "What do you mean 'you guys'?"

"Well, you both have to collaborate on the screenplay, of course. Trent, your wife has met Adam, right? I'm sure she'll want everybody she's ever met to be there for the blessed event anyway, so you'd might just as well get some work done at the same time."

Troma veteran ensemble player Rick Collins (*Class of Nuke 'Em High, Toxic Avenger III, The Last Temptation of Toxie, Troma's War, Citizen Toxie*, etc.) says: "You can check out anytime you want, but you can never leave."

"Jeez, I don't know . . ."

"Trent, if you're still sore about the whole digital video argument, I apologize. Your points are well taken. My preference for film is a personal thing. And who knows? Maybe I'll see a DV movie someday that will change my tune completely."

I could see Trent's attitude soften with my apology. "I know, Lloyd. I appreciate you letting me get my side of the argument across in the book."

"Trent, Adam, I know that making movies the Troma way is not easy. It's both physically and mentally painful and occasionally downright humiliating. But goddammit, we have to keep going! Without independent iconoclasts, art grows stale, boring, and stupid. We've gotta keep pushing the envelope and proving to the world that you don't have to sell your soul to the corporate entertainment factory to make movies. Film is an art and all art should be accessible to anybody, rich or poor. So whaddaya say? Are you with me?"

By this time, both of the guys were smiling again. "All right," Adam said. "I'm in."

Trent nodded along in agreement. "Okay, Lloyd. And y'know, I think I will name the kid after you. Stanley Lloyd Haaga isn't so bad. If the kid's going to be an independent movie geek like his dad, he'd better get used to having the shit kicked out of him anyway."

"Great!" I grabbed the guys and we shared the first nonerotic three-way hug anyone in the Troma Team had ever been involved in. "Now get back on that plane and get writing! This movie's going to be huge! Make sure it has a Rodney King scene and something to do with terrorism. And it's gotta have a scene in a rehab center. Kabukiman in L.A. has to go to a rehab center. And make sure it's funny, erotic, and exciting! All you guys have to do is give it a beginning, a middle, and an end!"

Trent and Adam headed back to the main terminal. Before they disappeared around the corner, they stopped and turned back.

"Wait one goddamn second," Adam said. "What the fuck is going on here? Lloyd, this is exactly the same way every single one of your movies ends. All the surviving characters suddenly reappear for some big, smiley, cathartic group hug. Did you actually drag us all the way across country just so we could come up with a literary equivalent of the typical—Lloyd Kaufman directed final scene?"

"Goddammit, quit stalling! Get on the plane and write the fucking screenplay! If we don't have a script by Monday, it's asshole time! You hear me? I'll blow my fucking brains out and it'll be all your fault!"

The two of them shook their heads at this and flipped me off. However, I believe they flipped me off good-naturedly.

Index